CONTENTS

Analysis for Crime Prevention

Nick Tilley

Editor

Crime Prevention Studies
Volume 13

Criminal Justice Press
Monsey, NY

Willan Publishing
Devon, UK

2002

CRIME PREVENTION STUDIES

Ronald V. Clarke, Series Editor

Crime Prevention Studies is an international book series dedicated to research on situational crime prevention and other initiatives to reduce opportunities for crime. Most volumes center on particular topics chosen by expert guest editors. The editors of each volume, in consultation with the series editor, commission the papers to be published and select peer reviewers.

© Copyright 2002 by
Criminal Justice Press.
All rights reserved.

ISSN (series): 1065-7029
ISBN: 1-881798-33-X (cloth)
ISBN: 1-881798-34-8 (paper)

INTRODUCTION: ANALYSIS FOR CRIME PREVENTION

by

Nick Tilley

Nottingham Trent University

The collected papers in this volume address analysis for crime prevention. Analysis *for* crime prevention differs from analysis *of* crime prevention. Analysis *of* crime prevention stands back from and comments on what has been and is being done to try to prevent crime. It may be concerned with effectiveness as part of a broad agenda of social reform, but is not concerned directly to inform efforts to identify and deal with specific crime threats at specific times and places (see, for example, Crawford, 1997, Gilling, 1997, Garland, 2001, and Hughes, 1998). Analysis *for* crime prevention is oriented directly to the formulation of preventive strategies. It does so in three ways. First, it identifies concentrations of either crime as a whole or single offences where there is a potential yield from preventive efforts. Second, it helps find the most efficient, effective and, perhaps, equitable means of prevention. Third, it can help forecast likely future crime problems with a view to developing preemptive strategies (Rogerson et al., 2000; Pease, 1997).

All the chapters included in this collection aim in one way or another to improve the conduct and use of analysis for crime prevention. Some are based in relatively "pure" research. Others turn on involvement in practical work. The relationship between research and practice is by no means straightforward, as various of the following chapters indicate. The application of established research findings in new settings is often highly problematic. Moreover, general patterns and their explanation have often emerged from scientific work attempting to target specific practical problems — "pure" research has not always come first in crime prevention or, for that matter, as we shall see in an exemplary case, in other fields either. The following sections introduce and set in context contributions to this volume, that identify general crime patterns, that apply research in practical settings, that explore the appropriate use of past research, and that consider the relationship between research, policy and practice.

ANALYSING GENERAL PATTERNS

One contribution of generic analysis for crime prevention has been to identify characteristic problem patterns that might form the focus of preventive interventions.

Hot products have been shown to be those that are CRAVED (Concealable, Removable, Available, Valuable, Enjoyable and Disposable) (Clarke 1999), or those that have VIVA attributes (Value, Inertia, and Visibility of target to likely offender, alongside Accessibility to the offender) (Felson 1998). These features make objects especially vulnerable to theft. Think of cash, cars, jewelry, and small, lightweight, anonymous high-value electronic goods. Defining attributes that make products hot is to define their criminogenic potential. Anticipating what is likely to become hot helps concentrate efforts to incorporate preemptive design attributes (U.K. Department of Trade and Industry, 2000).

Hot places are those that attract criminals because of the rich crime pickings available there or which generate crime because of the numbers of targets and offenders drawn in because of where they are or what else goes on (Brantingham and Brantingham, 1995).

Notwithstanding the normality of occasional offending (Gabor 1994), hot offenders are those who are prolific, in some instances due to drug use and drug dependency (Johnson et al., 2000; Bennett et al., 2001).

Hot victims suffer crime repeatedly, either because particular offenders learn that they offer reasonable returns at reasonable effort and reasonable risk (Farrell et al., 1995), or because the victims have attributes that make them especially vulnerable (Spelman, 1995).

Crime surveys have identified those at particular risk of crime victimisation. For example it has been found in Britain that age, income, ethnicity and employment status of the head of household, number of security devices fitted, type of neighborhood, and household structure are associated with variations in vulnerability to domestic burglary (Kershaw et al., 2000; Budd, 1999). Other research literature has identified attributes of those most likely to become involved in committing crimes (Cashmore et al., 1999).

There is, thus, a substantial volume of research findings that can inform the targeting of preventive efforts, in terms of victims, products, places, and offenders. In this collection three chapters contribute to this literature. The first, by Farrell et al., takes forward methods of analysing patterns of repeat victimisation. The second, by

Groff and La Vigne, reviews ways in which geographical information systems (GIS) can be deployed to predict crime patterns, on the basis of which decisions about allocation of preventive efforts can be made. The third, by Townsley and Pease, helps identify those longer-term hot spots where a sustained preventive focus may have a substantial potential yield. These three chapters break new ground in developing methods that can be used in local analysis to inform preventive work.

A second contribution of generic analysis to crime prevention has been the identification of causal mechanisms generating and changing crime patterns. The manipulation of these mechanisms provides the means to reduce crime problems.

Clarke's analyses have clearly been seminal here. His study of changes in the toxicity of domestic gas supplies and suicide rates, with Mayhew, is a classic (Clarke and Mayhew, 1988). It opened the way to understanding how convenient opportunity could be crucial even to the most serious decisions we can make about our futures (or lack of them), and how its reduction could lead to substantial changes in behavioural patterns. Developments since then (notably Laycock 1985, 1997) have highlighted the importance of *perceived* opportunity. Clarke's classification of crime prevention techniques in the first and second editions of his collection of *Successful Case Studies* (Clarke 1992, 1997) reflects recognition that the active mechanism in prevention is often perceived opportunity. The headings "increased risk," "increased effort" and "decreased reward," are replaced, respectively, by "increased perceived risk," "increased perceived effort" and "decreased perceived reward."[1]

In this collection, the contribution by Smith et al. develops further the notion that changed perceptions can comprise a crucial mechanism producing changed crime patterns associated with the introduction of crime prevention measures. The notion of "anticipatory benefit" captures the ways in which crime prevention programs can often begin to bite prior to implementation. The paper outlines mechanisms whereby this form of benefit diffusion may be generated.

APPLYING ANALYSIS IN PRACTICE

Particular efforts to reduce or forestall crime require bespoke analysis involving the identification and definition of problems, and determination of what might be done to address them. Reviews of problem-oriented policing on both sides of the Atlantic find this work generally to be done poorly (Scott, 2001; Read and Tilley, 2000). The pioneering Newport News project was distinctive in involving talented researchers (Eck and Spelman, 1987). In the absence of strong analytic capacity at problem level, there is more commonly a swift transition from presumed problem to presumed solution, followed, where there is any assessment, by selective use of data to show that the response has been successful.

A good starting point for local analysis will often be the sorts of crime patterns identified nationally. National crime surveys identify risk factors that face classes of victims; or products that are frequently stolen. Local analysts concerned with particular areas can draw on these to check whether the results are also found in their circumstances. In some cases variations are found. For example, though the elderly in Britain are a relatively low crime-risk-group (Kershaw et al., 2000), there are circumstances where this is not the case. In an analysis to inform burglary reduction work in an area of North Wales, elderly residents in sheltered accommodation were found to suffer more than twice the national domestic burglary rate (Curtin et al., 2001).

The chapter by Clarke and Goldstein in this volume shows what is involved in adopting an analytic approach in a local area to the definition of a problem, and the development of a strategy to deal with it. Clarke and Goldstein highlight the ways in which the contours of a practically addressable problem emerged only through sustained analysis, working alongside local police practitioners. Once a problem with some specific definable and modifiable commonality had been detected and measured, and its conditions specified, thinking about methods of dealing with it became much clearer. Yet the initial analysis was crucial, and the findings far from self-evident at the start. The presenting problem, theft from construction sites in Charlotte-Mecklenburg, was too loose to be open to targeted intervention. The analysis had to move to a sharper specification of a problem — theft of household appliances from newly completed homes. Data collection in relation to this opened the way to working out a solution — removing targets for theft by postponing installation of the targeted appliances.

There are other cases in the literature showing similar features. One example is Boston's Operation Ceasefire. Here, Kennedy et al., working with a "line level" practitioner group, assembled data on shootings, victims and youth gangs. They used this analysis to inform a strategy that spoke to the particular conditions generating the carrying and use by gang members of firearms and other weapons (Braga et al., 1999). They defined the problem not as one of dissolving gangs per se, but of reducing injuries through undermining the conditions generating the availability and use of weapons. Another example, this time from Britain, is the Kirkholt burglary prevention project. This again began with analysis, identifying aspects of the underlying problem that had hitherto lain hidden, in this instance the high rates of repeat victimisation The analysis informed the choice and targeting of preventive measures (Forrester et al., 1988, 1990). In each of these cases, imaginative analyses, aimed at identifying essential but modifiable aspects of the problems addressed, were conducted alongside practitioners. In each case, the analyses threw up critical features of the problem that were not already being actively considered in developing responses.

Using Past Research

There are significant methodological issues at stake in determining what comprises "good practice" and what comprises good use of past practice. One of the main reasons for evaluating programs is to learn lessons for the future. Yet, even where past initiatives are found to have been successful, determining when and where they can appropriately be drawn on, and also what about them should be adopted or adapted, and how, remain tricky issues (Tilley, 1996).

The problems of replicating the apparently successful Boston and Kirkholt projects already mentioned illustrate the point. What was crucial to the Boston project? Was it the problem-oriented approach, the application of targeted leverage to groups, the interagency co-operation, the disruption of weapons supply, the focus on shootings and gangs, the formation of a line-level working group, the strong and supportive mayor, or the analysis by Harvard academics? Was it all of these features or a specific subset? What exactly would need to be included to reproduce Boston's achievements? Those planning to draw on Boston have to make decisions.

In Kirkholt, was it the analytic starting point, the removal of pre-payment meters, the small relatively self-contained housing project, the focus on repeat victimisation, the leadership by Police Inspector David Forrester, the involvement of some inspiring English academics, the interagency approach, the cocoon home watch, the focus on domestic burglary, all or some of these? What would be needed to reproduce the achievements? Again, those planning to draw on Kirkholt had to make decisions. In the Kirkholt case, there is evidence that different decisions were made by different groups over what to try to reproduce and what would comprise replications (Tilley, 1996). The same may befall the Boston gun project. In the event, for Kirkholt the focus on repeats appears now to have been crucial. For Boston, the use of targeted specific leverage has been seen by Kennedy to be portable and particularly important (Kennedy, 1997).

One recent trend has been the development of databases that capture past experience and their provision to practitioners so that they can avoid "reinventing the wheel," or worse, "reinventing the flat tyre."

What, though, comprises good practice, and how do we emulate it? How do we use what we know? As Ekblom argues in his wide-ranging contribution, the fact that a measure has proved successful in the past in specific circumstances is insufficient to guarantee its appropriateness in the future. The circumstances may be different, meaning that the measure may trigger different causal mechanisms, bringing about different outcomes. Moreover, in the case of complex packages of measures, which are increasingly used in crime prevention work, the active ingredients may be far from self-evident. Finally, even where there is strong evidence that a particular measure has brought about a reduction in crime, changed capacities are liable to supersede it. For example, a given safe design may be enough to resist even well-organised, skilful safe-breakers at one time. Given new technology and the invention of new methods of penetrating safes, however, this capacity successfully to resist may not last indefinitely (see Ekblom, 1997).

Rather than drawing on specific projects that have been found once to work to deal with a specific problem, it may make more sense, as Ekblom argues, to distil principles that have been successful in informing the choice of interventions, from previous projects. This calls for a different "reading" of past initiatives — less that of looking at surface attributes and associations, and more an understanding of their underlying logic. Rolling out projects or mimicking projects is liable to disappoint.

ANALYSIS, PRACTICE AND POLICY RELATIONSHIPS

It might at first sight seem that general analysis will yield findings to be used in practical analysis, and that findings from previous research can be applied in a more or less mechanical way. In practice, the relationship has been more multi-directional than this. The point has already been made that findings of effectiveness in one context cannot mechanically be transposed to another situation with expectations that precisely the same results will occur. More than that, local analysis has sometimes preceded more general analysis and informed it. For example, the identification of patterns of repeat victimisation and their use as a way of shaping preventive work in the Kirkholt burglary reduction project, preceded and stimulated a widespread international research and development programme. The latter has included national initiatives to find patterns of repeats across countries and crime types (Farrell and Pease, 2001). This, in turn, is feeding back into quite widespread routine local analysis of repeats and strategies to reduce them (Farrell et al., 2000; Laycock, 2001).

Research funding bodies may be tempted to invest in blue skies research in the belief that it is mainly this that will yield the general lessons that can then be applied in practice. This is not how matters have proceeded in situational crime prevention (Laycock and Clarke, 2001). It is also not how matters have always proceeded in the natural and medical sciences either. In both, the work on specific practical issues by an engaged practitioner-researcher has often yielded insights that have turned out to be crucial both for understanding and for policy and practice. The history of science yields many examples. One, from the medical field, will suffice here.

Ignaz Semmelweis's starting problem was this. In the Viennese hospital, where he was working as a physician, there were two maternity divisions with different mortality rates for mothers from puerperal fever (or childbed fever), as shown in Table 1.

Table 1: Mortality Rates for Puerperal Fever

Maternity Division mortality rate from puerperal (childbed) fever			
	1844	1845	1846
First	8.2%	6.8%	11.4%
Second	2.3%	2.0%	2.7%

Semmelweis's problem was, "Why the difference and what could be done about it?" He collected the following series of folk explanations, considered them critically in the light of available evidence and a series of trials, and rejected them:

(1) "Epidemic influences," also known as "atmospheric-cosmic-telluric changes," which were spreading over all districts and causing childbed fever to women in confinement. Semmelweis reasoned, however, that this did not make sense of the divisional differences, or of the relatively low level of death from childbed fever from those giving birth outside hospital.
(2) Overcrowding. Semmelweis reasoned, however, that division 2 was more crowded, partly because mums try to avoid the dangerous division 1.
(3) Rough examination from medical students. Semmelweis reasoned, however, that injuries from birth were more extensive than those caused by rough examination. Moreover, when the

number of medical students was halved, after a brief fall mortality rates rose again to a higher level than previously.
(4) Shock at seeing a priest bearing last sacraments walking through First Division ward with a bell ringing. Semmelweis found, however, that when the priest was persuaded to arrive discreetly, and without a bell and without parading through First Division ward, the mortality rate did not fall.
(5) Giving birth on the mum's back in the First Division as against on her side in the Second Division. Semmelweis found, however, that when women in a First Division trial gave birth in the lateral position the mortality rate did not fall.

In 1847, Semmelweis came up with an explanation that opened the way to prevention. A colleague cut his finger during an autopsy, and then died after an agonising illness with symptoms similar to childbed fever victims. Semmelweis thought poisonous "cadaveric matter" might have been transmitted. Perhaps, given that the first division was staffed by physicians and trainees whilst the second was staffed by midwives and trainees, women in the first had died from similar blood poisoning which he and colleagues introduced after doing dissections in the autopsy room. Physicians therefore began washing their hands in solution of chlorinated lime before examining women as a way of testing the theory. There was an instant fall in the mortality rate (in 1848 it fell to 1.27% in the first division, compared to 1.33% in the second).

So hand-washing in chlorinated lime was introduced to avoid passing on poisonous cadaveric matter. The theory, however, was subsequently refined. Semmelweis and his associates washed their hands in the chlorinated lime, then examined 13 women. The first had festering cervical cancer. The doctors then just washed their hands again, but this time without doing so in chlorinated lime, since the prevailing theory did not suggest this was needed. Eleven of the twelve women subsequently examined died of childbed fever. It was not matter from dead bodies, as such, that was causing the problem. Poisonous matter could be passed on from living bodies also. Thorough washing in disinfectant needed to be more general.

Semmelweis was a talented action-researcher in medicine. He identified a problem pattern, and refined his definition of it. He elicited, developed and tested theory to address specific problems. Out of his work more general issues of disease patterns, hospital practice and infection emerged. Concentrating on what began as a small particular problem, much larger issues emerged and were illuminated. Semmelweis bridged research, practice and policy, doing what might be called problem-oriented medicine.

In her contribution to this volume, Laycock discusses the ways in which researchers, policy makers and practitioners need to learn to work more closely if we are to move towards evidence-based practice and policy. Researchers and analysts, in particular, need to attune their ways of working to the realities of policy and practice. If useful contributions are to be made to problem-solving and crime reduction, adjustments to conventional presentational styles, methodologies, and forms of engagement with practitioners are needed. The chapter by Clarke and Goldstein nicely illustrates the benefits that can accrue from researchers working with practitioners. Their roles describe one way in which academics can help build local capacity for an analytic approach to problem-solving and crime prevention. They also, as they point out, identify a specific problem and potential response that may be relevant far beyond the local confines of the specific project in Charlotte-Mecklenburg.

There is, thus, a two-way track between problem-oriented analysis, addressing local or specific pressing problems, and basic research, identifying general attributes of problems and mechanisms lying behind them. In both cases, the translation into new practice conditions will require a close grasp of the underlying theory or principles and an ability to recognise their relevance.

There is also a two-way track between concrete problem analysis at different levels of jurisdiction/or potential intervention (Read and Tilley, 2000). In some cases, early indications of problems may come from local analysis, for further and wider interrogation at a "higher" level of administration. In other cases, patterns identified at a higher level will be checked out for their relevance at a lower level.

Constructive and innovative uses of suites of analyses and evaluations are able sometimes to identify new patterns and new mechanisms that can be put to use in preventive strategies. The contribution by Smith et al. (this volume) exemplifies ways in which theoretically informed secondary analysis of series of studies can yield new insights of potential use to crime prevention practitioners.

IMPLICATIONS

There is clearly a critical need for crime analysts in crime prevention. The role of the expert analyst is to sharpen definitions of problems — to identify crime sets in relation to which well-targeted preventive efforts have real scope for success. This is a high-level activity, requiring imagination and a firm grasp of research-based prevention paradigms. Only with creativity, informed by an understanding of well-developed and tested theory, will analysts be able to figure out constructive ways of looking at data sets to discern patterns open to preventive interventions. Such analysts will also be able to help devise promising strategies and tactics, drawing on research-based principles. There appear to be few jurisdictions where this currently occurs. There also appears to be a serious shortage of personnel who have the education, skills and disposition effectively to deliver the analytic services that are needed. It is not clear that many jurisdictions are configured in ways that are hospitable to the forms of analysis that might inform effective preventive strategies. Whilst progress is being made in refining techniques of analysis, in crime prevention theory, and in understanding what is involved in the appropriate application of that theory, the potential pay-offs can only be realised if the environment into which strong analytic capacity is inserted is capable to making good use of it. This will require the sort of ways of working described here by Clarke and Goldstein, Laycock, and Ekblom.

Address correspondence to: Nick Tilley, Department of Social Sciences, Nottingham Trent University, Burton Street, Nottingham NG1 4BU. E-mail: <tilley@home-office.swinternet.co.uk>.

REFERENCES

Bennett, T., K. Holloway and T. Williams (2001). *Drug Use and Offending: Summary Results from the First Year of the NEW-ADAM Research Programme.* (Findings #148.) London, UK: Home Office.

Braga, A., D. Kennedy and A. Piehl (1999). *Problem-Oriented Policing and Youth Violence: An Evaluation of the Boston Gun Project.* (A Final Report Submitted to the U.S. National Institute of Justice.) Cambridge, MA: Kennedy School of Government, Harvard University.

Brantingham, P.L. and P.J. Brantingham (1995). "Criminology of Place: Crime Generators and Crime Attractors." *European Journal of Criminal Policy and Research* 3(3):5-26.

Budd, T. (1999). *Burglary of Domestic Dwellings: Findings from the British Crime Survey.* (Home Office Statistical Bulletin 4/99.) London, UK: Home Office.

Cashmore, J., L. Gilmore, J. Goodnow, A. Hayes, R. Homel, J. Lawrence, M. Leech, J. Najman, I. O'Connor, T. Vinson and J. Western (1999).

Pathways to Prevention — Developmental and Early Intervention Approaches to Crime in Australia. Canberra, AUS: Commonwealth Attorney General's Department.

Clarke, R. (1999). *Hot Products: Understanding, Anticipating and Reducing Demand for Stolen Goods.* (Police Research Series, Paper No. 112.) London, UK: Home Office.

—— (1997). "Introduction." In: R. Clarke (ed.), *Situational Crime Prevention: Successful Case Studies* (2nd ed.). Guilderland, NY: Harrow and Heston.

—— (1992). "Introduction." In: R. Clarke (ed.), *Situational Crime Prevention: Successful Case Studies.* Guilderland, NY: Harrow and Heston.

—— and P. Mayhew (1988). "The British Gas Suicide Story and its Criminological Implications." In: M. Tonry and N. Morris (eds.), *Crime and Justice: A Review of Research,* vol. 10. Chicago, IL: University of Chicago Press.

Crawford, A. (1997). *The Local Governance of Crime.* Oxford, UK: Oxford University Press.

Curtin, L., N. Tilley, M. Owen and K. Pease (2001). *Developing Crime Reduction Plans: Some Examples from the Reducing Burglary Initiative.* (Crime Reduction Research Series, Paper No. 7.) London, UK: Home Office.

Eck, J. and W. Spelman (1987). *Solving Problems: Problem-Oriented Policing in Newport News.* Washington, DC: Police Executive Research Forum.

Ekblom, P. (1997). "Gearing up against Crime: A Dynamic Framework to Help Designers Keep up with the Adaptive Criminal in a Changing World." *International Journal of Risk, Security and Crime Prevention* 2(4):249-265.

Farrell, G. and K. Pease (eds.) (2001). *Repeat Victimization.* (Crime Prevention Studies, vol. 12.) Monsey, NY: Criminal Justice Press.

—— A. Edmunds, L. Hobbs and G. Laycock (2000). *RV Snapshot: UK Policing and Repeat Victimisation.* (Crime Reduction Research Series, Paper 5.) London, UK: Home Office

—— C. Phillips and K. Pease (1995). "Like Taking Candy: Why Does Repeat Victimisation Occur?" *British Journal of Criminology* 35(3):384-399.

Felson, M. (1998). *Crime and Everyday Life.* Thousand Oaks, CA: Pine Forge Press.

Forrester, D., S. Frenz, M. O'Connell and K. Pease (1990). *The Kirkholt Burglary Prevention Project: Phase II.* (Crime Prevention Unit Series, Paper No. 23.) London, UK: Home Office.

—— M. Chatterton and K. Pease (1988). *The Kirkholt Burglary Prevention Project.* (Crime Prevention Unit Series, Paper No. 13.) London, UK: Home Office.

Gabor, T. (1994). *"Everybody Does It!" Crime by the Public.* Toronto, CAN: University of Toronto Press.

Garland, D. (2001). *The Culture of Control.* Oxford, UK: Oxford University Press.

Gilling, D. (1997). *Crime Prevention: Theory, Policy and Politics.* London, UK: UCL Press.

Hughes, G. (1998). *Understanding Crime Prevention.* Buckingham: Open University Press.

Johnson, B., A. Golub and E. Dunlap (2000). "The Rise and Decline of Hard Drugs, Drug Markets, and Violence in Inner-city New York." In: A. Blumstein and J. Wallman (eds.), *The Crime Drop in America.* Cambridge, UK: Cambridge University Press.

Kennedy, D. (1997). "Pulling Levers: Chronic Offenders, High Crime Settings, and a Theory of Prevention." *Valparaiso University Law Review* 13(2):449-484.

Kershaw, C., T. Budd, G. Kinshott, J. Mattinson, P. Mayhew and A. Myhill (2000). *The 2000 British Crime Survey.* (Home Office Statistical Bulletin 18/00.) London, UK: Home Office.

Laycock, G. (2001). "Hypothesis-based Research: The Repeat Victimization Story." *Criminal Justice* 1:69-82.

—— (1997). "Operation Identification, or the Power of Publicity?" In: R. Clarke (ed.), *Situational Crime Prevention: Successful Case Studies.* Guilderland, NY: Harrow and Heston.

—— (1985). *Property Marking: A Deterrent to Domestic Burglary?* (Crime Prevention Unit Series, Paper No. 3.) London, UK: Home Office.

—— and R. Clarke (2001). "Crime Prevention Policy and Government Research: A Comparison of the United States and United Kingdom." *International Journal of Comparative Sociology* XLVI(1-2):235-255.

Pease, K. (1997). "Predicting the Future." In: G. Newman, R. Clarke and S. Shoham (eds.), *Rational Choice and Situational Crime Prevention.* Aldershot, UK: Ashgate.

Read, T. and N. Tilley (2000). *Not Rocket Science? Problem-solving and Crime Reduction.* (Crime Reduction Research Series, Paper No. 6.) London, UK: Home Office.

Rogerson, M., P. Ekblom and K. Pease (2000). "Crime Reduction and the Benefit of Foresight." In: S. Ballintyne, K. Pease and V. McLaren (eds.), *Secure Foundations: Key Issues in Crime Prevention, Crime Reduction and Community Safety.* London, UK: Institute for Public Policy Research.

Scott, M. (2001). *Problem-Oriented Policing: Reflections on the First 20 Years.* Washington, DC: U.S. Department of Justice, Community Oriented Policing Services.

Spelman, W. (1995). "Once Bitten, Then What?" *British Journal of Criminology* 35(3):366-383.

Tilley, N. (1996). "Demonstration, Exemplification, Duplication and Replication in Evaluation Research." *Evaluation* 2:35-50.

U.K. Department of Trade and Industry (2000). *Turning the Corner. Report of Foresight Programme's Crime Prevention Panel.* London, UK: author.

NOTES

1. It may, of course, be that "real effort increase" comprises a mechanism separate from, and additional to "perceived effort increase"?

THE TIME-WINDOW EFFECT IN THE MEASUREMENT OF REPEAT VICTIMIZATION:
A Methodology for its Examination, and an Empirical Study

by

Graham Farrell
University of Cincinnati

William H. Sousa
Rutgers University

and

Deborah Lamm Weisel
University of North Carolina

Abstract: *Crime control strategies and criminological theory have been increasingly informed by developments in the study of repeat victimization in recent years. As a consequence, the measurement of repeat victimization is an important issue. The outcome of the measurement of repeat victimization can influence the manner in which police and other agencies develop, implement and evaluate crime control efforts. In addition, the results of measurement can influence the theories and explanations that derive from empirical study. Among the several measurement issues that have been identified to date in relation to repeat victimization, a key issue is that of the "time-window effect." The term refers to the fact that the length of the period of observation directly affects the proportion of repeat victimization that is "captured." The present study has two key aims. First, it presents a method to measure the size of the time-window effect. Second, it tests this method em-*

pirically with residential burglary data from three cities. The implications for criminological research and crime control practice are then discussed.

INTRODUCTION

While the phenomenon of repeat victimization has long been recognized, it is only in the decade and a half since the publication of the Kirkholt project in Britain in the late 1980s (Forrester et al., 1989, 1990) that its significant implications for crime control and criminological study have been developed. This renewed interest in repeat victimization has led to a growing exploration of the implications for theories of crime, the understanding of crime and offending patterns in different areas, and the development of policy implications for agencies, including the police and victims services. There are several recent reviews of repeat victimization (Davis et al., 1997; Friedman and Tucker, 1997; Pease and Laycock, 1996; Pease, 1998). There is variation in the extent to which repeat victimization has been incorporated into crime control practice and crime research: a recent national-level review of policing practices in the U.K. observed that all police forces in that country had a policy on repeat victimization and were beginning to integrate that work into routine policing practice (Farrell et al., 2000). The study of repeat victimization is rapidly gaining ground in Australia (Criminal Justice Commission, 1997; Mukherjee and Carcach, 1998; Townsley et al., 2000; Morgan, 2001), in the Netherlands (Hakkert and Oppenhuis, 1998; Kleemans, 2001), and in relation to cross-national comparative study (van Dijk, 2001; Farrell and Bouloukos, 2001).

Despite significant developments in the understanding of repeat victimization and its prevention, many questions remain unanswered. Among these are methodological issues related to measurement, including what has been termed the "time-window effect." This issue is addressed here using police data relating to residential burglaries occurring in three large cities. The "time-window effect" is the term used to denote the fact that the proportion of crimes that appear to occur against the same targets will change with the length of the period during which crime is observed. The issue has received little study since it was outlined in 1993 in the following terms:

A study of crime in an area for a one week period will show virtually no repeat victimization. This is because crimes which are noted during the observed week may be repeats of crime the week before, or may be precursors of crimes in the subsequent week. Even though some of the crimes are in fact repeat crimes or linked to future repeat crimes, by research of this kind they are observed as "single-incident" crimes. Even if there are only six days between one incident and the next, only those where the prior crime took place on the first day of the study would have the repeat recorded as such.

Repeat victimization is therefore under-counted, and single-incident crimes are over-counted. The extent of the problem of the "time-window" of the research is proportional to the length of the period of observation. A study with a long reporting or recording period — perhaps several years of crime with dates and times of occurrence — will have virtually excluded this problem. A study with a very short time period has this problem acutely. In the study of school burglary and property crime mentioned [elsewhere in the monograph], this problem was tackled using a simple weighting formula to account for the under-estimate (Farrell and Pease 1993:19).

Despite this recognition of the time-window effect, it has received little theoretical or empirical attention. Yet two examples should demonstrate its importance and give justification to the present study. The first example relates to victim surveys. Enormous insight into crime and victimization has been gained in recent decades from crime victim surveys of the local, national and international variety. Typically, such surveys utilize a one-year reference period over which victimization experiences are measured. But what if this is not the optimal period in which to measure repeat victimization? The effect could be that, since it is already evident that repeat victimization plays such an important role in the make-up of crime, our current understanding of crime victimization patterns is significantly distorted.

The second example relates to the development, implementation and evaluation of local crime prevention projects by the police and other agencies. The authors have encountered many instances where practitioners have concluded that "There is no repeat victimization in my data," or that "Repeat victimization does not occur in my area." In some instances this may be true (although we have yet to encounter this to any significant extent), but in others it may be because many local crime audits utilize a data set that covers only a short period of time, to the extent that repeat victimization is virtually excluded. Our colleague Ken Pease tells of an instance when a police department "suddenly found" a significant level of repeat victimization in their crime data where none had previously existed — the day before he was due to visit them. The anecdote embodies the general notion that more than a cursory examination of data is necessary to reveal the rate of repeat victimization. Issues in the measurement of repeat victimization will influence the manner in which crime prevention efforts are developed, implemented and evaluated, at the local, national and international levels. It is not inconceivable that, in the longer term, these measurement issues could influence the rate of initiation of efforts to prevent repeat victimization. Hence, while the present study is primarily methodological in nature, it is evident that it has implications that are directly related to, and potentially significant for, policing and crime prevention practice and, more broadly speaking, for the manner in which crime is studied.

DATA AND METHOD

The present study uses data relating to residential burglaries reported to the police in Baltimore, Dallas and San Diego. These three large cities were selected in part because they had computer information systems that utilized a "justified" address field or an address "lookup table." This meant that the typing and spelling errors typical of many police data sets should not be encountered since each new burgled address entered into each system is automatically cross-referenced with a list of known street names for the city. This is a separate methodological issue that has been identified, but will be briefly rehearsed here. If, for example, the property at 23 Washington Place is burgled and entered in the computer as "23 Washington Place," then burgled again and entered as "23 WASHINGTON PL." (that is, using upper rather than lower case, and/or the truncation of the street name), analysis of the aggregate data may not recognize these burglaries as occurring at the same address. We therefore sought to minimize this possible source of methodological error from the outset. Data were collected from each city for a three-year period, producing data sets of between 20,000 and 40,000 burglary incidents for each.

This paper has two aspects. The first is a methodology for measuring the time window. The second is a case study in the use of that methodology. This statement of the nature of the methodology is important since it may prove that empirical studies using different data sources and crime types produce different findings. The development and utilization of a standardized methodology however, should allow knowledge in this area to develop with transparency. The methodology for the measurement of the time-window effect is conceptually simple: we compared rates of repeat victimization captured using data for different periods of time. More specifically, we split each three-year data set into 36 one-month data sets, and measured changes in the rate of repeat victimization as increasingly longer time windows were used. First we measured the proportion of repeats found in one month's data, then that found in two months' of data etc., up to 36 months' worth. Although conceptually simple, translating the concept into practice was somewhat more laborious. It involved writing algorithms to produce 36 separate analytic runs for each of the data sets, prior to the transformation and analysis of the results.

FINDINGS

As the work progressed, not only was the importance of using a longer period of data apparent, but the monthly incremental or marginal effect could be measured. The extent of repeat burglaries measured in only a few months' data was typically small and increased gradually, with similar patterns for each city. The findings are presented in full below, but two of the key findings were that, on average across the three cities:

(1) A one-year time window captures 42% more repeats than a six-month window;

(2) A three-year window captures 57% more repeats than a one-year window.

The percentage of burglaries observed to be repeats for time-windows of different numbers of months, for each city, is shown in Table 1, indexed to 100 at 12 months. Twelve months is probably the most commonly used and understood measurement period, since crime rates are typically annual, whether from victim surveys or other sources. The table shows that, for the present data sets, when only one month's worth of data are used, repeat burglaries constituted 33%, 38% and 38%, in Baltimore, Dallas and San Diego, respectively, of the number of repeats that were captured in that city's one-year study. When three years or 36 months of data were examined, it was found that repeat burglaries constituted 162%, 146% and 163% percent of the total city burglaries in comparison to a one-year time window.

Table 1: Volume of Repeat Burglaries Observed Using Different Time Windows, by City
(Indexed to 100 at 12 months)

Months	Indexed to 100 at 12 months		
	Baltimore	Dallas	San Diego
1	32.5	38.1	37.5
2	38.6	47.2	37.0
3	43.1	56.9	49.4
4	54.3	63.5	54.9
5	62.2	67.4	62.4
6	69.6	72.7	69.0
7	75.4	76.7	74.0
8	81.3	81.1	80.3
9	87.5	86.1	85.2
10	91.0	90.9	92.0
11	95.3	94.6	95.1
12	100.0	100.0	100.0
13	103.6	102.8	105.4
14	107.4	106.5	108.4
15	110.0	109.3	112.5
16	113.9	112.6	115.3
17	116.8	116.2	119.9
18	119.0	117.7	122.6
19	121.3	119.7	125.5
20	121.4	121.4	128.8
21	124.7	122.6	133.6
22	127.3	123.8	137.0
23	130.2	125.2	138.8
24	133.2	127.3	140.6
25	135.5	128.7	142.0
26	137.7	130.1	143.8
27	140.5	132.0	145.7
28	143.1	133.7	149.0
29	146.5	135.8	151.0
30	149.6	137.3	152.3
31	151.5	138.8	153.1
32	153.8	140.5	155.7
33	156.0	142.0	157.0
34	158.1	143.0	158.0
35	159.4	144.5	160.7
36	161.5	146.1	163.2

The results are more visually compelling when presented graphically. Whereas marginal revenue curves are common in the study of Economics, Figure 1 shows what are effectively marginal capture curves for the measurement of repeat burglary. The shape of the curve for each city reflects the marginal change in the rate of repeat burglaries captured for different time periods of study. The curves are clearly non-linear, demonstrating a diminishing marginal increase in the rate of repeats captured after a period of approximately 18 months. What proved quite surprising to the authors was that the shape of the curve was perhaps less pronounced than expected. While the increase in the rate of repeats begins to slow after around 18 months, it does not slow quickly, and the curve is still rising quite steeply after three years. Simple extrapolation from the curves suggests that even more repeats would be captured if even longer periods of data were available. It is possible that this is a factor inherent to the present data sets that may not prove generally replicable, and is a point returned to later as part of the discussion.

DISCUSSION

Issues are raised both by the general and specific shape of the time window effect in Figure 1. The amount of repeat burglaries captured increases rapidly at first, then becomes less as the time window expands. These diminishing marginal returns are as might be expected for two reasons. The first is that the cut-off effect of the study period at either end (failing to measure precursors and subsequent burglaries related to ones within the study period) will have less overall significance. They tend to produce an absolute rather than a relative effect. The second is that because repeats are known to occur quickly after victimization, then, after an optimal study period or time window has been reached, the overall effect of this phenomenon will diminish.

It is possible that the shape of the curves in Figure 1 may be steeper at the three-year point than those which future studies will show. This may occur since some of our present data combines residential burglaries from individual dwellings with that from multiple-dwelling apartment complexes where burglaries in individual apartments are grouped together at the same address. We propose that distinguishing between these different categories of residential burglary in future work may produce a more rapid decrease in the slope of the curves. This is for future replications to determine. For the present purposes, we conclude that while the specific effect of the time window may be slightly overstated, its general shape and nature (and hence the implications of the study) should be correct — despite the acknowledged limitation of the data sources. Future studies may find that the time-window effect tails off more quickly if apartment-specific data contain repeats that occur more quickly on average than those in the present data sets.

Figure 1

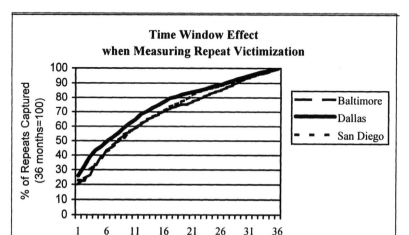

A preliminary interpretation of the findings can be attempted in terms of event dependency and risk heterogeneity. Event dependency is when one residential burglary leads to another at the same dwelling. This may be because the offender realized it was a suitable target, informed associates of such, or because something about the dwelling changed to make it visually more attractive to other offenders (such as a broken lock not having been replaced). Risk heterogeneity in this context refers to when the same dwelling is more attractive in comparison to others and remains so, attracting different burglars to commit otherwise unrelated burglaries. Event-dependency is the most compelling explanation of the fact that many repeats occur within a short period of time of the first crime. Crimes occurring for reasons related to risk heterogeneity would be more randomly distributed in time since they are unrelated. The time-window effect in the present study seems to lend support to both explanations. The time-window effect is greatest at first, concurrent with an event-dependent explanation of repeat burglary. However, the longevity of the time-window effect, although at a lower level, is concurrent with risk-heterogeneic explanations. As mentioned previously, the fact that some multiple-dwelling addresses are included in the data sets under the same street number may slightly influence these findings. Recording such burglaries as repeats would tend to overstate risk heterogeneity since burglaries at these separate dwellings would be more likely to have a more random distribution in time.

Although we have utilized data for three cities by means of demonstrating a general applicability of the findings, we propose that the present work needs replicating on different data sets and for different crime types before we can make wholesale generalizations. A call for replication of a study and recognition of its limitations is standard practice, however. It should not let us preclude the possibility of discussing possible implications for research, policy and crime prevention practice based upon the expectation that the findings will for the most part prove to be robust.

The present findings make a strong case that the rates of repeat victimization uncovered by crime surveys are gross underestimates. The typical one-year time-window of crime surveys may measure at least 50% less repeat victimization than actually occurs. If this is true, our understanding of crime patterns in general may be significantly skewed.

We would not expect that analyzing crime surveys that ask questions with a longer recall period than one year, such as the International Crime Victims Survey, will resolve the issue of the time window. This is because the memory-decay effect of interviewees when asked about crime occurring several years ago will almost certainly produce disproportionately low rates of repeat victimization. It is possible that the U.S. National Crime Victims Survey may shed some light upon these issues through the analysis of a three-year recall period data set compiled from repeated panel surveys. Such a data set was recently constructed by Brian Wiersema and Richard Titus (see Titus, 1997). However, though police crime records embody problems due to underreporting of crime, they are independent of memory problems, and as such may be preferable for the present purposes.

The present findings suggest the possibility that local crime audits, or any crime analysis that uses data covering only a short period of time such as a few months, may produce such grossly misleading findings as to be totally misleading. The implication of the present study is that, the longer the time window, the better.

The present findings lend further credence to the development of the prevention of repeat victimization as a crime prevention strategy. Levels of repeat victimization may well be significantly greater than has been recognized in most studies to date. However, the measurement of repeat victimization that is used to develop and evaluate crime prevention projects needs to be conducted with caution and with appropriate consideration given to methodological issues that may otherwise be assumed to be negligible.

Repeated residential burglary appears to be explained by both event dependency and risk heterogeneity. It also seems reasonable to expect that an interaction effect between the two will occur. Thus, an attractive residential property that is burgled will be more likely to be burgled again soon thereafter if the offender finds it to be a suitable target. Burglary due to risk heterogeneity should lead to event-dependent burglary.

For crime control strategies, utilizing victimization as a flag that triggers the placement of crime prevention resources will remain an efficient means of resource allocation. This is particularly true if risk heterogeneity is caused at least partly by simple visual cues to offenders that cause them to think a property is attractive. Such otherwise enduring cues of attractiveness might be altered at low cost if recognized during a police security survey of the property. Allocating police officers responsible for security surveys to properties that have proven vulnerable may thus be a simple means by which such resources could be used more effectively.

Repeat victimization prevention strategies that are able to reduce event dependent burglary in combination with those that address issues of risk heterogeneity (by the same or different tactics) may thus prove the most effective over all. When the possibility of detecting offenders who return to replicate a recent burglary is considered, then event-dependent burglaries become of greater practical significance.

There is a need for replication of the methodology used here with different burglary data sets, and also with different types of crime. The data used here were aggregated to the building level rather than the individual-address level. We would anticipate that the finding would change depending on the level of aggregation of the data. Although prediction is tricky and treacherous, we might anticipate some of the findings if this analysis were conducted at the individual-address level: we would expect the frequency of short-term repeats to increase, since repeats at the same address are more likely to be related repeats than those at different addresses within the same building. Consequently, we might anticipate that the time window is of lesser influence over longer periods (greater than a year) than was found in the present study. In terms of the graphical curve, we would expect it to level off more quickly, so that the marginal returns to extending the observation period decreased more rapidly after the first year. This is a hypothesis that future research might seek to test.

CONCLUSION

Methodological issues relating to the measurement of crime rates can be of importance for policy, practice, and crime theory. They can influence substantive knowledge about crime patterns and the way in which crime prevention strategies are developed. Such methodological issues should not be neglected in favor of the rush towards grandiose social theories, with which much criminological research is unfortunately concerned. We would propose that in the study of repeat victimization, continued attention to methodological issues of measurement should continue to inform theory, crime control, and policing practice.

Address correspondence to: Dr. Graham Farrell, Division of Criminal Justice, University of Cincinnati, PO Box 210389, Ohio 452221-0389. E-mail: <GrahamFarrell@compuserve.com>.

Acknowledgments: We would like to acknowledge the contributions of John Stedman and Ronald V. Clarke. In the three-cities studies, data collection in the police departments was undertaken by Katrina Okoli, Donald Smith and Elizabeth Perkins.

REFERENCES

Criminal Justice Commission (1997). *Hot Spots and Repeat Break and Enter Crimes: An Analysis of Police Calls for Service Data.* Brisbane, AUS: Research and Coordination Division, Criminal Justice Commission.

Davis, R.C., B.G. Taylor and R.M. Titus (1997). "Victims as Agents: Implications for Victim Services and Crime Prevention." In: R.C. Davis, A.J. Lurigio and W.G. Skogan (eds.), *Victims of Crime* (2nd ed.). Thousand Oaks, CA: Sage.

Farrell, G. and A. Bouloukis (2001). "International Overview: A Cross-national Comparison of Rates of Repeat Victimization." In: G. Farrell and K. Pease (eds.), *Repeat Victimization.* (Crime Prevention Studies, vol. 12.) Monsey, NY: Criminal Justice Press.

—— A. Edmunds, L. Hobbs and G. Laycock (2000). *RV Snapshot: UK Policing and Repeat Victimisation.* (Crime Reduction Research Series, Paper No. 5.) London, UK: Home Office.

—— and K. Pease (1993). *Once Bitten, Twice Bitten: Repeat Victimization and its Implications for Crime Prevention.* (Crime Prevention Unit Paper #46.) London, UK: Home Office.

Forrester, D., S. Frenz, M. O'Connell and K. Pease (1990). *The Kirkholt Burglary Prevention Project: Phase II.* Crime Prevention Unit Paper 23. London, UK: Home Office.

—— M. Chatterton and K. Pease (1988). *The Kirkholt Burglary Prevention Project, Rochdale.* (Crime Prevention Unit Paper 13.) London, UK: Home Office.

Friedman, L.N. and S.B. Tucker (1997). "Violence Prevention Through Victim Assistance: Helping People Escape the Web of Violence." In: R.C. Davis, A.J. Lurigio and W.G. Skogan (eds.), *Victims of Crime* (2nd ed.). Thousand Oaks, CA: Sage.

Hakkert. A. and E. Oppenhuis (1996). *Herhaald slachtofferschap.* (Repeat Victimization.) The Hague, NETH: Dutch Ministry of Justice.

Kleemans, E.R. (2001). "Repeat Burglary Victimization: Results of Empirical Research in the Netherlands." In: G. Farrell and K. Pease (eds.), *Repeat Victimization.* (Crime Prevention Studies, vol. 12.) Monsey, NY: Criminal Justice Press.

Morgan, F. (2001). "Repeat Burglary in a Perth Suburb: Indicator of Short-term or Long-term Risk?" In: G. Farrell and K. Pease (eds.), *Repeat Victimization.* (Crime Prevention Studies, vol. 12.) Monsey, NY: Criminal Justice Press.

Mukherjee, S. and C. Carcach (1997). *Repeat Victimisation in Australia: Extent, Correlates and Implications for Crime Prevention.* Canberra, AUS: Australian Institute of Criminology.

Pease, K. (1998). *Repeat Victimisation: Taking Stock.* (Crime Detection and Prevention Series, Paper No. 90.) London, UK: Home Office.

—— and G. Laycock (1996). *Revictimization: Reducing the Heat on Hot Victims.* (National Institute of Justice, Research in Action series.) Washington, DC: U.S. Department of Justice, National Institute of Justice.

Titus, R. (1997). "Segment-level Analysis of Residential Burglary Victimization." Paper presented to the American Society of Criminology, San Diego, November.

Townsley, M., R. Homel and J. Chaseling (2000). "Repeat Burglary Victimisation: Spatial and Temporal Patterns." *Australian and New Zealand Journal of Criminology* 33(1):37-63.

van Dijk, J. (2001). "Attitudes of Victims and Repeat Victims toward the Police: Results of the International Crime Victims Survey." In: G. Farrell and K. Pease (eds.), *Repeat Victimization.* (Crime Prevention Studies, vol. 12.) Monsey, NY: Criminal Justice Press.

FORECASTING THE FUTURE OF PREDICTIVE CRIME MAPPING

by

Elizabeth R. Groff
National Institute of Justice

and

Nancy G. La Vigne
The Urban Institute

Abstract: *While the use of mapping in criminal justice has increased over the last 30 years, most applications are retrospective – that is, they examine criminal phenomena and related factors that have already occurred. While such retrospective mapping efforts are useful, the true promise of crime mapping lies in its ability to identify early warning signs across time and space, and inform a proactive approach to police problem solving and crime prevention. Recently, attempts to develop predictive models of crime have increased, and while many of these efforts are still in the early stages, enough new knowledge has been built to merit a review of the range of methods employed to date. This chapter identifies the various methods, describes what is required to use them, and assesses how accurate they are in predicting future crime concentrations, or "hot spots." Factors such as data requirements and applicability for law enforcement use will also be explored, and the chapter will close with recommendations for further research and a discussion of what the future might hold for crime forecasting.*

INTRODUCTION

Methodological rigor in crime prevention initiatives has increased significantly in the last two decades. This is a result of partnerships between researchers and practitioners as well as the introduction of more user-friendly analytic software programs, including Geographic Information Systems (GIS) (Crime Mapping Laboratory, Police Foundation, 2000; Report of the Task Force on Crime Mapping and Data Driven Management, 1999; Weisburd and McEwen, 1997). GIS is often credited for providing a valuable analytic tool for the identification and analysis of crime problems as well as the development and assessment of crime prevention programs (Groff, 1996; Groff et al., 2000; La Vigne and Wartell, 1998, 2000). GIS has been used to produce maps depicting crime "hot spots" as well as to conduct spatial analyses that suggest relationships between crime and characteristics of the social and physical environments in which crime concentrations occur (Rich, 1995; Sherman and Weisburd, 1995; Weisburd and McEwen, 1997).

The use of GIS in law enforcement has increased significantly, and the variety of applications for crime control and prevention is quite broad (Dunworth et al., 1998; La Vigne and Groff, 2001; Mamalian and La Vigne, 1999; Crime Mapping Laboratory, Police Foundation, 2000). Most applications, however, are retrospective – that is, they examine criminal phenomena and related factors that have already occurred. While such retrospective mapping efforts are useful, the true promise of crime mapping lies in its ability to identify early warning signs across time and space and inform a proactive approach to police problem solving and crime prevention. Such efforts necessitate predictive models that identify "hot spots" of crime and disorder, as well as areas where crime is abating.

Recently, attempts to develop predictive models of crime have increased,[1] and while many of these efforts are still in the early stages, enough new knowledge has been built to merit a review of the range of methods employed to date. This chapter identifies the various methods, describes what is required to use them, and assesses how accurate they are in predicting future crime concentrations, or "hot spots."[2] This review covers methods ranging from simple predictions based on the locations of past events to highly sophisticated modeling methods employed by researchers. Factors such as data requirements and applicability for law enforcement use will also be explored, and the chapter will close with recommendations for further research and a discussion of what the future might hold for crime forecasting.

It should be noted that it is beyond the scope of this paper to provide detailed information and accompanying algorithms for the methods reviewed herein. Rather, the intent is to describe these methods with an emphasis on data requirements, ease of use, and applicability to crime prevention. Each method is appropriately cited to enable the reader to obtain more specific information and provide guidance to those wishing to employ the methods themselves.

WHY PREDICT CRIME?

The ability to predict the locations of future crime events can serve as a valuable source of knowledge for law enforcement, both from tactical and strategic perspectives. From a traditional policing perspective, predictive mapping can inform a police department's deployment efforts, helping to allocate patrols more efficiently and reduce response times. Despite the increased emphasis on proactive policing, the core of police work remains that of responding to calls for service, making effective deployment strategies paramount to a well-functioning police department.

From a more proactive standpoint, problem-oriented policing efforts may be enhanced by a more accurate scanning of areas with crime problems, in that one can examine both distributions of past crimes and predictions of future concentrations. As detailed below, some of these predictive methods also provide information on "leading indicators," or explanatory variables, which can aid in the analysis stage of problem-oriented policing. Such indicators offer the ability not only to predict future crimes, but to identify underlying causes of those future hot spots. Thus, predictive mapping can assist in the identification of crime problems and enable officers to target intervention efforts to very narrowly defined geographic areas.

Predictive mapping holds promise for improving the identification of areas in which to focus interventions, but it also may improve the way those interventions are implemented. A common criticism of crime prevention efforts is that crime is simply displaced — most often geographically — rendering the intervention ineffective. Studies have demonstrated that displacement is not at all inevitable, and that when it does occur 100% of crime is not displaced (Eck, 1993; Hesseling, 1995). Nonetheless, successful crime prevention strategies consider potential displacement possibilities and craft interventions based upon those considerations. Thus, predictive mapping can help law enforcement to anticipate areas of displacement, and may lead to targeting the intervention in a broader geographic area in order to reduce the possibility of its occurrence. Likewise, predictive mapping may be used to enhance the potential "halo" or "diffusion of benefits" of an intervention, whereby it has a beneficial effect beyond the places that were targeted. Clarke and Weisburd (1994) offer ways in which diffusion of benefits may be enhanced, including the concentration of resources on highly visible or attractive targets to give the impression to potential offenders that the intervention is more widespread that it actually is. Predictive mapping can help identify those attractive targets, thus bolstering this spillover effect.

This discussion of the potential uses of predictive mapping is by no means exhaustive, but it is designed to illustrate the valuable contributions that predictive models might offer, and emphasizes the importance of this relatively new area of inquiry. Before reviewing the various predictive methods that have been employed, it is important to examine the theoretical underpinnings of this topic.

THE ROLE OF THEORY IN PREDICTIVE MAPPING

As described in detail below, various means of forecasting crime events and locations exist, and not all of them can be considered "modeling." Some methods are strictly atheoretical, relying on past events to predict future ones. Other methods, however, are developed by modeling the behavior of likely offenders, making it important to review the theory underlying these efforts because theory can play an important role in guiding the selection of independent variables, or leading indicators.

Perhaps the most germane theories for forecasting purposes are the rational choice perspective and routine activities theory. Both assume that crime is purposive and that individuals are self-determining: when people commit crime, they are seeking to benefit themselves, and certain calculations are involved in determining whether the criminal act will yield positive results (Clarke, 1997). Thus, offenders are influenced by situational and environmental features that provide desirable — or undesirable — offending opportunities. These theories are based upon the belief that criminals engage in rational (if bounded) decision-making (Becker, 1968; Cornish and Clarke, 1986), and that characteristics of the environment offer cues to the offender that promising opportunities for crime exist (Brantingham and Brantingham,1978, 1981; Newman, 1972; Cohen and Felson, 1979; Harries, 1980; Wilson and Kelling, 1982).

The practical implications of these theories are that even motivated criminals may nonetheless be deterred from committing crime if they perceive a potential target to be too risky, to involve too much effort, to yield too meager a profit, or induce too much guilt or shame to make the venture worthwhile (Clarke, 1997; Clarke and Homel, 1997). From a predictive modeling perspective, then, these theories have the potential to guide the selection of independent variables with a focus on those that characterize desirable targets — and in turn, desirable locations — of crime. Further, theory-based modeling enables us to identify which factors influence crime target selection, and thus inform crime prevention efforts. The models described below include an assessment of whether they are supported by theory, and the extent to which they inform prevention efforts.

THE ROLE OF GIS IN PREDICTIVE MODELING

While geographic information systems (GIS)[3] are most often associated with data aggregation and display, the technology is capable of serving a variety of purposes. In terms of crime forecasting, GIS can be used at the front end, as a data manipulator; in the analysis phase as a spatial analysis engine; at the back end, for display purposes; or throughout the research project. Currently, GIS is used most frequently in the front end as a geocoder and data aggregator. The ability to geocode[4] records in a database to coordinates on the earth's surface unlocks the potential for spatial analysis of phenomena. Once these locations can be displayed, they can be aggregated to whatever boundary is appropriate for the analysis. On the back end, GIS is most often used as a visualization tool. The crime forecasts that are generated by statistical models can be displayed both on the screen to facilitate interactive analysis and in the form of hard copy maps, which are more portable. Both types of output can be used to visually identify concentrations and patterns and to communicate those findings. Finally, GIS has great potential as a data analysis tool in and of itself. The rest of this section describes how spatial analysis and "map algebra" can be used in a GIS to develop spatial models to predict crime.

A layer of polygon grids in a vector GIS or a raster GIS are required in order to take advantage of grid cell-based modeling.[5] In both types of GIS, the study area is divided into a series of equal-sized cells that together form a grid. Each cell is assigned a value based on the quantity of the variable being measured that it contains. A grid is created for each attribute to be used in the model. One advantage to raster GIS is that it is easy to represent continuous data such as distance from another cell (e.g., distance from a major road) or degree of concentration (e.g., density of crime). Once the individual layers are calculated, they can then be used as parameters in a mathematical equation.

Another capability of a raster GIS is the ability to incorporate the effects of neighboring grid cell values on a grid cell. In ArcView's Spatial Analyst Extension, this is known as a "focal function" (ESRI, 1998). The focal function computes a new value for each cell in a grid based on the "neighborhood of cells" defined.[6] This is analogous to a spatial lag using the queen pattern since all cells that share a side or a corner are included up to the specified neighborhood size. These new "smoothed" cell values can then be used in the final model.

The use of methods that involve GIS tends to require both broader and more in-depth skill sets. While only a basic level of GIS knowledge is needed to display the results of a statistical technique on a map, geocoding requires more skill, and using extensions such as Spatial Analyst® to build models requires even more specialized knowledge. Encouragingly, there have been enhancements to Spatial Analyst® that have made it easier to learn and to use (Ormsby and Alvi, 1999).[7] There are several major advantages to using GIS in developing a model for forecasting crime. As mentioned before, a GIS can use data in a spreadsheet and spatially enable it through geocoding. Once spatially enabled, those data can then be aggregated to whatever areal unit is most appropriate to the analysis. These functions of a GIS are important whether or not the model is implemented in GIS. Finally, the ability to visualize patterns in the data cannot be overstated and makes GIS a valuable tool for communicating the results of an analysis. Thus, the phrase "predictive crime mapping" used throughout this chapter is broadly applied to a variety of methods that use GIS in any number of points throughout the forecasting process.

REVIEW OF METHODS

Hot Spots

The most common method of "forecasting" crime in police departments is simply to assume that the hot spots of yesterday are the hot spots of tomorrow. Crime analysts prepare maps of crimes that have already occurred and those maps are used to deploy officers and to identify areas in need of intervention. While surprisingly scant research exists to test this assumption, the few studies we have identified suggest that the effectiveness of this approach depends upon the time period employed. Spelman (1995) found that examining past crimes over a one-month period is not a particularly powerful predictor — hardly better than chance, yet one year of data predicts with 90% accuracy.[8] This suggests that hot spots may flare up and diminish over relatively short time periods, but that these flare-ups nonetheless occur in the same places over time, creating longer-term trends. Thus, law enforcement agencies that examine last week's crime statistics to deploy patrols may find it more useful to identify hot spots based on an entire year's worth of data.

One means of testing the persistence of hot spots is to analyze the extent to which they coincide over the course of several years. Adams-Fuller's (2001) examination of hot spots of homicide in three U.S. cities found that the vast majority of homicide hot spots persisted over time,[9] suggesting that past history may indeed be an accurate predictor of future hot spots, at least in the long-term.

Adams-Fuller (2001) also attempted to understand the root causes of hot spots by examining their socio-economic and environmental characteristics. She found that most historical homicide hot spots had public housing, were located in economically depressed sections of cities, contained drug markets, and had major thoroughfares running through them, providing easy access into and out of the area. Her research clearly illustrates the ability to integrate theoretical explanations of crime with the search for hot spots. In fact, hot spot methods are one-dimensional without the inclusion of contextual variables.

There are many ways in which researchers and analysts identify hot spots (for a thorough review, see Jefferis, 1998). The most simplistic approach is to use GIS to create graduated circles, the radii of which reflect the number of events. While this method requires minimal GIS skills, it also has its drawbacks, in that these circles can often overlap, making it difficult to visually discern patterns of concentrations. A more commonly applied hot spot method among researchers is the use of spatial statistical software such as STAC[10] or CrimeStat.[11] These methods generate a set of ellipses that represent the highest concentrations of points.

In recent years, methods for visualizing hot spots have increasingly relied on a raster GIS to interpolate a surface of crime based on reported crime events. The analysis results have the look of a "weather map," and are extremely popular for communicating crime patterns for a jurisdiction. However, this type of hot spot identification treats the known crime events as a sampling of the continuous surface of all crime. In other words, it creates data points in geographic locations where crimes have not occurred, based on averages between actual data points. As a consequence, large-scale maps (e.g., at the neighborhood level) often depict higher crime rates than were reported to the police. This disconnect between reported crime and interpolated crime has yet to be adequately resolved. An additional caveat with any of these methods is that the output is based upon user-defined criteria (e.g., band width and search area) and there are no standard guidelines for what those criteria should be.

The popularity of these methods stems from their relative ease of implementation — at least as compared to other methods discussed in this chapter — as well as their ease of interpretation. The ease of implementation is directly attributable to the existence of software to automate the algorithms for identifying clusters and drawing an ellipse. The methodology for this was outlined almost 25 years ago by Getis and Boots (1978), but languished until incorporated in a software product. Since 1998, several other free software programs have automated the creation of hot spots using ellipses.[12] Thus the current popularity of hot spots may be due to the fact they are relatively easy to generate and understand.

Repeat Victimization

The above research indicates that temporally aggregated hot spots may serve as accurate predictors of crime, but that relying on shorter previous time periods for predictive purposes is less effective. The exception to these research findings relates to "hot dots" (Pease and Laycock, 1996) rather than hot spots: that is, the repeat victim rather than the high-crime area. The concept of repeat victimization is now well established in the criminological literature (for an early review, see Farrell, 1995): those individuals or places that have been victimized once are likely to be victimized again, and the time course to subsequent victimization is a few short months (Anderson et al., 1995; Farrell and Pease, 1993; Polvi et al., 1990). This research suggests that past victimizations of individual addresses, places, and businesses can be very accurate predictors of future victimizations, even when relying on the previous month's victimization.

The crime prevention benefits of focusing on repeat victims to prevent subsequent crimes is well established (for a summary of the preventive impact of repeat victimization strategies on crime, see Pease, 1998), and raises the question: Can repeat victimizations of individuals and places be used to predict not just hot dots, but hot spots? Very few researchers to date have examined the extent to which hot spots are composed of repeat victimizations, except for those who have focused on residential burglary. Both Bennett (1996) and Townsley et al. (2000) found that one-third of all burglaries reported in the hot spot areas under study were repeat burglaries. While Morgan (2001) found a lower degree of repeat victimization concentration within high-crime areas, the areas under study combined multiple census districts and thus were larger than the average hot spot. In his research, Morgan also found what he terms "near repeats": residences close to repeat victims were likely to be victimized. Finally, a recent publication by Farrell and Sousa (2001) concludes that while repeat victimizations and hot spots do coincide, some hot spots experience more repeat victimization than others and may vary based upon crime type.

The research on repeat victimization suggests that much more could be learned from further examination of the composition of hot spots and the extent to which repeat victimizations could be used to predict not just future victimizations, but future hot-spot areas. Such studies should explore this question across different sized hot spots as well as different types of crime problems, and should explore the "near repeat" concept in further detail. Depending on future research findings in this area, repeat victimization has the potential to provide a simple method that could be employed by users of all skill levels and does not require the use of GIS. The limitation of this approach is that it does not tell us specifically what it is about the predicted hot spots that makes them hot, limiting the extent to which the method would inform prevention efforts.

Univariate Methods

There are a variety of univariate methods available to predict crime. These methods use previous values of one variable to predict its future value. They are attractive because of their straightforwardness: univariate methods require a minimum of data collection since they involve only one variable. Additionally, they are atheoretical and thus do not demand any thought about which variables should be included in the analysis. These methods range from simple random walk and naïve lag 12 to more sophisticated models that incorporate both seasonality and time trends. Among police practitioners the most frequently used crime prediction methods are so-called "naïve" univariate ones (Gorr et al., 2002; Gorr and Olligschlaeger, 2001). The two naive univariate methods used by police are the random walk[13] or and the naïve lag 12.[14] The random walk method is a good predictor of series in which there are frequent pattern changes (e.g., to predict stock market behavior) because it reflects those changes immediately. However, it is a poor predictor when the series to be forecasted has seasonality or time trends (Gorr et al., 2002; Gorr and Olligschlaeger, 2001). While these basic univariate methods are by far the most straightforward methods of predicting crime, they are also unfortunately by far the least accurate (Gorr et al., 2002; Gorr and Olligschlaeger, 2001).

More sophisticated univariate methods are available that more accurately predict crime levels by including seasonality in the model,[15] accounting for time trends using exponential smoothing[16] and pooling data[17] (Gorr et al., 2002; Gorr and Olligschlaeger, 2001). However, the addition of these steps also makes the methods more complicated for the user.

While all the more sophisticated univariate methods offer improvements over the simpler ones, the exponential smoothing methods have two main advantages as tools for crime forecasting. First, they offer the ability to account for changes in crime over time rather than relying on the current period to forecast the next period. Second, they are the most accurate type of method when the goal is to forecast "small to medium-level" changes in crime (Gorr and Olligschlaeger, 2001)

While the univariate techniques outlined above share many characteristics, they vary in the sophistication of both the software employed and the skills required to use them (Table 1). All of the techniques use area-level data and the results can be displayed easily in a desktop GIS. Both the random walk and the naïve lag 12 are very easy to compute and can be calculated within standard spreadsheet packages. The classical decomposition model and the exponential smoothing models are more sophisticated and are most easily calculated using a standard desktop statistical package (e.g. SPSS® or SAS®). The more sophisticated models also require an analyst with more advanced statistical training. Consequently, the investment in personnel and equipment is higher for the more sophisticated models than the simpler ones.

In an effort to shed some light on the comparative accuracy of these forecasting methods and others, Gorr et al. (2001) employed a rolling-horizon experimental design to test 10 different combinations of data-driven methods and univariate models to account for seasonality and time trends (Gorr et al., 2002; Gorr and Olligschlaeger, 2001). Of the techniques tested, the Holt exponential smoothing with pooled seasonality was the most accurate, and the simple exponential smoothing model with pooled seasonality was second best. These results clearly demonstrate that using citywide, pooled measures of seasonality offers more accuracy regardless of the exponential smoothing method used. Their findings that the random walk and Naïve Lag 12 methods were the least accurate at forecasting crime is of immense importance because these statistics are widely used in the field (Gorr et al., 2002; Gorr and Olligschlaeger, 2001).

The good news from Gorr and Olligschlaeger's (2001) study is that the more sophisticated univariate methods predict as well as the far more complicated multivariate methods for cases with small to medium changes in crime levels. Specifically, they note that while the pooled exponential smoothing model is not typically used in police agencies, the model is relatively simple to implement and, if used to forecast in areas with an average of 30 or more events per month, it offers good forecast accuracy. Given that simple exponential smoothing methods have already been recommended in one of the most frequently cited crime analysis books (Gottlieb et al., 1998), the real challenge may be in encouraging widespread adoption of these methods by analysts. One strategy for achieving this goal would be to make the methods easier for crime analysts to implement.

Table 1: Comparison of Methods

Method	Unit of Analysis	Data Require-ments	Software Requirements	Skill Requirements	Advantages	Disadvantages
Past Hot Spots	Hot spot	Address level data	GIS, possibly spatial statistical software or raster-based GIS to identify hot spots	Basic GIS skills required Knowledge of spatial statistical softer or Raster-based mapping helpful	Easy to compute and interpret	Assumes hot spots persist over time Uncertain what level of temporal aggregation is appropriate Does not inform prevention strategies re: what makes targets desirable
Repeat Victimization	Address	Address level data	Spreadsheet. GIS helpful but not necessary	Basic	Easy to compute and understand	Assumes "hot dots" correspond with hot spots Does not inform prevention efforts re: what makes targets desirable
Random Walk	Precinct or some other areal unit	Area level data	Spreadsheet or Statistical Program to Compute Forecast and desktop GIS to aggregate data and display results	Basic spread-sheet/statistical knowledge Basic desktop GIS knowledge	Easy to compute and understand Very sensitive to changes	Does not use a series of historical figures (just previous month) Does not account for seasonality

Method	Unit of Analysis	Data Requirements	Software Requirements	Skill Requirements	Advantages	Disadvantages
Naïve Lag 12	Precinct or some other areal unit	Area level data	Spreadsheet or statistical program to compute forecast and desktop GIS to aggregate data and display results	Basic spreadsheet/statistical knowledge Basic desktop GIS knowledge	Easy to compute and understand Very sensitive to changes	Does not use a series of historical figures
Classical Decomposition by Individual Areal Unit	Precinct or some smaller areal unit if N>30	Area level data	Statistical Program that does classical decomposition and seasonal indices Desktop GIS to aggregate data and display results	Knowledge of forecasting techniques Basic desktop GIS knowledge	Use of district level seasonality measure had mixed effectiveness at increasing accuracy	Requires specialized software to compute statistics Requires knowledge of forecasting techniques Does not forecast large and/or sudden changes in crime well
Classical Decomposition Pooled for Entire Jurisdiction	Precinct or some smaller areal unit if N>30	Area level data	Statistical Program that does classical decomposition and seasonal indices Desktop GIS to aggregate data and display results	Knowledge of forecasting techniques Basic desktop GIS knowledge	Use of pooled seasonality measure across the entire jurisdiction increases homogeneity of data that, in turn, improves prediction accuracy Accurate in forecasting incremental crime changes	Requires specialized software to compute statistics Requires knowledge of forecasting techniques Does not forecast large and/or sudden changes in crime well

Method	Unit of Analysis	Data Require-ments	Software Requirements	Skill Requirements	Advantages	Disadvantages
Exponential Smoothing	Precinct or some smaller areal unit if N>30	Area level data	Statistical program that does exponential smoothing Desktop GIS to aggregate data and display results	Knowledge of forecasting techniques Basic desktop GIS knowledge	Use of exponential smoothing allows statistic to take into account changes over time Most accurate in forecasting small or moderate changes in crime	Requires specialized software to compute statistics Requires knowledge of forecasting techniques Does not forecast large and/or sudden changes in crime well
Leading Indicator Models: Linear Regression	Areas as small as 4000 by 4000 foot grid cells as long as N>30 for each grid cell	Grid level data	Spatial statistical program (e.g. Space-Stat, Splus Spatial Stats module, or PC SAS 7) that is able to compute a spatial lag Desktop GIS to aggregate data and display results	Intermediate knowledge of statistics Intermediate desktop GIS knowledge	Can incorporate sudden changes in crime rates in forecasts Can be used to forecast crime changes that are significantly different from normal variation	Requires specialized software to compute statistics Requires intermediate knowledge of statistics and software to implement the models

Method	Unit of Analysis	Data Requirements	Software Requirements	Skill Requirements	Advantages	Disadvantages
Point Process Model	Police precincts	Census data at block group level Reported crime data at precinct lvel	C plus programming language	Advanced knowledge of programming to create customized model Advanced knowledge of algorithms/processes underlying point process models	Indicates which independent variables are good predictors	Difficult to replicate Use of large areal units limits precision Narrows areas for future deployment rather than targeting specific areas for interventions
Artificial Neural Networks		Address-level calls-for-service data	Requires custom programming (Olligschlaeger used C programming language) and significant computing power	Advanced knowledge of neural networks, programming	Potentially more robust than other methods	Very data intensive Requires significant computing power and time Requires a high degree of expertise No statistical tests of significance Unable to determine which inputs (independent variables) are providing predictive power

Method	Unit of Analysis	Data Requirements	Software Requirements	Skill Requirements	Advantages	Disadvantages
Raster GIS Models	Grid Cells	Point or area level data	Raster GIS	Intermediate to advanced knowledge of statistics and forecasting* Advanced GIS knowledge*	Variables used in the model are theory-driven Great visualization tool both for indicator variables and crime predictions Ability to include spatial relationships in model	Requires specialized GIS software Can require advanced knowledge of statistics and forecasting. Model used as example was better at predicting low risk areas than high risk ones

*Depending on the complexity of the model

Leading Indicators

"Leading indicator" multivariate methods focus on using current and past values of independent variables to predict the future value of the dependent crime variable (Gorr and Olligschlaeger, 2001). The "leading indicators" term in the title of the model refers to specific characteristics of areas or neighboring areas (e.g., shots fired, calls for service, disorderly conduct offenses, etc.) for which their rise or fall in current and previous months can be used to predict future values of the dependent crime variable.

There are three issues that must be addressed when specifying a "leading indicator" model related to crime (Gorr and Olligschlaeger, 2001). First, leading indicator methods require the identification of leading indicator variables before the model can be used. Identification of the appropriate leading indicator variables requires a thorough review of the literature, and grounds this method in theory. Developing theory-based leading indicators is a time consuming task that is critical to the success of the model.[18]

Second, because crime forecasts are typically done for short time periods and across smaller areas, often there are not enough events to develop robust model parameters. Thus, it is important to pick an areal unit that is large enough to provide adequate numbers of observations. In general, the greater the volume of crime the more reliable the forecasts will be, and the smaller the volume of crime the more variable the data will be and the more unreliable the forecasts. Gorr and Olligschlaeger (2001) determined that a grid with 4,000-foot cells was the smallest grid cell that would still provide reliable forecasts.

The third issue when specifying this type of model concerns the development of leading indicator measures at the same geographic and time scales as the dependent variable (e.g., grid cell data that vary by month). Geographic information systems (GIS) have made the spatial issue much less problematic than in the past, since a GIS enables automated aggregation of points to customized areas. Thus, both crime types and leading indicator variables can be aggregated to the same areal units easily. Furthermore, Gorr and Olligschlaeger found that selected Part 2 crimes and CAD calls are leading indicators of Part 1 dependent variable crimes. Hence police are among the few organizations fortunate enough to generate their own leading indicators.

One advantage of this technique is the ability to use spatial econometric methods that enable the inclusion of spatial and temporal lags in the model. Spatial lags allow the explicit modeling of the effects of the values in neighboring cells on the value of the subject cell.[19] Temporal lags allow the modeling of the effects during previous time periods on the study time period.

Over all, leading indicators show great promise since they are the only method that has the ability to "see pattern changes coming" (Gorr, 2001 and Gorr and Olligschlaeger, 2001). Thus, they are very good at predicting large changes in crime levels, while extrapolative methods are better for small to medium changes. Gorr (2001) recommends that police agencies routinely use both extrapolative methods, such as the Holt two parameter exponential smoothing method with pooled seasonality and a leading indicator model. He recommends that if the leading indicator model forecasts a large change, one should use it because the technique forecasts correctly about half the time. If it does not forecast a large change, then one should use the extrapolative method's results.

While promising, these methods require significant expertise on the part of the end user. The analyst must be familiar with multivariate statistical methods and have access to statistical or spreadsheet software programs to calculate the statistics. A geographic information system is necessary to aggregate the chosen leading indicator measures to the areal unit used in the study, whether it is a grid cell or some other area such as a police beat.

Point Process Model

A new method being employed by Brown (2001) and his colleagues is based on the theory of point patterns and multivariate density estimation, and can best be described as a point process model (Brown, 2001). The modeling is akin to neural networks in that there is training involved, and past data are used to predict future events. In essence, this approach glues multivariate models together and uses notions from kriging and density estimation (Brown, 2001).

Brown et al. (2000) developed this predictive model based upon the preferences of offenders, or what they term "event initiators": past behavior illustrating the preferences of offenders is used to model both when and where future crimes will occur: "...we do not regard the past crime intensity at a site as a direct factor to influence how soon criminals are going to strike again. However, this past behavior does tell us about the preferences of site selectors and we directly model those preferences..." (Brown et al., 2000:4). The output of the model is a probability surface indicating likely areas of future crimes.

Brown and colleagues compared their point process model's predictive powers to that of using past hot spots to predict future ones, testing both models by plotting commercial and residential burglaries. For all but one comparison, the point process model statistically outperforms the comparison model at the 90% confidence level. Mean percentile scores are calculated to demonstrate how well the model performs, essentially indicating more about how the model performs over all than about its ability to forecast at a particular location. The model narrows down at-risk areas to 15-25% of all potential areas, thus enabling law enforcement to better target resources. The smaller the percent, the better the model, because police can more narrowly focus resources. According to Brown (2001), the model is limited from producing smaller percentages because explanatory data were generated from census block groups, which do not provide enough variation across space.

While this method shows promise, in its current form it is not possible for others to replicate and apply it because it was custom programmed for a specific research purpose. Furthermore, the approach requires both high-level programming skills as well as knowledge of kriging and density estimation. Nonetheless, this method has distinct advantages over others in that it is informed by theory (rational choice) and identifies which variables have explanatory power.

Artificial Neural Networks

One of the earliest efforts to do predictive crime mapping was that of Olligschlaeger (1997), who employed a "feed-forward network with backpropogation" to predict areas where future drug markets will emerge. Best known to laypeople as artificial intelligence, the type of neural network model employed by Olligschlaeger is capable of learning extremely complex space-time patterns (Olligschlaeger, 1997). According to Olligschlaeger, "The goal is to map the input units to a desired output similar to the way in which the dependent variable is a function of the independent variables in a regression analysis. The difference is that regression analysis uses linear direct mapping whereas multi-layer feed-forward networks use non-linear direct mapping" (Olligschlaeger, 1997:325). In essence, the network is trained by feeding it past data and adjusting the weights assigned to the input units; when the network is processed, the error signal is fed back, or "backpropogated" through the network to adjust the weights until, ultimately, the error signals are minimized (Olligschlaeger, 1997). GIS was employed in conjunction with this model in order to process spatial and temporal data, including data aggregation and determination of spatial and temporal lags. This was accomplished by overlaying a grid and summing the data points that fall into each cell, as well as employing contiguity measures.

The network was used to predict drug markets. Inputs included 35 months of weapon-related, robbery, and assault-related calls-for-service; the relative proportions of residential and commercial properties in each cell; and a seasonality index. The model's performance was tested against Ordinary Least Squares (OLS) regression analysis and the random walk method. A comparison of R-squareds indicated that the network's forecasting abilities were superior (Olligschlaeger, 1997). In more recent work, Olligschlaeger and Gorr (2001) found that neural networks outperform multiple regression leading indicator models when the set of leading indicators is rich and numerous.

While this method holds promise, there are no statistical tests of significance associated with it, precluding the ability to determine which inputs (independent variables) are providing predictive power. The model is somewhat atheoretical and the method requires a high degree of expertise, making it difficult to replicate.

Polygon Grid/Raster GIS Methods

As stated earlier, GIS can be used throughout a research project to incorporate spatial relationships in the crime forecast. In Groff and La Vigne (2001), we used a combination of polygon grid cells and raster-based GIS to generate an opportunity surface for residential burglary. We identified a set of variables based on the theories of routine activities, rational choice and environmental criminology, and used GIS to operationalize those variables.

We were very interested in modeling the effects of the values of surrounding properties on a particular property. For example, we wanted to model the effect of having a substandard housing unit or vacant unit nearby. In order to incorporate the effect of surrounding grid cell's values, each layer was recalculated using a focal neighborhood function within the GIS.[20] Map algebra was used to combine the new grid cell values in each layer to produce an overall risk index surface for residential burglary. Reported burglaries were then plotted on top of this new opportunity surface to determine how well the model predicted. The percentage of cells that were accurately predicted was used to empirically compare the actual burglaries with the opportunity surface. Two categories of burglaries were examined: any burglary event and repeat burglaries.

Interestingly, the model predicted repeat burglaries better than locations with both single and repeat burglaries. This finding leads to questions about the strength of the predictive power of repeats: could the repeat-address locations serve as a proxy for all of these other variables used to create the opportunity surface? If so, it would support the use of past repeat victimization addresses to predict future hot spots. There is a definite need for more research to test the validity of this line of reasoning. However, even if repeat burglaries are good predictors of future hot spots we still do not know why they are more likely to be future hotspots.

The method outlined above can be used with any point data or with polygon data. However, the amount of data available definitely determines the level of detail that can be incorporated in the model. Thus, in relation to methods discussed above, this approach has the potential to be data-intensive if used at the micro level. Most data sets that are routinely collected do not have the level of detail required to do this type of modeling. For instance, our analysis required specific characteristics of houses/properties and their surrounding areas that may be difficult to obtain (e.g., housing quality, incivilities, lighting level, etc.). The model can also be used with less specific data sets and at a macro level of analysis, but its results are likely to be less accurate.

In addition to having GIS skills, an analyst employing grid-based methods must understand how to build models. The level and breadth of statistical knowledge required will depend upon the sophistication of the model. In the case of the example above, the model was designed for use by law enforcement agencies, so it was purposely kept straightforward and simple. However, as the field evolves, the demand for more complex and more accurate models will continue to grow. This growth is evident in the demand for the integration of spatial statistics and GIS. If achieved, this integration would enable an analyst to combine statistical rigor with effective modeling of context to produce more accurate crime forecasts.

CONCLUSIONS

As mentioned at the beginning of this chapter, our purpose was to review the current methods employed for predictive crime mapping, from basic approaches currently used by crime analysts, to sophisticated models developed by researchers. Our method was to assess each forecasting approach on the basis of accuracy, data requirements, hardware and software requirements, and ease of use. What we learned is that in many respects, this review is premature. The more sophisticated approaches described in this chapter are still very much in the development stages and can best be considered "alpha versions" that have yet to be tested by the end users. Our review also suffers from the fact that there are few published, refereed works on these methods. Furthermore, the variability of the methods themselves precludes a head-on comparison of the accuracy of one versus another. Nonetheless, this is an appropriate point in which to take stock of both current practice and future development, as this review may inform mid-course corrections.

Perhaps the most important finding from this review is that, while technology has improved our ability to create, maintain and manipulate data, there is still much work to be done before we can effectively forecast crime trends. GIS has enabled the creation of geographic data (both crime and crime-related) and the integration of data from a variety of sources. However, the most frequently used methods for evaluating the data are the same ones that have been in use for about 30 years. In fact, the current state of knowledge seems to indicate that at least two of the existing and relatively straightforward methods (those based on exponential smoothing) are as effective — if not more so — than more advanced ones.

This is not to say that further examination of new methods should be abandoned. Recent innovations have yet to gain widespread acceptance and we will not be sure of their accuracy until further research is conducted. Specifically, in order to better evaluate the methods that have been created, the field needs more head-to-head comparisons of some of the newer, more sophisticated methods versus the more traditional, univariate ones. These comparisons must also consider the question of what qualifies as an "accurate" prediction, both in relation to the scale of the predicted area and the quality of the prediction itself. Is a 500-foot grid cell necessary, or will a 4,000-foot area (such as the one used by Gorr et al.) suffice? How accurate does the spatial prediction have to be in order to inspire confidence by police officers? If we can identify that there will be an increase in crime, how accurate does the prediction really need to be for effective intervention? Finally, how small does the unit of analysis need to be in order to be practically useful? These are important questions for further investigation; until they are answered, individual researchers and analysts will continue to experiment with their own methods — possibly reinventing the wheel — rather than learning from each other.

One troubling aspect of many of the methods reviewed here is the lack of guiding theory, which not only can help develop better models but also helps us interpret a model's performance so that prevention efforts are improved. The accuracy of the multivariate methods depends upon the appropriateness of the variables included in the model. Since the identification of appropriate variables is grounded in theory, one without the other will only have limited utility. Many of these methods are also very complicated, requiring a high level of specialized statistical and modeling expertise as well as a large volume of data that are not often easily available on a micro level. Ultimately, our goal is to find relatively a simple method that is both accurate and can tell us something about why future hot spots are likely to emerge in certain locations, so as to inform prevention efforts.

Once effective crime forecasting methods are identified, perhaps the most important challenge will be educating practitioners so they can employ them. There is a significant leap that must take place before crime analysts begin to use even the simplest of these methods, and this leap may well be achieved through the automation of forecasting techniques into a user-friendly software program. A parallel can be drawn with the diffusion of statistical techniques and GIS. With the advent of cheap, easy to-use software, the use of statistical software (e.g., SPSS®) increased. The same scenario occurred with GIS software. Recent history suggests that the adoption of sophisticated crime forecasting software would follow the same trajectory if automated tools were available. However, the development of a new set of analytical skills will still be necessary in order to use these new methods.

There are several conclusions to be drawn from this review of crime forecasting methods. First, the more complicated methods are not always better predictors. More research is needed that evaluates the relative performance of methods. Second, many questions surrounding the choices made in sophisticated models must be empirically answered before the models will accurately and consistently perform (e.g., size of grid cell size and spatial lag). Third, additional research is needed to identify the input variables in the multivariate models. Choice of variables is critical to the success of the model and must be informed by theory. Finally, the connection between the output of models and how they translate into practice is extremely important. In fact, perhaps the most important measure of a crime forecasting technique may be whether it aids in crime control and prevention.

Note: Points of view are those of the authors and do not necessarily represent the views of the U.S. Department of Justice or the National Institute of Justice, or the Urban Institute.

Address correspondence to: Nancy G. La Vigne, The Urban Institute, Justice Policy Center, 2100 M Street, NW, Washington, DC 20037. E-mail: <NLaVigne@ui.urban.org>.

Acknowledgments: We would like to thank Professor Wilpen Gorr for his thoughtful and constructive comments on an earlier version of this manuscript. Any errors, misrepresentations or inaccuracies are the fault of the authors.

REFERENCES

Adams-Fuller, T. (2001). "Historical Homicide Hot Spots: The Case of Three Cities." Doctoral dissertation, Howard University, Washington, DC.

Anderson, D., S. Chenery and K. Pease (1995). *Biting Back: Tackling Repeat Burglary and Car Crime.* (Home Office Crime Prevention Unit Series, No. 58.) London, UK: Home Office.

Anselin, L. (1999). Spatial Data Analysis with SpaceStat™ and ArcView®. Ann Arbor, MI: SpaceStat (http://www.spacestat.com).

—— Cohen, D. Cook, W.L. Gorr and G. Tita (2000). "Spatial Analysis of Crime." In: D. Duffee (ed.), *Measurement and Analysis of Crime and Justice, Criminal Justice 2000,* vol. 4. Washington, DC: Office of Justice Programs, National Institute of Justice.

Antenucci, J., K. Brown, P. Croswell and M. Kevany, with H. Archer (1991). *Geographic Information Systems: A Guide to the Technology.* New York, NY: Van Nostrand Reinhold.

Bailey, T.C. and A.C. Gatrell (1995). *Interactive Spatial Data Analysis.* Essex, UK: Addison Wesley Longman Ltd.

Becker, G.S. (1968). "Crime and Punishment: An Economic Approach." *Journal of Political Economy* 76:169-217.

Bennett, T. (1996). "Identifying, Explaining, and Targeting Burglary Hot Spots." *European Journal of Criminal Policy and Research* 3:113-123.

Brantingham, P.J. and P.L. Brantingham (1981). "Notes on the Geometry of Crime." In: P.J. Brantingham and P.L. Brantingham (eds.), *Environmental Criminology.* Prospect Heights, IL: Waveland Press.

—— and P.L. Brantingham (1978). "A Theoretical Model of Crime Site Selection." In: Krohn and Akers (eds.), *Crime Law and Sanctions.* Beverly Hills, CA: Sage Publications.

Brown, D.E. (2001). Conversation with Professor Donald E. Brown, Chair, Systems and Information Engineering Department, University of Virginia. August 3, 2001.

—— H. Liu and Y. Xue (2000). "Mining Preferences from Spatial-Temporal Data." Paper presented at First SIAM International Conference on Data Mining, Chicago, IL, April.

Brown, R.G. (1963). *Smoothing Forecasting and Prediction of Discrete Time Series.* Englewood Cliffs, NJ: Prentice Hall.

Clarke, K.C. (1997). *Getting Started with Geographic Information Systems.* Upper Saddle River, NJ: Prentice-Hall.

Clarke, R.V. [1992] (1997). *Situational Crime Prevention: Successful Case Studies* (2nd ed.). Albany, NY: Harrow and Heston.

—— and R. Homel (1997). "A Revised Classification of Situational Crime Prevention Techniques." In: S.P. Lab (ed.), *Crime Prevention at a Crossroad.* Cincinnati, OH: Anderson.

—— and D. Weisburd (1994). "Diffusion of Crime Control Benefits: Observations on the Reverse of Displacement." In: R.V. Clarke (ed.), *Crime Prevention Studies* (vol. 2). Monsey, NY: Criminal Justice Press.

Cohen, L.E. and M. Felson (1979). "Social Change and Crime Rate Trends: A Routine Activities Approach." *American Sociological Review* 44:588-608.

Cornish, D.B. and R.V. Clarke (1986). *The Reasoning Criminal: Rational Choice Perspectives on Offending.* New York, NY: Springer.

Crime Mapping Laboratory, Police Foundation (2000). "Integrating Community Policing and Computer Mapping: Assessing Issues and Needs Among COPS Office Grantees." Final Report. Washington, DC: Department of Justice, Office of Community Oriented Policing Services (http://www.usdoj.gov/cops/pdf/toolbox/computer_mapping/e032k0046.pdf).

Dunworth, T., G. Cordner, J. Greene, T. Bynum, S. Decker, T. Rich, S. Ward and V. Webb (1998). "Police Department Information Systems Technology Enhancement Project: ISTEP." Washington, DC: Department of Justice, Office of Community Oriented Policing Services (http://www.usdoj.gov/cops/cp_resources/pubs_ppse/istep.htm).

Eck, J.E. (1993). "The Threat of Crime Displacement." *Criminal Justice Abstracts* 25:527-46.

ESRI (1998). *Working with Spatial Analyst: Three Day Course Notebook with Exercises and Training Data.* Redlands, CA: ESRI.

Farrell, G. (1995). "Predicting and Preventing Revictimisation." In: M. Tonry. and D.P. Farrington (eds.), *Building a Safer Society.* (Crime and Justice, vol. 19.) Chicago, IL: University of Chicago Press.

—— and K. Pease (2001). *Repeat Victimization.* (Crime Prevention Studies, vol. 12.) Monsey, NY: Criminal Justice Press.

—— and W. Sousa (2001). "Repeat Vicitimization and Hot Spots: The Overlap and Its Implications for Crime Control and Problem-Oriented Policing." In: G. Farrell and K. Pease (eds.), *Repeat Victimization.* (Crime Prevention Studies, vol. 12.) Monsey, NY: Criminal Justice Press.

—— and K. Pease (1993). *Once Bitten, Twice Bitten: Repeat Victimization and its Implications for Crime Prevention.* (Home Office Crime Prevention Unit Series No. 46.) London, UK: Home Office.

Getis A and B. Boots (1978). *Models of Spatial Processes.* Cambridge, UK: Cambridge University Press.

Gorr, W.L. (2000). "Approaches to Crime Predictive Modeling." Paper presented at annual Crime Mapping Research Conference, San Diego, December.

—— (2001). Conversations with Professor Wilpen Gorr, H. John Heinz III School of Public Policy, Carnegie Mellon University. August 16 and 17, 2001.

—— A. Olligschlaeger and Y. Thompson (forthcoming in 2002). "Assessment of Crime Forecasting Accuracy for Deployment of Police." *International Journal of Forecasting.*

—— and A. Olligschlaeger (2001). *Crime Hot Spot Forecasting: Modeling and Comparative Evaluation.* (Draft Final Report.) Washington, DC: Office of Justice Programs, National Institute of Justice.

Gottlieb, S., S. Arenberg and R. Singh (1998). *Crime Analysis: From First Report to Final Arrest.* Montclair, CA: Alpha Publishing.

Groff, E. (1996). "Information Systems for Community Policing: A Micro-Analysis of Crime." *Proceedings of the Urban and Regional Information Systems Association.* Park Ridge, IL.

—— and N.G. La Vigne (2001). "Mapping an Opportunity Surface of Residential Burglary." *Journal of Research in Crime and Delinquency* 38(3):257-278.

—— J.K. Fleury and D. Stoe (2000). "Strategic Approaches to Community Safety Initiative (SACSI): Enhancing the Analytic Capacity of a Local Problem-Solving Effort." Washington, DC: National Institute of Justice (http://www.ojp.usdoj.gov/nij/sacsi/index.html).

Harries, K.D. (1980). *Crime and the Environment.* Springfield, IL: Charles C. Thomas.

Hesseling, R.B.P. (1995). "Displacement: A Review of the Empirical Literature." In: R.V. Clarke (ed.), *Crime Prevention Studies,* vol. 3. Monsey, NY: Criminal Justice Press.

Jefferis, E. (1998). "A Multi-method Exploration of Crime Hot Spots." Presented at the Academy of Criminal Justice Science's Annual Conference (http://www.ojp.usdoj.gov/cmrc/pubs/hotspot/intro.pdf).

La Vigne, N.G. and E. Groff (2001). "The Evolution of Crime Mapping in the United States: From the Descriptive to the Analytic." In: A. Hirschfield and K. Bowers (eds.), *Mapping and Analysing Crime Data: Lessons from Research and Practice.* London, UK: Taylor and Francis.

—— and J. Wartell (2000). *Crime Mapping Case Studies: Successes in the Field* (vol. 2). Washington, DC: Police Executive Research Forum.

—— and J. Wartell (1998). *Crime Mapping Case Studies: Successes in the Field.* Washington, DC: Police Executive Research Forum.

Makridakis, S., S.C. Wheelright and V.E. McGee (1983). *Forecasting: Methods and Applications* (2nd ed.) Chichester, UK: Wiley.

Mamalian, C.A. and N.G. La Vigne (1999). "The Use of Computerized Crime Mapping by Law Enforcement: Survey Results." (National Institute of Justice Research Preview.) Washington, DC: National Institute of Justice.

Mathsoft, Data Analysis Division, (1999). *S-Plus Guide to Statistics* vol. 1. Seattle, WA: Mathsoft.

Morgan, F. (2001). "Repeat Burglary in a Perth Suburb: Indicator of Short-term or Long-term Risk?" In: G. Farrell and K. Pease (eds.), *Repeat Victimization.* (Crime Prevention Studies, vol. 12.) Monsey, NY: Criminal Justice Press.

Newman, O. (1972). *Defensible Space: Crime Prevention Through Urban Design.* New York, NY: Macmillan.

Olligschlaeger, A.M. (1997). "Artificial Neural Networks and Crime Mapping." In: D. Weisburd and T. McEwen (eds.), *Crime Mapping and Crime Prevention.* Monsey, NY: Criminal Justice Press.

Ormsby, T. and J. Alvi (1999). *Extending ArcView GIS.* Redlands, CA: ESRI.

Pease, K. (1998). *Repeat Victimisation: Taking Stock.* (Home Office Crime Prevention and Detection Series, Paper No. 90.) London, UK: Home Office.

—— and G. Laycock (1996). *Reducing the Heat on Hot Victims.* Washington, DC: Bureau of Justice Statistics.

Polvi. N., T. Looman, C. Humphries and K. Pease (1990). "Repeat Break and Enter Victimisation: Time Course and Crime Prevention Opportunity." *Journal of Police Science and Administration* 17:8-11.

Rengert, G. F., S. Chakravorty, K. Henderson and T. Bole (2000). *Evolution of Drug Markets: an Analysis of Susceptibility, Accessibility, Opportunity, and Police Action. Draft Final Report.* Washington, DC: Office of Justice Programs, National Institute of Justice.

Report of the Task Force on Crime Mapping and Data Driven Management (1999). *Mapping Out Crime: Providing 21st Century Tools for Safe Communities.* Washington, DC: U.S. Department of Justice and National Partnership for Reinventing Government (http://www.npr.gov/library/papers/bkgrd/crimemap/content.html).

Rich, T. (1995). *The Use of Computerized Mapping in Crime Control and Prevention Programs.* (National Institute of Justice Research in

Brief.) Washington, DC: Office of Justice Programs, National Institute of Justice.

Sherman, L.W. and D. Weisburd (1995). "General Deterrent Effects of Police Patrol in Crime 'Hot-Spots': A Randomized Controlled Trial." *Justice Quarterly* 12:625-648.

—— P.R. Gartin and M.E. Buerger (1989). "Hot Spots of Predatory Crime: Routine Activities and the Criminology of Place." *Criminology* 27:27-55.

Spelman, W. (1995). "Criminal Careers of Public Places." In: D. Weisburd and J. Eck (eds.), *Crime and Place*. (Crime Prevention Studies, vol. 4.) Monsey, NY: Criminal Justice Press.

Townsley, M., R. Homel and J. Chaseling (2000). "Repeat Burglary Victimisation: Spatial and Temporal Patterns." *The Australian and New Zealand Journal of Criminology* 33(1):37-63.

Weisburd, D. and T. McEwen (1997). "Introduction." In: D. Weisburd and T. McEwen (eds.), *Crime Mapping and Crime Prevention*. (Crime Prevention Studies, vol. 8.) Monsey, NY: Criminal Justice Press.

Wilson, J.Q. and G.L. Kelling (1982). "Broken Windows: The Police and Neighborhood Safety." *The Atlantic Monthly* 249(3):29-38.

NOTES

1. The National Institute of Justice has funded a number of grants to develop predictive models, drawing on spatial regression analysis, environmental modeling, neural network analysis and other methods, and having the capability of being displayed within a GIS (www.ojp. usdoj.gov/cmrc).

2. This paper is limited to predictions of geographic concentrations of crimes; assessments of "geographic profiling" and other predictive methods to identify the location and time of future serial crimes are beyond the scope of this paper.

3. A GIS consists of hardware, software, and peripherals to create, store, analyze and output geographic data.

4. The term geocode refers to the process of assigning coordinates on the earth's surface to an address or some other location identifier (e.g. zip code, census tract etc.).

5. The terms raster and vector refer to the two main types of geographic information system data models. In a vector GIS all features are repre-

sented as points, lines or polygons. While a raster GIS is grid cell based. For more information on basic GIS concepts please see K.C. Clarke (1997) and Antenucci et al. (1991).

6. The neighborhood size can be defined by distance from the target cell (e.g., 200 feet) or by specifying a number of cells to use (e.g., 10 cells).

7. Spatial Analyst is a raster GIS extension to ArcView. Version 2.0 of the software includes a visual model builder that allows models to be created and saved so that parameters can be changed and the model run again automatically (i.e., in a "batch" mode). This is a vast improvement over previous versions, for which each layer had to be created in raster form and recreated every time the analyst changed a parameter of the model.

8. It should be noted that this assessment was based upon an examination of hot spots at specific types of locations — high schools, public housing projects, subway stations, and parks and playgrounds — rather than all hot spots distributed throughout the study area.

9. Persistence was defined as the intersection of five or more hot spot ellipses (based on annual data) over a ten-year period.

10. The software began as a DOS-based program, and was under the auspices of the Illinois Criminal Justice Information Authority (ICJIA). The Spatial and Temporal Analysis of Crime (STAC) is available from the ICJIA's website (http://www.icjia.org/public/index.cfm?metaSection= Data&metaPage=StacFacts).

11. CrimeStat is a suite of spatial statistical software tools that is available from NIJ's Crime Mapping Research Center at http://www.ojp. usdoj.gov/cmrc/tools/welcome.html#crimestat.

12. Three free software programs that contain a hot spot routine using ellipses are ReCAP (http://www.sys.virginia.edu/research/crime.html), RCAGIS (http://www.databasefiles.com/_dbf/0000007e.htm), and Crime Stat (see footnote 11).

13. The random walk method simply uses the current time period to predict the next time period. One example of this method is when the number of Burglaries in May is used to predict the number of Burglaries in June.

14. In the Naïve Lag 12 model the value for the same time period in the previous year is used to predict the value for the current year. Using the above example, Burglaries in June of 2000 would be used to predict Burglaries in June of 2001.

15. Classical decomposition is used to calculate a seasonal index for each month in relation to other months in the series using multiplicative adjustments to the trend model.

16. Exponential smoothing methods are typically used to forecast short-term changes in a series and to try and balance sensitivity to structural changes against accuracy of forecasts. Simple exponential smoothing utilizes past values of a series and averages them with exponentially decreasing weights. This method takes into account both the trends and variability in a data series. Recent values in data series with a high degree of variability receive less weight than recent values in series that show a definitive trend. This method "smoothes" out variability in the data series and makes it easier to distinguish actual trends in the data. Another method is Holt's Two-Parameter Linear Exponential Smoothing method (Gorr et al., 2002; Gorr and Olligschlaeger, 2001), which integrates a smoothed time trend model with the generation of two smoothing constants (one for level and one for trend) to create a more accurate forecast of crime. The smoothing constants for both techniques are generated using a grid cell search.

17. Pooling involves combining the data for areas and then computing a common index across all those areas. Pooling provides more homogenous data that, in turn, improve the accuracy of predictions. In Gorr et al.'s (2002) tests they identified the best model for predicting crime as the one that used classical decomposition to calculate pooled seasonal indices by crime type for the whole city (Gorr et al., 2002; Gorr and Olligschlaeger, 2001). Gorr (2001) notes that one potential enhancement to the pooling method he used in his previous research would be to pool the crime data by type of land use (e.g., several categories of residential vs. commercial, etc.). This method has both enough homogeneity in the data and a large enough sample size to get more accurate predictions than those achieved when the pooling was by crime type across the city.

18. Gorr and Olligschlaeger (2001) identified 25 measures of drug calls, 17 measure of property crime and 27 measures of violent crime that they used as leading indicators in their work (Figures 4-6).

19. For more information about incorporating spatial and temporal lag techniques into research see Anselin, 1999; Bailey and Gatrell, 1995 and Mathsoft, Data Analysis Division, 1999.

20. For instance, we accounted for the influence of nuisance violations in neighboring grid cells by having the values in those cells be used in the calculation of the target cell.

HOT SPOTS AND COLD COMFORT: THE IMPORTANCE OF HAVING A WORKING THERMOMETER

by

Michael Townsley
University of Liverpool

and

Ken Pease
University College, London

Abstract: *The effective deployment of police resources is heavily de-pendent on the quality of analysis available. Over the past decade, the term "hot spots" has come to be commonplace in policing, and it is rare to find a police agency that cannot or does not identify spatial cluster-ing of criminal incidents. Equally rare is the consideration of any other type of clustering. The following study highlights the existence of other dimensions that may provide more accurate tactical directives for the deployment of resources ("hot groups") or at least qualify the spatial clustering ("hot times").*

INTRODUCTION

The spatial distribution of crime has been of interest to criminolo-gists for the entire life of the field. While the level of interest has waxed and waned according to the prevailing theoretical perspective, in the last decade both the technological and theoretical advances have made micro-level spatial analyses possible.

One area of intense activity has been the identification of crime "hot spots," i.e., areas of spatial concentration of crime. Their appeal lies in the promise that crime is so prevalent in certain locales that concentrating police resources there will lead to greater impact on crime levels than targeting other areas. If crime is spatially skewed, so, the argument goes, should police attention.

Of somewhat less prominence in the literature has been temporal variation of hot spots (notable exceptions are Ratcliffe [2000] and Rengert [1997]). Understanding temporal variation is self-evidently crucial to policing hot spots, not least in choosing when to apply resources. This paper looks at one aspect of analysing temporal variation, namely the temporal stability of hot spots relative to the point of their designation as such. Some analysis focused on that point is followed by a wider discussion of how temporal issues should or could inform the policing of places consistently or intermittently high in rates of crime.

Allocation of Police Resources To Designated Hot Spots

The context for this article is provided by the authors' work in a Basic Command Unit (BCU) of a British police force. In common with other BCUs in the force area, the practice has been to designate sub-areas as hot spots, and to address the problems thereby highlighted. Our role was to facilitate the development of evidence-led policing as part of day-to-day operations. Members of the command team wished to know how effective actions taken after hot-spot designation were in reducing levels of crime. The most common response was High Visibility Policing (HVP) — deployment of extra patrols in the troubled area. Hence, the issue which they wished to be addressed concerned trends in crime around the point of hot-spot designation.

Data

The set of hot spots examined were identified between May and November 2000. Typically the designated hot spot was a beat, and a type of crime was identified as the problem. Where the area circumscription was more specific (e.g., the Smith Street area) the hot spot was not included in the analysis reported here because of problems in knowing where the Smith Street area ended.

Officers learned about their local hot spots primarily by means of an internal document designed to disseminate information and analyses to BCU staff. During the six month period in question, 62 issues of the internal document were produced. To restate, these set out both current hot spots and the crimes that made them hot.

Recorded crime data for the BCU were extracted and aggregated by week, beat and crime type. The time period spanned March 2000 to January 2001, overlapping the hot-spot range at both ends to allow the scrutiny of pre- and post-hot spot crime levels.

Method

Having identified beats and periods designated as hot spots, the next step was to look at trends in crime before, during and after the point of hot-spot period. While there was no consistent tendency for crimes to fall after hot-spot designation, the variation in numbers of crimes per unit time (some very small), and the number of different patterns, taken together, made it difficult to detect any overall reduction. It was decided to aggregate by crime type. This was done by indexing the first week of hot spot in an area as week zero, and summing the number of relevant crime events in that week, the week before hot-spot designation, and so on, across designated hot spots. The choice was made to separate crime types because hot-spot designation may well have effects which differ according to the crime type addressed.

A period of seven weeks before and seven weeks after the week of hot-spot designation was chosen to depict any trends. Thus, levels of crime were measured for 15 weeks for each hot spot.

RESULTS

The analysis thus yielded three graphs, for autocrime, domestic burglary and violence. In addition, all 42 hot spots were combined to measure overall trends.

Figure 1 shows the trend in crime around the designation of an area as an autocrime hot spot. That is to say, each area designated as an autocrime hotspot has the first week of the designation set to 0, and the number of autocrimes seven, six, five etc., weeks before and after the hot-spot designation plotted. Week 0 reflects different calendar weeks for each of the areas, whose data are aggregated to yield the graph. It will be noted that the decline after hot-spot designation appears to be merely the continuation of a decline that had started some weeks earlier, the bulk of which occurred before hot-spot identification.

Figure 1: Autocrime Trends around Designation of Autocrime Hot Spot (N=20)

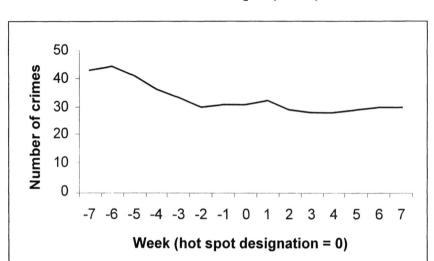

Figure 2 shows the aggregate level of domestic burglary hot spots pre- and post-hot-spot designation. In a similar way to autocrime hot spots, there was a decrease in burglary counts before hot-spot identification. The decrease continued after hot-spot designation, but at a more modest rate. Unlike pre-hot spot patterns for autocrime, domestic burglary started to decline quite close to hot-spot designation.

Figure 3 shows the aggregate level of violence hot spots pre- and post-hot-spot designation. Levels of violence are lower than the preceding crime classifications, and consequently are susceptible to fluctuation to a greater extent. This makes interpretation of pre- and post-hot spot levels less straightforward. Nonetheless, the weeks immediately prior to violence hot-spot designation enjoyed declining crime levels.

Figure 2: Domestic Burglary Trends around Designation of Hot Spot (N=13)

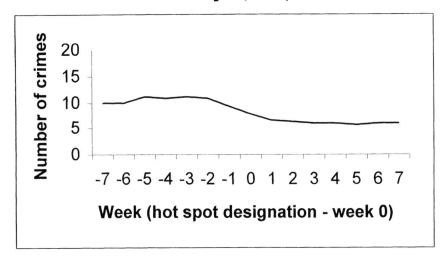

Figure 3: Violent Crime Trends around Designation of a Violence Hot Spot (N=9)

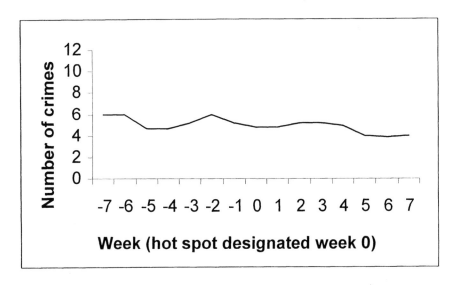

Figure 4 shows the aggregate crime level of all hot spots pre- and post-hot-spot designation. Given the consistent trends for the separate crime types, it is not surprising that similar pre-hot-spot levels were observed. The maximum weekly crime level was observed at six weeks prior to hot-spot identification.

Figure 4: Crime Trends Around Designation of Hot Spot (N=42)

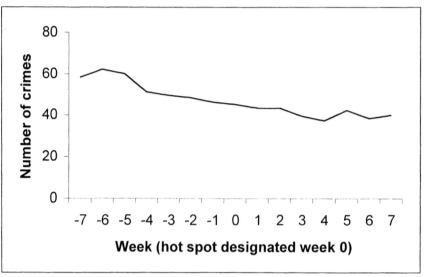

What does this analysis amount to? The conclusions tentatively reached are:

- When the number of crimes involved is low, their rate is volatile. It may be less helpful for police operational purposes to designate hot spots than to describe other kinds of regularities and predictability in crime rates.

- Hot spots, when designated, are on average cooler than they had been a few weeks before. This is possibly a consequence of the phenomenon known as regression to the mean. When something is chosen because of its extremity, it will tend to become less extreme. Alternatively, officers on the streets may have already identified a cluster of crime, and so the pre-designation decline can be ascribed to good police work.

- There is no indication that designation of a hot spot speeds the decline of crime already in place.

DISCUSSION

Good police work and regression to the mean provide alternative accounts of the pre-designation crime decline that seems common across crime types. Distinguishing between these alternatives is difficult, but could be addressed by finding how well neighbourhood officers know current hot spots in advance of their designation. If they were good at this task, good police work would be the leading explanatory account. If they were not, regression would be favoured.

The Designation of Hot Spots

The exercise reported above led to a renewed consideration of hot-spot designation. There is a fairground game in which figures pop up from holes randomly, the player having to strike the figures with a mallet before they retreat into the hole. This is a good metaphor for the designation and policing of transient hot spots. To anticipate, the work reported above led to a process where areas are selected for special consideration on the basis of their enduring high rates of crime.

There are many different techniques to calculate hot spots, each having strengths and weaknesses over rival methods. It is important to emphasise that no single method has found universal approval.

There are two main ways of designating hot spots: (a) the relative method, hot-spotting places that are high in crime compared to themselves at all times, and (b) the absolute method, hot-spotting places that are high in crime compared to all places at all times. The difference between the relative and absolute methods can be likened to the comparison of winter in Barbados and summer in Alaska. Barbados has a high average temperature. Local minima exceed the majority of local maxima of other areas (absolute method), whereas the latter has a low average temperature such that local maxima (considered Alaskan heat waves), would barely be registered by other areas (relative method).

Before the exercise reported above, hot-spot designation tended to be by the relative method outlined. Discussion in the light of the exercise had the effect of de-emphasising hot spots generally in resource allocation in favour of the SARA (Scanning, Analysis, Response and Assessment) process central to problem-oriented policing.

Although the hot spots which comprised the data in the analysis reported above were not entirely systematic in their calculation, the method of analysis which was being developed at the time, and which reflected the current thinking, was as follows. A hot spot is a police beat where the weekly level of a crime type is one standard deviation above the mean for that area calculated over the last 52 weeks. In other words, beats with high crime counts relative to themselves were to be deemed hot spots. In this way, an area will, in any week, have a .165 probability of having a crime level that high, assuming the normal distribution is an appropriate choice in this context. The number of standard deviations can be changed to lower or heighten the threshold at which hot-spot designation takes place. The higher the number of standard deviation units above the mean which triggers hot-spot designation, the more confident we can be that a real problem has been identified, and the fewer spurious hot spots will be designated. In the following table, the number of hot spots identified at different thresholds has been calculated, using the beat as the geographical unit of a hot spot, that would be expected by chance alone.

Table 1: Number of Hot Spot Beats Produced Using Different Thresholds

Hot spot threshold	Expected number of beats identified as hot spots[a]
Avg + 0.5 standard deviations	15.73
Avg + 0.75 standard deviations	11.56
Avg + 1 standard deviation	8.08
Avg + 2 standard deviations	1.19
Avg + 3 standard deviations	0.09

[a] Based on an area containing 50 beats

Table 1 demonstrates that changing the threshold for identifying hot spots alters the number of hot spots inversely. We would expect to see about 8 beats every week with a crime count that exceeds average +1 standard deviation, due purely to random variation. Increase the threshold to two standard deviations, and the number of hot spots falls to a little over one hot spot (again, due to random variation).

If ten beats (the force norm) were identified exceeding the one standard deviation threshold, about eight would be due to random variation alone.[1] The remainder would be considered actual high-crime areas and therefore hot spots. Identifying the "random" hot spots may be achieved through looking at the recent history of the area or the magnitude of the crime problem. Areas with low crime counts find it comparatively easy to become a hot spot because proportional increases are great compared to absolute increases.

There are a number of problems with this method used to identify hot spots. The principal one is that if random variation is driving the beat's high crime rate, it will diminish of its own accord. Two implications arise from this scenario: a false success rate (crime goes down, but not due to analytical work), and wasted resources (which could have been allocated to areas in legitimate need).

Absolute hot spots — those areas with high crime levels with respect to all areas at all times — are now to be dealt with through a SARA process, the problem-solving model developed by Eck and Spelman (1987) in the well known Newport News project and used by many police agencies around the world. Briefly, it is characterised by a cycle of analysis, intervention and assessment with clear objectives to indicate when the problem is solved. Hot spots that do not respond to the usual High Visibility Policing tactic, or are clearly complex from the outset, will be assigned SARA status.

The primary advantage of the SARA process is that it is not constrained by geography. A geographically defined absolute hot spot may frame the problem to which a SARA may be applied, but place is only one of a range of variables in terms of which a problem may be framed. In short, crime concentration is not purely spatial. Other useful, but rarely mentioned dimensions that display crime concentration include the temporal ("hot times") and the demographic ("hot groups"). Repeat victims are a hot group not necessarily constrained by spatial concentration; there is evidence to suggest that repeat victimisation occurs at higher levels within geographically defined hot spots (Johnson et al., 1997 and Townsley et al., 2000). By focusing on prior victims, reductions in future victimisation may be possible at levels far greater than focussing on hot spots.

Targeting vulnerable groups (young, ethnic minorities, aged) may provide an alternative strategy to the conventional spatial approach. The following table, reproduced from Budd (1999), shows the relative risk of household type for domestic burglary victimisation.

The figures can be multiplied, so that (for example) where head of household is aged 16-24 and is Asian, the burglary risk is 2.71 x

1.77 = 4.79 times the national average. In this way, manageably small high risk groups can be identified. The rationale for doing this is identical to that for identifying hot spots in the first place. If crime risk is skewed, so should police attention be. The mistake made by some is to assume that spatial skewness will be greater than temporal or demographic skewness. Restricting attention to geographically defined hot spots is to neglect people at individually high risk of crime victimisation in areas of low risk, and to unnecessarily support people at low risk in areas of high risk.

Table 2: Risks of Domestic Burglary by Household Type

Household is...	Relative Risk
Head of household 16-24	2.71
One adult living with children	2.00
Head of household is single	1.73
Head of household is separated	1.63
Respondent is Asian	1.77
Head of household is unemployed	1.80
Head of household is economically inactive	1.70
Home is privately rented	1.73
Respondent resident for less than one year	1.75
Home has no security measures	2.71
Home in inner city	1.52
Home in an area with high levels of physical disorder	2.14

Source: Budd (1999).

Address correspondence to: Dr. Michael Townsley, Department of Civic Design, University of Liverpool, P.O. Box 147, Abercrombie Square, Liverpool, UK L69 3BX. E-mail: <mtownsle@liverpool.ac.uk>.

REFERENCES

Budd, T. (1999). *Burglary of Domestic Dwellings: Findings from the British Crime Survey.* (Home Office Statistical Bulletin 4/99.) London, UK: Home Office Research and Statistics Directorate.

Eck, J.E. and W. Spelman (1987). *Problem Solving: Problem Oriented Policing in Newport News.* Washington, DC: Police Executive Research Forum.

Johnson, S.D., K. Bowers and A. Hirschfield (1997). "New Insights in the Spatial and Temporal Distribution of Repeat Victimisation." *British Journal of Criminology* 37(2):224-241.

Ratcliffe, J.H. (2000). "Aoristic Analysis: The Spatial Interpretation of Unspecific Temporal Events." *International Journal of Geographical Information Science* 14(7):669-679.

Rengert, G. (1997). "Auto Theft in Central Philadelphia." In: R. Homel (ed.), *Policing for Prevention: Reducing Crime, Public Intoxication and Injury.* (Crime Prevention Studies, vol. 7.) Monsey, NY: Criminal Justice Press.

Townsley, M, R. Homel and J. Chaseling (2000). "Repeat Burglary Victimisation: Spatial and Temporal Patterns." *Australian and New Zealand Journal of Criminology* 33(1):37-63.

NOTES

1. Interestingly, this is the reason given for the use of a one standard deviation buffer around the mean, rather than the conventional two. In the words of one police officer, "it gave us about the right number of hot spots that we needed."

ANTICIPATORY BENEFITS IN CRIME PREVENTION

by

Martha J. Smith
Cardiff University

Ronald V. Clarke
Rutgers University

and

Ken Pease
University College, London

Abstract: *This chapter seeks to achieve three things, in decreasing order of importance: (1) To point out the basic phenomenon, i.e., the prematurity of many crime prevention effects relative to the point at which they would occur if they were the product of their presumed mechanism. This is termed anticipatory benefits. (2) To trawl published literature for instances of possible and probable anticipatory benefits. (3) To classify possible reasons for anticipatory benefits and to set out their implications.*

INTRODUCTION

For almost 70 years, social science students have been lectured about events in the bank wiring room of the General Electric Company's factory in Hawthorne, Michigan (see Mayo 1933). In summary, changes in working conditions, duration of rest periods and the like all yielded increases in productivity, whatever the nature of the change. Thus, lengthening rest periods increased productivity, as did shortening rest periods. Extra illumination increased productivity, as did less illumination. The active ingredient in the change was not its specifics, but the attention directed at the employees in the bank wiring room. For present purposes, the precise psychological process involved matters little. It could have been fear of dismissal or pleasure at being the centre of attention, or any combination of these and other reactions. However, the central conclusion remains robust, namely that social processes are complex, and capable of giving rise to substantial unforeseen effects masquerading as the effects of the "real" variables manipulated.

Three points from the Hawthorne study are relevant to crime reduction:

- The manipulation of working conditions took place along lines that should have worked. It makes intuitive sense that better working conditions would improve productivity. In the same way it is clear that street lighting or closed-circuit television (CCTV) should work by increasing surveillability. Plague reduction should work by drowning witches, and fever should be reduced by the extraction of overheated blood. We have been too ready to assume that how crime prevention *should* work is the way crime prevention *does* work.

- It took time in the Hawthorne study to work out that the active ingredient was change itself, not the specifics of the change. In crime reduction, we have scarcely begun to look at matters from that perspective, even though change itself seems a clear means of dissuading offenders from repeatedly targeting the same place or person (Ashton et al., 1998) .

- The Hawthorne Effect has typically been characterised as a problem, not a solution. Yet deploying such effects is arguably the most cost-effective crime prevention technique possible.

Seeking to deploy such effects requires some understanding of the mechanisms by which crime reduction achieves its effects (Pawson and Tilley 1997). Ultimately, all crime reduction, with the exception of incapacitating offenders, works by changing a potential offender's or victim's construction of a presenting opportunity. Successful rehabilitation programmes would work by the erstwhile offender ceasing to register a criminal opportunity, or ceasing to regard it as personally relevant. Successful deterrent programmes operate through change in the presumed consequences of acting on a recognised opportunity. Successful opportunity reduction programmes reconfigure environments so that opportunities are removed or are no longer recognised. Opportunity itself does not inhere in the external world. It is a perception, more or less realistic, of circumstances which make an action opportune. Insofar as crime reduction tactics work at all, they work through changes in perception. The centrality of offender per-

ceptions to the effectiveness of situational prevention is well understood, and these form the basis of Clarke and Homel's (1997) classification of 16 opportunity reducing techniques. For example, denying
benefits is effective as crime reduction only insofar as a would-be offender is able to learn from experience to construe a presenting
situation in a changed way.

If crime control is contingent on the perception of changed circumstances, it may (and frequently does) confer *anticipatory benefits*,
as we have chosen to call it. As this chapter goes on to suggest, such
anticipatory benefits are not uncommon.

ANTICIPATORY BENEFITS IN THE LITERATURE

How widespread is the phenomenon? The literature was trawled
for examples of crime reduction initiatives. These were classified as
detailed enough or not detailed enough for anticipatory benefits to be
discerned. Criteria for inclusion were that reports were:

(1) in English;
(2) published (although unpublished reports submitted to local
    authorities or funding bodies were included, if a copy could be
    located);
(3) included an initiative that had been implemented, permitted
    some assessment about when it appears to have been initi-
    ated, and could be coded using the 16-category SCP technique
    classification of Clarke and Homel (1997);
(4) had some measure of crime (even if these were not official po-
    lice records).

Some 142 pieces of research met the criteria set out above, involving
prevention projects at 211 sites.[1]

The next step was to classify the research according to whether it
was sufficiently detailed to discern anticipatory benefits. A study was
deemed detailed enough if four sets of criteria were met. First, the
date (or month) when the initiative was implemented must be given.
Second, the study must set out time-series data that cover enough of
the period prior to the initiative so that factors that might account for
anticipatory benefits are included. Third, the time-series data points
must be frequent enough to be meaningful given the type of initiative
involved and the base rates of the crimes to be prevented. Fourth, it
must be possible to separate the effects of the present initiative from
previous crime prevention initiatives in the area and from other initiatives being carried out at the same time in the same place. Of the
211 cases reported, 52 met the above criteria. That only one in four
evaluation reports allowed consideration of anticipatory benefits

should be remarked. At first blush, it suggests that most evaluation reports are not drafted with issues of effect onset in mind.

The 52 "sufficiently detailed" reports were further classified. *Prima facie* anticipatory benefits were noted if a pre-initiative drop in a crime measure was observed. A study was considered as reflecting "probable" anticipatory benefits if the study noted some factor that could plausibly operate as a mechanism for it, even if the authors themselves did not draw this conclusion. Prima facie and probable anticipatory benefits studies differ less in the likelihood of anticipatory benefits as in the prominence and self-consciousness with which explanatory variables to account for it are addressed. Put crudely, if evaluators do not speculate or more rigorously account for anticipatory effects, it makes those effects no less real.

Rather than duplicate lists of references in the body of the chapter and the bibliography, each reference marked:

"+" reports a case that is sufficiently detailed but which shows no evidence of anticipatory benefits;

"++" shows prima facie evidence; and

"+++" shows anticipatory benefits for reasons set out in the paper.

Of the 52 cases, 22 showed prima facie evidence of an anticipatory effect, of which seven stated reasons for it (or set out enough information for constructing a putative mechanism). Looked at in this way, around 40% of those studies reviewed which were capable of demonstrating anticipatory benefits showed at least prima facie evidence of them. Crude as this trawl is, it suggests that anticipatory benefits are not rare phenomena, and that, as a minimum, evaluation studies should contain enough information to allow these effects to show themselves.

Some Examples

In what follows, some sense of what anticipatory benefits look like is provided (see also Table 1).

Barclay et al. (1997), studying the effects of security cycle patrols on parking lot crime, showed (Figure 1) that announcing the scheme (at highlighted point 1) was followed by a reduction in crime before foot was ever laid to pedal (at highlighted point 2). Ending the scheme (at highlighted point 3) was not immediately followed by an increase in crime.

Table 1: Published Evaluations of Crime Prevention Initiatives with Recorded Anticipatory Benefits

Study	Location	Intervention	Anticipatory Benefits	Possible Explanation
Armitage et al. (1999)	Burnley, Lancashire, UK	CCTV system	Vehicle crime and other property crime – March 1995	First camera became operational in April 1995. Publicity associated with planned camera installation.
Barclay et al. (1996)	Vancouver, Canada	Bike patrol	Vehicle thefts – late March 1995.	Publicity campaign began March 11, 1995. Bike patrol implemented on April 1, 1995. Offenders unsure when bike patrol began.
Brown (1995)	Newcastle-upon-Tyne, UK	CCTV system	Burglary — Dec. 1992 Criminal damage & Other theft – Jan. 1993	Cameras installed in Nov. 1992. Cameras fully operational in March 1993. Offenders may have thought cameras were working as soon as they were installed.
Poyner et al. (1986)	Pepys Estate, Lewisham, London, UK	Physical improvement and clean-up	Thefts of cars – Oct. 1981 Thefts from cars – July 1982	Consultation on Estate began in Sept. 1981. Action Plan agreed June 1982. Offenders may have altered their offending patterns due to uncertainty over changes to Estate.
Ross (1973)	Great Britain	Legislation on compulsory testing of blood alcohol levels of drivers	Failing to stop after an accident – dropped in 1965, remained stable in 1966 and dropped again in 1967	Proposed legislation on compulsory testing of blood alcohol levels presented in Dec. 1965. Law became effective in Oct. 1967. Drivers may have thought that the law had gone into effect when the legislation was discussed in 1965.

Study	Location	Intervention	Anticipatory Benefits	Possible Explanation
Squires (1998b)	Burgess Hill, Sussex, UK	CCTV system	Criminal damage – Jan. 1997 Shoplifting & All crime – Feb. 1997	CCTV operational April 1997. "All crime" drop attributed to the visibility of the CCTV installation work. Sharp pre-operational drop in shop- lifting attributed to other policing factors (not CCTV).
Tilley and Hopkins (1998)	Belgrave, Leicester, UK	Tailored alarm or detection mea- sures or security advice	Non-domestic burglary dropped in fourth quarter 1995	Princess Anne announced initiative designed to assist small businesses in third quarter 1995. The initiative began during second quarter 1996. Offenders may have thought initiative began when announced.

This anticipatory effect seems also to be a feature of CCTV schemes. Figure 2 shows such an effect in Burnley (see Armitage et al., 1999). The two lines in that figure represent the proportion of projected cameras not installed (solid line) and the amount of recorded crime (dashed line), both indexed to 100 at the scheme's inception. It will be seen that the bulk of the crime decline coincided with the first few cameras installed, the last 75% being associated with only a trivial further decline. The crime decline anticipated the first camera installation by a month. Similar pre-operational declines appeared in Newcastle-upon-Tyne (Brown, 1995) and Burgess Hill (Squires, 1998b) (see Table 1).

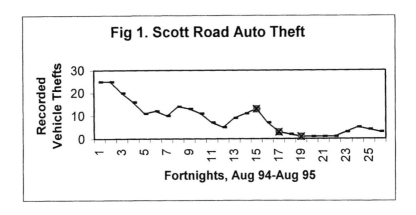

Fig 1. Scott Road Auto Theft

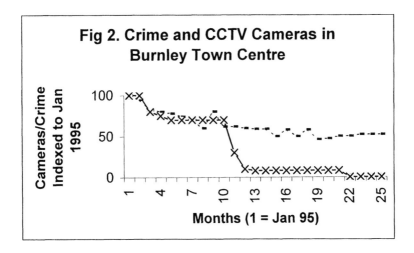

Fig 2. Crime and CCTV Cameras in Burnley Town Centre

The evaluation of a Home Office burglary reduction programme across many sites shows strong anticipatory benefits (Northern Consortium, 2001).[2] The Consortium studied 21 burglary reduction initiatives, of which 19 showed reductions. Of this 19, seven showed steep reductions in burglary levels prior to projects being launched.

In the Northern Consortium report (2001) some post hoc suggestions are made about the reasons for the anticipatory decline, (such as a survey of the public that provided police with a fuller understanding of presenting crime problems), but in no case are they exhaustive or made with confidence.

Among other studies, Tilley and Hopkins (1998) showed a crime decline coinciding with the announcement of the initiative in the Belgrave section of Leicester. Poyner et al. (1986) recorded a crime decline following public consultation about crime reduction on the Pepys Estate. Ross (1973) showed a decline in the number of charges of failing to stop after an accident after breath test legislation was discussed in the media.

WHY DO ANTICIPATORY BENEFITS ACCRUE?

What are the possible reasons for anticipatory effects. They include:

(1) *Effects caused by the smoothing of curves using moving averages.* Such effects would be limited to very short-run anticipations and can be discounted as a major factor;

(2) *Changes caused by over-recording crime levels* in expectation of gaining funding to reduce the crime levels thus inflated. Such effects should be detectable by contrary changes in events uprated to the crime of focal concern (e.g., a decrease in the numbers of criminal damage crimes as those events are "promoted" to attempted burglary);

(3) *Seasonal effects masking the absence of change*; where an initiative takes effect at the same time as a seasonally predictable decline. This is possible because action is likely at a time when matters are at their worst;

(4) *Regression effects*, where a place chosen for intervention because it is extreme relative to other places is also extreme relative to itself at other times, and will thus tend to experience declines over time;

(5) *Creeping implementation*, where some elements of a programme are put in place before an official start date;

(6) *Preparation-disruption effects*, where surveillance is a by-product of installation of crime-reductive hardware, such as street lighting;

(7)   *Preparation-training effects*, where planning, population surveys, etc. render officers better equipped personally to understand and reduce local crime;

(8)   *Motivation of officers involved to make an initiative a success*, which translates itself into better performance in advance of the initiative itself;

(9)   *Preparation-anticipation effects*, where equipment is deemed by motivated offenders to be operational before it is;

(10) *Publicity/disinformation effects*, whereby covert measures are presumed to exist as a result of publicity or hearsay.

PUBLICITY/DISINFORMATION EFFECTS

In the limited scope of this chapter, we should direct our attention to the alternative which, were it true, would have the most profound implications. This is number 10 on the list above, namely the publicity/disinformation alternative. We should be clear that we are not here talking about generalised publicity campaigns, whose effect has typically been found to be meagre (Burrows and Heal 1980; Riley 1980), but of information that the police or other agencies are taking action of specific kinds in circumscribed places.

First, an anecdote illustrates the possible effect (Laycock 2001), discussing the effects of property marking:

...as the year wore on it was clear that the burglary rate was starting to creep up again and I expected it to carry on going to its previous level. I was not therefore best pleased to be told by my then boss that he wanted a second year follow up. I knew what would happen.

But I uncharacteristically did as I was told and in the second year the rate went down even further, but all the reduction was concentrated in the second half of the year. In fact it was almost zero from June. What happened? Well, it was June of the second year before the report of the first year was published. And the fact that crime had gone down was heavily reported in the local and national press. There were TV crews and press interviewers. The project was written up in the Times as a big success. Despite all my careful caveats, property marking was declared "to work." And the burglars read the newspapers and saw the Chief Constable on TV like everyone else.

A study of police decoy vehicles (Sallybanks, 2000) has the unusual feature of deployment of such vehicles in advance of publicity. Figure 3 summarises the results.

It shows that vehicle crime in Stockton, where the initiative ran, was marginally below that elsewhere in the Cleveland force area (April '97-March '98). The drop lines showed where the action and the publicity kicked in respectively. It will be seen that the crime control effect became more marked when publicity alone took place. Taken at face value, this may suggest that publicity about a police initiative is more effective than the substance of the project. This is probably an oversimplification, since the initiative itself (with the communication of arrests effected as part of it) may have sensitised the community to activity, which enhanced the effect of later publicity. Put crudely, the Stockton experience perhaps shows that publicity may be effective only insofar as levels of activity make it plausible.

SO WHAT?

The perceptual underpinnings of prevention have been too little reflected in its evaluation. If perception is indeed central, change in crime rates will coincide with changed perception rather than changed practice, when these are not coincident in time. In the typical crime reduction initiative, crimes committed before and after the introduction of a reductive programme has been introduced are summed and contrasted. This approach is almost universally the design to which an evaluator is reduced when the scale of the initiative is limited, since any graphed representation, being based on small numbers of crimes, is erratic. However, as shown above, in those examples where a curve has been calculated, a common sequence is for the crime decline to begin before it becomes possible that it is an effect of the supposed active ingredient. In such cases, the reduction may better be regarded as the result of changes in perception.

We have demonstrated:

- that many crime reduction programmes exhibit effects too early for them to be attributed to the "obvious" active ingredient;

- that the conventional form of before-after analysis brought to bear on crime reduction initiatives serves to disguise such anticipatory effects, which seem to be very widespread;

- that there exists a variety of possible reasons for anticipatory effects; and

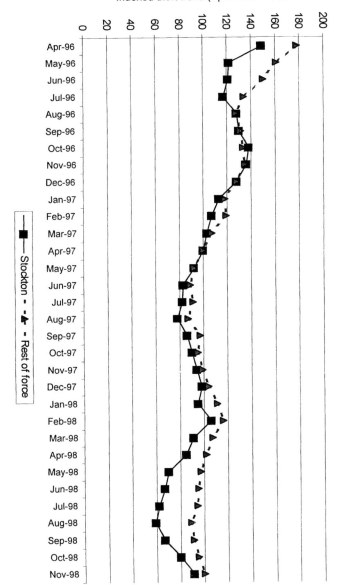

Figure 3. The Effects of Decoy Vehicles in Stockton

- that although the design of programmes does not typically allow one to distinguish among the range of possible explanations, some studies appear to have effects driven by publicity/disinformation.

The reader should know that the authors agonised about what to call the phenomenon whereby crime reductive benefits occur "too early." The primary reason for the choice of "anticipatory benefits" is to make explicit the parallel with diffusion of crime control benefits, which refers to:

...the spread of the beneficial influence of an intervention beyond the places which are directly targeted, the individuals who are the subject of control, the crimes which are the focus of intervention or the time periods in which an intervention is brought (Clarke and Weisburd 1994:169).[3]

The advantage of the chosen term is that the practical implication of anticipatory benefits is identical to that of diffusion of benefits generally, namely:

Recognition of diffusion ... provides an opportunity for maximising crime control benefits. If the processes that lead to diffusion could be identified, crime prevention programmes designed to harness this phenomenon could be more clearly defined (Clarke and Weisburd 1994:169).

The term's disadvantage lies in its lack of neutrality with respect to the presumed mechanism of change. "Anticipatory benefits" fail to call into question the assumption that the initiative whose effects were diffused incorporated the active ingredient in the change. The reader, in accepting the term "anticipatory benefits" should remain aware of its crucial distinguishing characteristic, namely that it *does* call into question the assumed mechanism of change in a way that other types of diffusion of benefit do not. To say that a crime prevention initiative lowers crime earlier than it "should" is to say nothing about the mechanism whereby it does this, other than that the realisation of plans was not a necessary condition for crime control. In this respect, anticipatory benefits are far more threatening to settled beliefs about what reduces crime than are other diffusion types.

What should we now do? Insofar as crime reduction can be achieved before one has done anything, how much crime prevention can be achieved without doing anything beyond triggering anticipatory benefits? Answering this question requires a different kind of prevention research, where the active ingredient is explicitly preparation, assertion or publicity. Imagine a campaign asserting that decoy cars will be deployed on the basis of their thievability, with illustrations of three vehicles known to be frequently stolen and described as decoy vehicles, with an account of the use of one such car to effect an arrest. An intending car thief would be in an approach-avoidance conflict. He selects a car to steal. In the very act of selecting it, it is defined as a thievable car and therefore one which may be a decoy. Testing the effectiveness of an approach such as this would be a first step. The programme following the success of such an approach would entail work on how far one can stretch the schedule of reinforcement, i.e., how often one could get away with saying decoy vehicles are deployed in relation to actually mounting such operations.

One illustration of how little the police think in terms of disinformation is their use of the word "informant." The word is in principle direction-neutral. It does not say who is being informed about the actions of whom. In practice, the understanding of the word is unidirectional. The informant tells the police what putative offenders are doing. It could be the other way round, telling putative offenders about what the police wish them to think is happening. Similarly the cliché used to describe the work of Neighbourhood Watch is that it forms extra "eyes and ears" for the police. This too depicts the policing enterprise as an information sponge, rather than as a dispenser of information.[4] This contrasts with espionage, where a more sophisticated, layered approach to the deliberate supply of (dis)information goes along with intelligence gathering.

The underlying ethical question needs to be addressed squarely. This approach involves the police in lying or exaggeration. Whether that is defensible is no doubt a matter for debate. How different it is from disguising the true state of affairs in covert operations is also worthy of discussion. To allow the argument to be developed, the position is taken here that dissembling is here justified in that it presents a closer approximation to a state of affairs to which the public would choose to subscribe. It thus goes along with deceits which exaggerate police strengths covering an area, or levels of usage of forensic investigation.

Effects around a programme's onset should be considered alongside effects around its termination. In the same way that effects antedate onset, so they extend beyond offset. Sherman's (1990) review of police crackdowns suggests, to simplify, periods of quiescence after the crackdown which approximate the crackdown in length. We may speculate that, in the same way as anticipatory effects presume preventive measures to be already in place, residual effects after crackdowns lead people to assume that measures remain in place. We may thus speculate on the perfect, virtually cost-free, crime reduction tactic, in which false information yields anticipatory crime prevention, and reduction is maintained after the fictional initiative would realistically have ended. This post (fictional) crackdown period can be used to consolidate effects achieved.

Address correspondence to: Martha J. Smith, Cardiff University, School of Social Sciences, Glamorgan Building, King Edward VII Avenue, Cardiff, Wales CF10 3WT, UK. E-mail: <SmithM8@cardiff.ac.uk>.

REFERENCES

Each reference marked:

"+" reports a case that is sufficiently detailed but which shows no effects of anticipatory diffusion;

"++" shows prima facie evidence; and

"+++" shows anticipatory diffusion for reasons set out in the paper.

+++Armitage, R., G. Smyth and K. Pease (1999). "Burnley CCTV Evaluation." In: K. Painter and N. Tilley (eds.), *Surveillance of Public Space: CCTV, Street Lighting and Crime Prevention.* (Crime Prevention Studies, vol. 10.) Monsey, NY: Criminal Justice Press.

Ashton J., B. Senior, I. Brown and K. Pease (1998). "Repeat Victimisation: Offender Accounts." *International Journal of Risk, Security and Crime Prevention* 3:269-280.

+++Barclay, P., J. Buckley, P.J. Brantingham, P.L. Brantingham and T. Whinn-Yates (1997). "Preventing Auto Theft in Commuter Parking Lots: A Bike Patrol in Vancouver." In: R.V. Clarke (ed.), *Situational Crime Prevention: Successful Case Studies* (2nd ed.). Guilderland, NY: Harrow and Heston.

++Bennett, T. and L. Durie (1999). *Preventing Residential Burglary in Cambridge: From Crime Audits to Targeted Strategies.* (Police Research Series, Paper 108.) London, UK: Home Office.

++Braga, A.A. and R.V. Clarke (1994). "Improved Radios and More Stripped Cars in Germany: A Routine Activities Analysis." *Security Journal* 5:154-159.

+Bridgeman, C. (1997). "Preventing Pay Phone Damage." In: M. Felson and R.V. Clarke (eds.), *Business and Crime Prevention*. Monsey, NY: Criminal Justice Press.

+++Brown, B. (1995). *CCTV in Town Centres: Three Case Studies*. (Crime Prevention and Detection Series, Paper No. 73.) London, UK: Home Office.

Burrows J. and K. Heal (1980) "Police Car Security Campaigns." In: R.V. Clarke and P. Mayhew (eds.), *Designing Out Crime*. London, UK: Her Majesty's Stationery Office.

Canter, P. (1998). "Baltimore County's Autodialer System." In: N. LaVigne and J. Wartell (eds.), *Crime Mapping Case Studies: Successes in the Field*. Washington, DC: Police Executive Research Forum.

+Chaiken, J.M., M.W. Lawless, and K.A. Stevenson (1992). "Exact Fare on Buses." In: R.V. Clarke (ed.), *Situational Crime Prevention: Successful Case Studies*. Albany, NY: Harrow and Heston.

++Challinger, D. (1997). "Refund Fraud in Retail Stores." In: R.V. Clarke (ed.), *Situational Crime Prevention: Successful Case Studies* (2nd ed.). Guilderland, NY: Harrow and Heston.

Clarke, R.V. and R. Homel (1997). "A Revised Classification of Situational Crime Prevention Techniques." In: S.P. Lab (ed.), *Crime Prevention at a Crossroads*. Cincinnati, OH: Anderson Publishing.

—— and D. Weisburd (1994). "Diffusion of Crime Control Benefits." In: R.V. Clarke (ed.)., *Crime Prevention Studies*, vol. 2. Monsey, NY: Willow Tree Press.

+—— and G. McGrath (1990). "Cash Reduction and Robbery Prevention in Australian Betting Shops." *Security Journal* 1:160-163.

+—— and P. Mayhew (1989). "Crime as Opportunity: A Note on Domestic Gas Suicide in Britain and the Netherlands." *British Journal of Criminology* 29:35-46.

+Diener, E. and R. Crandell (1979). "An Evaluation of the Jamaican Anti-Crime Program." *Journal of Applied Social Psychology* 9:135-146.

++Ditton, J. and E. Short (1999). "Yes, It Works, No, It Doesn't: Comparing the Effects of Open-Street CCTV in Two Adjacent Scottish Town Centres." In: K. Painter and N. Tilley (eds.), *Surveillance of Public Space: CCTV, Street Lighting and Crime Prevention*. (Crime Prevention Studies, vol. 10.) Monsey, NY: Criminal Justice Press.

+Eck, J. and W. Spelman (1992). "Thefts from Vehicles in Shipyard Parking Lots." In: R.V. Clarke (ed.), *Situational Crime Prevention: Successful Case Studies*. Albany, NY: Harrow and Heston.

++Gabor, T. (1981). "The Crime Displacement Hypothesis: An Empirical Examination." *Crime & Delinquency* 27:390-404.

++Griswold, D.B. (1992). "Crime Prevention and Commercial Burglary." In: R.V. Clarke (ed.), *Situational Crime Prevention: Successful Case Studies.* Albany, NY: Harrow and Heston.

+Honess, T. and M. Maguire, with E. Charman (1993). *Vehicle Watch and Car Theft: An Evaluation.* (Crime Prevention Unit Series, Paper No. 50.) London, UK: Home Office Police Department.

++Husain, S. (1990). *Neighbourhood Watch and Crime: An Assessment of Impact.* London, UK: The Police Foundation.

+Knutsson, J. (1984). *Operation Identification — A Way to Prevent Burglaries?* Stockholm, SWE: The National Council for Crime Prevention.

+Landes, W.M. (1978). "An Economic Study of U.S. Aircraft Hijacking, 1961-1976." *Journal of Law and Economics* 21:1-32.

Laycock, G (2001). "Scientists or Politicians — Who Has the Answer to Crime?" Inaugural lecture at University College London, 26 April 2001, <www.jdi.ucl.ac.uk>.

+Matthews, R. (1993). *Kerb-crawling, Prostitution and Multi-Agency Policing.* (Crime Prevention Unit Series, Paper No. 43.) London, UK: Home Office.

+Mayhew, P., R.V. Clarke, and D. Elliot (1989). "Motorcycle Theft, Helmet Legislation and Displacement." *Howard Journal* 28:1-8.

Mayo, E. (1933). *The Human Problems of an Industrial Civilisation.* New York, NY: Macmillan.

+Mazerolle, L.G. and J. Roehl (1999). *Controlling Drug and Disorder Problems: Oakland's Beat Health Program.* (Research in Brief.) Washington, DC: National Institute of Justice.

Northern Consortium (2001). "Home Office Burglary Reduction Initiative North East, North West and Merseyside Regions: Interim Outcome Report." Available from Dr. Shane Johnson, Department of Civic Design, Abercrombie Square, University of Liverpool, Liverpool L69 3BX, UK.

Pawson R. and N. Tilley (1997). *Realistic Evaluation.* London, UK: Sage.

+Poyner, B. (1992). "Video Cameras and Bus Vandalism." In: R.V. Clarke (ed.), *Situational Crime Prevention: Successful Case Studies.* Albany, NY: Harrow and Heston.

+++Poyner, B., B. Webb, and R. Woodall (1986). *Crime Reduction on Housing Estates: An Evaluation of NACRO's Crime Prevention Programme.* London, UK: The Tavistock Institute of Human Relations.

++Press, S.J. (1971). *Some Effects of an Increase in Police Manpower in the 20th Precinct of New York City* (R-704-NYC). New York, NY: New York City Rand Institute.

Riley D. (1980). "An Evaluation of a Campaign to Reduce Car Thefts". In: R.V. Clarke and P. Mayhew (eds.), *Designing Out Crime.* London, UK: Her Majesty's Stationery Office.

+++Ross, H.L. (1973). "Law, Science and Accidents: The British Road Safety Act of 1967." *Journal of Legal Studies* 4:285-310.

Sallybanks, J. (2000). *Assessing the Police Use of Decoy Vehicles.* (Police Research Series No. 137.) London, UK: Home Office.

++Sarno, C. (1996). "The Impact of Closed Circuit Television on Crime in Sutton Town Centre." In: M. Bulos and D. Grant (eds.), *Towards a Safer Sutton? CCTV One Year On.* London, UK: London Borough of Sutton.

+Schnelle, J.F., R.E. Kirchner, M.P. McNees, and J.M. Lawler (1975). "Social Evaluation Research: The Evaluation of Two Police Patrol Strategies." *Journal of Applied Behavior Analysis* 8:353-365.

+—— R.E. Kirchner, Jr., J.E. Casey, P.H. Uselton, Jr. and M.P. McNees (1977). "Patrol Evaluation Research: A Multiple-Baseline Analysis of Saturation Police Patrolling during Day and Night Hours." *Journal of Applied Behavior Analysis* 10:33-40.

Sherman, L.W. (1990). "Police Crackdowns: Initial and Residual Deterrence." In: M. Tonry and N. Morris (eds.), *Crime and Justice: A Review of Research* (vol. 12). Chicago, IL: University of Chicago Press.

++—— and D.P Rogan (1995). "Effects of Gun Seizures on Gun Violence: 'Hot Spots' Patrol in Kansas City." *Justice Quarterly* 12:673-693.

+Sivarajasingam, V. and J.P. Shepherd (1999). "Effect of Closed Circuit Television on Urban Violence." *Journal of Accident and Emergency Medicine* 26:255-257.

+Squires, P. (1998a). *An Evaluation of the Ilford Town Centre CCTV Scheme.* Brighton, UK: Health and Social Policy Research Centre, University of Brighton.

+++ —— (1998b). *CCTV and Crime Reduction in Burgess Hill Town Centre: An Independent Evaluation.* Brighton, UK: Health and Social Policy Research Centre, University of Brighton.

++ —— (1998c). *CCTV and Crime Reduction in Crawley: An Independent Evaluation of the Crawley CCTV System.* Brighton, UK: Health and Social Policy Research Centre, University of Brighton.

+ —— (1998d). *The East Grinstead Town Centre CCTV Scheme: An Independent Evaluation.* Brighton, UK: Health and Social Policy Research Centre, University of Brighton.

+Tilley, N. (1993). *Understanding Car Parks, Crime and CCTV: Evaluation Lessons from Safer Cities.* (Crime Prevention Unit Series, Paper No. 42.) London, UK: Home Office.

+++ —— and M. Hopkins (1998). *Business as Usual: An Evaluation of Small Business and Crime Initiative.* (Police Research Series, Paper No. 95.) London, UK: Home Office.

+Webb, B. (1997). "Steering Column Locks and Motor Vehicle Theft: Evaluations from Three Countries." In: R.V. Clarke (ed.), *Situational Crime Prevention: Successful Case Studies* (2nd ed.). Guilderland, NY: Harrow and Heston.

++ —— and G. Laycock (1992). *Reducing Crime on the London Underground: An Evaluation of Three Pilot Projects.* (Crime Prevention Unit Series Paper, No. 30.) London, UK: Home Office.

NOTES

1. Some studies contained more than one usable comparison.

2. A fuller account of this important work will be published, under authorship of Alex Hirschfield, Kate Bowers and Shane Johnson. These scholars have long been aware of anticipatory diffusion benefits.

3. The temporal diffusion of benefits discussed by Clarke and Weisburd concerns residual effects rather than anticipatory effects. They link this phenomenon with the carryover of the effect of police crackdowns (Sherman, 1990).

4. Of course, this is a simplification. There are examples of the police dispensing information about crime risks (see, for example, Canter, 1998).

REDUCING THEFT AT CONSTRUCTION SITES: LESSONS FROM A PROBLEM-ORIENTED PROJECT

by

Ronald V. Clarke
Rutgers University

and

Herman Goldstein
University of Wisconsin — Madison

Abstract: *A building boom in Charlotte, NC led to sharp increases in the number of kitchen appliances stolen from houses under construction. This paper describes a problem-oriented policing project, extending over a period of more than two years, that was undertaken by the Charlotte-Mecklenburg Police Department to address the problem. A detailed analysis of security practices and the risks of theft was made for 25 builders operating in one of the police service districts in the northern part of the county. This produced the recommendation that installation of appliances should be delayed until the new owners had taken up residence, thus effectively removing the targets of theft. Twelve of the larger builders agreed to experiment with this approach for a period of six months, though systematic checks made by police throughout the period found that builder compliance was variable. Despite this, analysis showed that delayed installation was an effective policy. Appliance theft declined in the district and there was no evidence of displacement of thefts to surrounding districts. The concluding discussion of the difficulties encountered by police in undertaking problem-oriented projects focuses on the vital role of crime analysis,*

Crime Prevention Studies, volume 13, pp.89-130.

and considers ways to strengthen analytic capacity in police departments.

INTRODUCTION

Problem-oriented policing was initially advanced as a way of focusing attention on the effectiveness, rather than just the efficiency, of the police. Advocates of problem-oriented policing contend that it is not enough to respond, however efficiently, to incidents as they occur. Rather, with effectiveness as the goal, it is essential that the police identify patterns in the incidents they routinely handle; subject these patterns (labeled problems) to in-depth analysis; and explore new ways of intervening earlier in the causal chain so that these incidents are less likely to occur in the future. These new strategies are not limited to standard police responses that traditionally depend on law enforcement — i.e., on efforts to identify, arrest and prosecute offenders. Rather, without abandoning the use of the criminal law when it is likely to be the most effective response, problem-oriented policing encourages a broad exploration of other potentially effective responses, alone or in partnership with others, with a high priority on prevention. Thus, by expanding the repertoire of possible responses and settling on a strategy that has the potential for reducing the problem, the ultimate and steadfast goal is to increase effectiveness (Goldstein, 1979, 1990).

Problem-oriented policing has its roots in the increased awareness, reinforced by continually accumulating studies, that substantial categories of crime have been generally resistant to traditional policing methods. For example, car and foot patrols can do little to deter crime occurring in private places. Crackdowns rarely have lasting effects on street crimes. Stakeouts produce few arrests when crimes occur at extended intervals. Fast response is usually of limited value when the offender has departed the scene. Criminal investigation is too laborious and unproductive for all but a minority of serious offenses. And the arrest and prosecution of minor property offenders is often not productive, given the overburdened court systems and the unavailability to a judge of effective sanctions or alternative forms of disposition. These limitations sometimes lead to labeling many of the categories of crime at which the cited strategies are directed as "non-suppressible."

The crimes addressed in this project, thefts from residential construction sites in Charlotte, NC, would fit the definition of non-suppressible crimes. As shown below, they were inherently difficult to deter and they did prove resistant to conventional police methods. However, they were reduced as the result of a problem-oriented project undertaken by the Charlotte-Mecklenburg Police Department (CMPD).

The initial purpose of the project was to illustrate a full, careful application of the problem-oriented policing concept. Once the decision was made to focus on theft from construction sites as the illustrative problem, the second purpose of the project was to enable the CMPD to deal with the problem more effectively by making use of the problem-oriented methodology. This paper reports on what was learned about the problem, describes the effort to reduce it, and presents data showing that the response implemented was effective. In the language of situational crime prevention (Clarke, 1997b), this response would be classified as a form of "target removal." Thus, this paper not only documents the success of the CMPD in using the problem-oriented methodology to reduce thefts from construction sites. It contributes as well, albeit modestly, to the literature on "target removal."

As the project evolved, it provided another benefit — of potential value to the larger world of policing — in the lessons learned about implementing problem-oriented policing. In name, problem-oriented policing has become quite popular, but the number of efforts that meet the original criteria of the concept is very small (Clarke, 1997a, 1998; Goldstein, 1994a, 1994b, 1996a, 1996b; Read and Tilley, 2000; Scott, 2000; Scott and Clarke, 2000). This is especially puzzling because the fundamental logic in problem-oriented policing is often, quite appropriately, described as simple or just plain common sense (Read and Tilley, 2000). This project afforded a unique opportunity to identify some of the factors that account for the small number of full applications of the concept — to identify the factors that, in practice, make a seemingly simple process complex. The opportunity was unique for three reasons: (1) the ambitious nature of the project; (2) the fact that the project had more than the usual support from within a police agency; and (3) the familiarity that the authors, involved as we were in the project, had with the concept (Goldstein with problem-oriented policing, and Clarke with situational crime prevention—a concept that in many ways parallels and complements problem-oriented policing). A major objective in preparing this paper, therefore, was to report on some of the complexities that were found in carrying out problem-oriented policing, to identify the barriers that were encountered, and to outline some measures that need to be taken if the benefits of problem-oriented policing are to be more fully realized.

BACKGROUND TO THE PROJECT

Wherever construction is underway, there will be related problems of theft, but these may assume significance for a particular police jurisdiction only during a construction boom. The form taken by the thefts will depend on the nature of the construction, which can range from enormous projects for new highways and airports to in-fill housing developments in suburbs. Construction site theft seems never to have been systematically studied, though occasional discussions of the problem can be found in trade journals such as *Construction Equipment*, "CONTRACTOR.mag.com," and *Constructor*, the latter being the house journal of the Associated General Contractors (AGC) of America (*Constructor*, 1999; Goldman, 1999; McGreevy, 1999; Snyder, 2000; Stewart, 1998, 2000). These discussions tend to focus on the organized theft of expensive equipment, such as bulldozers or backhoes (commonly known as "JCBs" in the U.K.). However, this literature draws attention to at least three other forms of construction site theft: theft by workers of tools and materials; after-hours pilfering of lumber and other materials by opportunist thieves, perhaps for their own use; and, in the case of homes under construction, thefts by habitual offenders and others of fixtures and appliances.

The present project started with a focus on the general problem of theft from construction sites, but, in the classic pattern of problem-oriented policing, it quickly became more tightly focused on just one of the specific sub-problems identified during analysis. This was the theft of household appliances, such as ranges (cooking stoves) and microwaves, from newly completed houses.

The project was located in the Charlie One service district, the geographically largest of 12 such districts of the Charlotte-Mecklenburg Police Department (CMPD) — an agency that provides police service to the City of Charlotte and to most of Mecklenburg County, in which the city itself is located. Charlie One covers most of the northern part of the county, an area with an estimated population in 1995 of just over 100,000. The southern part of the Charlie One district includes the Charlotte campus of the University of North Carolina and various office, mall and light industrial developments. To the north, the district is largely rural, with a scattering of separately incorporated small municipalities and lakeside developments. As a result of the booming regional economy, and because of its proximity to Charlotte, northern Mecklenburg County has experienced a large increase in population throughout the 1990s, and, as a consequence, a correspondingly large increase in housing. About one-third of the residential construction occurring in the entire area served by the CMPD was in Charlie One.

This construction was mostly in the form of single-family homes built in separate developments or "subdivisions" ("estates" in the U.K.), which were once farms or fields. In March 1999, 66 housing developments were underway, involving 48 different construction companies. This wave of building was expected to add more than 12,000 homes to the housing stock by 2002 and, by 2010, it is estimated that the population of northern Mecklenburg County would grow to about 180,000. This would be an 80% increase in population over a 15-year period.

During 1998, it became apparent to Captain E. Charles ("Chuck") Johnson, who was in charge of Charlie One, that construction site theft in the district was a large and growing problem. For example, of the 485 commercial burglaries recorded in Charlie One during 1998, 109 (22%) were break-ins to houses under construction, with an appliance taken.[1] Leaving aside the sheer volume of construction, it was not difficult to understand the reasons for this emergent crime wave in the district. The numerous subdivisions were scattered throughout a largely rural district, which made it next to impossible for the police to provide adequate patrol coverage at high-risk periods — in the evenings and weekends — when sites were usually deserted. Because of the high costs, few sites employed security guards or off-duty police and, to encourage casual inspection by potential buyers (and because it would have been difficult to secure entrances), the sites were generally left open. This afforded both the opportunity and the excuse for thieves openly to prowl for targets. When the first residents moved into their homes, they afforded only minimal guardianship of nearby properties because, in the evening, night and weekend hours, thieves could easily blend in with the employees of sub-contractors who sometimes worked in those hours. During the day, the large number of employees of sub-contractors, casual laborers on site, and delivery personnel made it difficult to maintain site security. Tools and materials were constantly at risk of theft. Finally, the large number of construction firms operating in the district, and the large number of site supervisors employed, could mean that thieves might be able to find ready purchasers for some of the appliances and home fixtures they stole. Altogether, in the terminology of routine activity theory (Felson, 1998), the construction sites ensured the convergence of many suitable targets for theft, an absence of capable guardians and a ready supply of likely offenders.

Two of Captain Johnson's officers, Daniel Cunius and G. Eric Rost, had been taking an interest in the problem and, on the basis of discussions with them, he assigned them part-time in May 1998 and then full-time in March 1999 to develop a workable solution. The plan they developed had three components:

- contacting all existing building site supervisors to discuss their crime prevention practices, provide them with crime prevention tips, and obtain after-hours contact numbers;

- establishing "community watch" schemes whereby new residents in subdivisions would be urged to report any suspicious vehicles or people; and,

- undertaking intensive patrols of the construction sites during the evenings, and working closely with other officers and investigators to identify and arrest suspects.

Elements of this plan — such as the move to a primarily proactive, preventive mode — reflected wider efforts that were being made at the time to establish problem-oriented policing within the CMPD. With grant support from the Office of Community Oriented Policing Services in the U.S Department of Justice (the COPS Office), Chief Dennis Nowicki had persuaded Goldstein to review these early efforts. As a result of that review, Goldstein argued that the CMPD could better develop its commitment to implementing problem-oriented policing if resources were focused on just a few projects in which a more intensive effort was made to address a specific substantive problem. It was suggested to him that, from among the many projects then underway, the Charlie One project on construction site theft would be a suitable candidate for the kind of intensive project he had proposed.

Accordingly, about six months into their project, Goldstein met with Captain Johnson and the two officers involved. The efforts the three police officers had already made to obtain a detailed picture of the problem, the relationship they had cultivated with the department's crime analysts, and, most important, the enthusiasm and openness they demonstrated were impressive, and it was therefore decided that the project merited the kind of concentrated attention that had been proposed. The offer to make their explorations the subject of a more intensive project was welcomed by Captain Johnson and the two officers. Despite the considerable efforts they had made to arrest offenders through intensive patrols, stakeouts and working with investigators, little tangible progress had been achieved. Both offenders and the stolen property seemed to vanish into thin air. In 1998, less than 2% of reported construction site thefts were cleared and, while the clearance rate was improving (it rose to about

6% in 1999), it was still at a low level. The few offenders arrested (most of whom were drug addicts) had refused to divulge how they disposed of goods they had stolen. In extensive checks of area pawn-shops and flea markets, not one appliance had been recovered out of the 159 stolen from houses under construction in 1998. The Charlie One team was anxious to consider any new ideas for dealing with the problem that might surface from the type of in-depth inquiry that had been proposed.

Soon after this first meeting at Charlie One, Goldstein invited Clarke to join him in advising the project. Clarke's help was sought particularly with the analysis and in identifying possible preventive measures. This was the beginning of a collaborative effort that extended over two years — the time frame greatly influenced by the need to collect data over an extended period and competing demands on the time of some of the project team members (the team now consisting of Captain Johnson, officers Cunius and Rost, and a crime analyst — a position filled during the project in succession by Carl Walter, Ryan Jackson, and Michael Humphrey). Goldstein and Clarke met with the team regularly in a series of short visits. The team was frequently joined in these meetings by Steve Ward, an assistant district attorney with senior status in that office, who had been assigned to work full-time with the CMPD. Conscious of the need to reduce the pressures on the criminal justice system, his constant involvement in the project proved vital to its success. The role played by Clarke and Goldstein was essentially consultative — analogous to that of coaches — to explain the process of problem-oriented policing, to help talk through problems, to raise points for further inquiry or action, and to make suggestions about data analysis. This work encompassed five main areas: refining the focus of the project; obtaining a better understanding of the problem; calculating risks (and relating these to builder practices); selecting and implementing a workable solution; and assessing its effectiveness.

DEFINING THE PROBLEM

In the initial meetings, much time was spent on defining the problem. It was decided early on to concentrate on sites being developed for housing and not to cover other kinds of construction sites. While relatively few, these other sites presented a greater variety of problems. Even the residential sites alone presented quite a variety of theft problems. While thefts of heavy equipment were rare, it appeared from the officers' analysis of crime reports and from talking to builders that there were at least three other common forms of theft:

theft of lumber and building materials, theft of tools, and theft of appliances from houses under construction. It was decided to concentrate on the latter, theft of appliances, not because this was the largest problem (the procedures for reporting and recording of construction site theft did not permit this to be determined), but for several reasons. It was a costly and common offense. It appeared that there were some potentially effective ways in which to secure the houses under construction. The large size of appliances and the fact they carry serial numbers afforded the possibility of retrieving those that had been stolen.

The other forms of theft seemed more intractable. Lumber and building supplies are often scattered around outside and they are almost impossible to identify as stolen. This is also true of tools. Even when they have serial numbers, the builders seemed not to keep records of them.

Added to these practical considerations, it seemed probable that if thefts of appliances could be reduced, then those of other less valuable property might also decline. This is because the increased risk or difficulty of stealing appliances might dissuade offenders from coming to the construction sites and picking up whatever else they could during their visits.

Once the decision to focus on appliances was made, the Charlie One team embarked on a closer study of the incidents. They quickly found that many of the thefts that they knew to have been reported had not been recorded under the correct category in the system used to collect crime statistics. This discovery required that they pull all the original incident reports of theft from construction sites and re-code those involving appliances — a major undertaking. Compared with the 55 incidents of break-ins to houses under construction reported officially for 1998, they found 109 such incidents, nearly double the number. They repeated the exercise for later years with similar results.

The team also found that thefts were particularly concentrated on ranges (cookers in the U.K.), microwaves and dishwashers. Of the 414 appliances stolen from houses under construction during 1998 and 1999 in the entire Charlie One district, 34% were ranges, 26% were microwaves and 22% were dishwashers. The remaining 18% were distributed among washing machines, dryers, refrigerators, ovens, stovetops, range hoods, air conditioners and garbage disposal units. Discussions with builders revealed that appliances that were "hard-wired" (i.e., that were directly wired into the electricity supply, were attached to plumbing, or were built into kitchen cabinets) were less likely to be stolen than "plug-in" appliances. This suggested that the thieves were not particularly well organized or determined, which was consistent with the fact that at least those apprehended had been habitual offenders with a problem of addiction.

As a result of these findings, the focus of the project was narrowed further to thefts of plug-in appliances from houses under construction.

THE NATURE AND SCOPE OF THE PROBLEM

Narrowing the focus of the project resulted in questions being raised about how seriously the problem, which consisted of just over 100 reported breaks-ins in the Charlie One district in one year (1998), ought to be taken, and whether it warranted the time that it was planned to devote to it. In particular, did the number of thefts present an unacceptably high risk of break-ins, given the volume of construction in Charlie One? To answer this question, the crime analyst initially assigned to the project (Carl Walter) sought to find information about the number of houses under construction. He obtained data from the county building inspector's office showing that building permits for 3,130 houses were issued for Charlie One in 1998. On the basis of this figure, he calculated that break-ins resulting in the theft of an appliance were experienced by 3.3% of houses under construction (104/3,130x100). This was little higher than the risk of reported burglary (2.8%) for all households in America in 1995 — the latest available comparative data (Farrington and Langan, 1998).

Another way to calculate risks is per builder, of whom there were several dozen operating in Charlie One during 1998. A risk of 3.3% translates into a risk of one break-in for every 30 houses. Only the contractors building as many houses as this per year (of which there were 25) could expect to be a victim of a break-in involving theft of appliances. The problem would in all likelihood be concentrated among the largest contractors in this group. There were eight who were building more than 100 houses per year (accounting between them for 82% of the building permits issued). Assuming a reasonably equal distribution of risk, each of these contractors might expect to suffer a minimum of three such break-ins per year. The largest contractor, who was issued 385 permits for the year, might expect to suffer 11 break-ins. Did these numbers represent an unacceptably high level of risk?

The answer to this question depends partly on the cost of break-ins, which, according to an analysis undertaken by Cunius and Rost of police reports for 1998, averaged just over $750 per incident. Of this amount, 66% represented the replacement costs for the stolen appliances, 13% was accounted for by the value of other items stolen at the same time and 21% consisted of the cost of damage repairs.

Direct costs of $750 per break-in are not high given the retail price of new houses in the area (averaging about $140,000) and given the 1% of the price that contractors are reported nationwide as generally budgeting for theft and other losses. In fact, Cunius and Rost had learned from talking with site supervisors while on patrol that the costs of break-ins were of comparatively little concern to most of them. Only the small builders, who saw their profits being eroded, were seriously concerned about the loss of the appliances and the costs of repairing the damage. For others, when losses climbed above budgeted amounts, these could be passed on to future customers in the form of higher prices.

Often more damaging than the direct costs of break-ins would be the administrative costs involved in putting the matter right: ordering a replacement appliance, being available to accept delivery, scheduling repairs, making a police report, and reporting for insurance purposes or for tax write-offs. Sometimes, theft of an appliance and a delay in replacement might also delay a house closing, with associated financial penalties. These indirect costs resulting from administrative action and other consequences of theft can easily account for "anywhere from two to ten times more than direct costs" (*Constructor*, 1999, page 1).

Another intangible cost of break-ins mentioned by some builders was that the neighborhood in which they were building might begin to acquire an unsavory reputation for crime, which could reduce demand for their houses. However, the concern did not seem to be justified given the large population growth and the relatively low rates of theft. Moreover, thefts at this stage in the development of a neighborhood, absent occupants, are not as productive of continuing fears as they would be in an established neighborhood. The reputation would evaporate with occupancy. Altogether, this analysis of costs gave little reason to think that an appeal to profits would help persuade builders to take preventive measures that were burdensome or expensive. While disappointing to the Charlie One team, this information was helpful in thinking about future action.

A major factor, internal to the police department, supporting increased attention to the problem was the contribution that the number of thefts made to the overall crime rate for the district. In varying degrees, district commanders and their personnel are held accountable for the incidence of crime and especially for substantial increases in crime The increase in thefts from construction sites was a big negative for a district that prided itself on the traditional measures of its performance. Moreover, the high volume of cases, along with the sense of frustration and futility in dealing with them, had become a source of annoyance to operating personnel. Thus, the desire to do something about theft from construction sites was probably stronger within Charlie One than from any source outside the CMPD.

RISK OF BREAK-INS AND BUILDER SECURITY

A benefit of calculating costs was that this focused attention on individual builders, their losses, and their security practices. Studying other aspects of risk was less fruitful. Hot spot analysis showed that break-ins tended to be concentrated in the southern part of the district, but this is where most construction was occurring. Construction in the more northerly parts of the county was in smaller, more upscale developments. Assuming that most of the thieves were habitual offenders taking advantage of the opportunities presented by the construction, they would have to travel further to reach these developments. Moreover, more of the appliances in these developments were built into the cabinetry in these more expensive homes. This made them both more difficult to steal and more difficult to sell.

Analysis by time of day, and day of week and month revealed patterns, such as an apparent rise in the spring and early summer and a heavy concentration around weekends, which were not unexpected or which were difficult to interpret because of small numbers. Three makes of appliances (GE, Whirlpool and Kenmore) accounted for about 75% of all appliances taken, but these were also the most commonly installed appliances. In few cases were more than one house broken-into and the appliances taken. Most often just one house would be targeted, which again suggests a low level of organization and planning.

There was a tantalizing suggestion that the amount of force used by thieves to gain entry varied among the different builders — thereby suggesting that some were more diligent about locking up — but small numbers of cases made it difficult to be sure of this point.

It was assumed, from the outset, that there would be substantial variation among builders in the risk of break-ins, and early analysis supported this assumption. But by this time in the project, the limitations of using building permits as a measure of the volume of construction in computing rates of theft were becoming more apparent. Building permits measure only planned construction, not that which is actually occurring. Thus, a builder might apply for permits to construct 100 homes in a particular subdivision, but only start to build a portion of the houses in that year. Indeed, very few houses in the subdivision might reach the stage of construction when appliances were installed and thus be at risk of break-ins.

Fortunately, the crime analyst involved in the project at this time (Ryan Jackson) learned that a "certificate of occupancy" (CO) had to be issued by the county before a new owner could take up residence. He also established that lists of COs could be provided which could be sorted according to builder and subdivision. Since these were only issued when a house was completed and ready for occupancy, they provided a much better, more timely basis for computing risk than the building permits.[2]

Calculations of the risk of break-ins based on COs substantially changed the project team's picture of the problem. Swayed by the large number of incidents reported by some of the large builders, the team had been assuming that lack of concern about break-ins on the part of these builders was one source of the problem. The more accurate measure showed that there was still considerable variation among builders in risks, but not necessarily of the same pattern they had previously discerned. The revised analysis revealed that while some of the large builders did in fact have a high rate of theft, others among them — like the smaller builders — experienced little theft. Accurate documentation of this variation considerably strengthened the team's hand when later they began to engage the builders in discussions about changing their practices.

While the laborious process of improving the measurement of risk was underway, Cunius and Rost were undertaking surveys of builder security practices. These surveys were undertaken at various times in the project, formally and informally, covering a variety of practices. The subjects that were covered gradually changed, as the needs of the project became clearer. Early on, the officers gathered information on: the use of gatekeepers, security guards or off-duty police officers; fencing and site-entrance gates; posted reward programs for information about offenders; and the use of temporary burglar alarms. Later, they focused on: the use of large dumpster-style locked containers on site for the storage of appliances prior to installation, thereby reducing opportunities for theft; removal of the door from appliances to make them less tempting targets; and delayed installation of appliances until close to occupancy. The surveys were coupled with explorations of individual builders' attitudes toward possible new initiatives, such as: establishing Neighborhood Watch schemes for new sites as houses began to be occupied; the use of electronic tracking devices concealed in appliances; and the use of video cameras to monitor the sites after hours.

It proved difficult to make precise determinations of security practices among particular builders because of the broad discretion allowed site supervisors. Thus, a particular supervisor might choose not to follow company policies (where these existed) about receiving and storing appliances prior to installation. It was also difficult to link security practices to particular sites, because supervisors quite frequently were reassigned to other sites or they left to take up employment elsewhere. Consequently, security practices at a particular site might change overnight without the contractor and his top managers becoming aware of the change. Indeed, Cunius and Rost were frequently able to inform senior managers that their beliefs about site security did not match what was actually occurring. This became a problem later in the project when builders were supposed to be changing their practices to conform to police advice.

SELECTING AND IMPLEMENTING THE PREVENTIVE MEASURES

When the improved risk measures had been developed, thought was given to repeating the surveys of contractor practices in a more systematic manner in an effort to identify "best practice." By then, however, the rather intensive mulling over of the newly acquired data led, rather naturally, to a growing consensus among team members as to what would constitute the most desirable "workable" solution. This was to delay installation of the appliances until the new owners occupied their new home. Adoption of this practice by the industry would effectively remove the opportunity for theft since the owners would provide "capable guardianship" of the appliances. Very few ordinary residential break-ins involve theft of appliances since these are difficult to carry away, and there are many other more tempting targets for theft in occupied homes, such as small electronic items, jewelry and cash (Clarke 1999).

The surveys of builder practices had shown that some smaller builders who were delaying installation of appliances reported no thefts, but this might have been because they were building too few houses to become statistically at risk. Some site supervisors for the larger builders also said they did this on occasion, but there was no real consistency of practice. In fact, many builders were at first hostile to the idea. Sales personnel believed that having all of the appliances in place made a home more saleable, and that the new owner wanted to see appliances in place before completing the paperwork for purchase. They also believed that the absence of appliances, if attributed to theft, might unnecessarily alarm purchasers about the kind of area they were moving into. Site supervisors felt that the logistics of accepting delivery and installing appliances individually as houses were occupied were considerably more complicated than batch delivery and installation. Some erroneously believed that COs would only be issued by the building inspectors if appliances — including the plug-ins — were in place. Others said that this was a requirement of obtaining a mortgage. Finally, individual installation would mean that builders could not take advantage of the greater likelihood of being able to arrange for tightly-scheduled building inspectors to visit a site and issue COs wholesale. Given the bottlenecks sometimes caused by the unavailability of inspectors, this was a substantial concern.

Instead of turning away from this proposed solution and investing more in exploring other means for securing appliances, the project team decided that the objections to delayed installation of appliances should be discussed with builders to see if answers could be found.[3] On deeper exploration, the problems proved not to be as intractable as they first seemed. Not all sales people were opposed to the idea of delaying installation until the new owners had occupied the premises, as long as the reasons for this could be properly explained. For some managers, the difficulties and extra costs of individual delivery and installation might be offset by the reduction in thefts and damage and in the resulting delays in closing. The COs could be issued without installation of the "plug-in" appliances, though problems would remain in the case of hardwired appliances. Even in the case of the latter, building inspectors thought these problems could be resolved. It was unlikely that difficulties would arise with the mortgage companies so long as a CO had been issued.

A decision was therefore made at the end of 1999 to seek agreement from the Charlie One builders to institute a policy of delaying installation of plug-in appliances until the new owners occupied the house. It might be difficult to sell this idea to every builder, but the project team would focus on a group of the largest and, to date, most cooperative builders. Builders not involved in this "natural experiment" would serve as controls, and their break-in rates could be compared with those who agreed to the change of policy.

Accordingly, a presentation was developed, which the project team would take to each builder whose agreement was being sought. The presentation, which served as a vehicle for succinctly summarizing the results of the project to date and which was fine-tuned after critiques by Clarke and Goldstein, consisted of several parts: an introduction to the nature and severity of the problem; a description of the routine, but intensive policing efforts that had been made to deal with the problem; an explanation of why these had met with relatively little success and the change of direction to a problem-oriented policing project; solutions considered but rejected; the need for assistance from the builders and the proposed solution; the expected benefits for builders, police and local communities; and the plan for monitoring and reporting on the results of the experiment.

It was recognized early on that it was important to gain the endorsement of key officials before going to individual builders and to the local builder's association. The presentation was therefore made to the City Manager, County Manager, City Council Public Safety Committee, the District Attorney and the Chief Building Code Administrator. Their endorsement was incorporated into the presentation.

In seeking the builders' agreement to the experiment, they were told that:

- Hardwired appliances would be exempted.

- The CMPD would publicly acknowledge responsibility for the delay in appliance installation.

- The experiment would begin on May 1 and end on October 31, 2000.

- Compliance with the agreement would be monitored by police through checks made on houses close to completion.

- If the experiment did not succeed in reducing the rate of break-ins, the experiment would be discontinued.

As builders agreed to participate,[4] their names were added to the list of those supporting the proposal when the presentation was made subsequently to other builders. An important part of the presentation was a bar chart enabling builders to compare their break-in risks with those of their competitors. (Prepared specifically for each presentation, it did not include the identity of competitors.) The presentation and especially the bar charts invariably impressed the builders with the depth of the police analysis and, according to the project team, helped persuade many to participate in the experiment.[5]

MONITORING COMPLIANCE

Ten builders agreed at once to participate in the experiment by delaying installation of appliances until occupancy. Two other builders who had been asked to participate, but who had not formally agreed, were found from the beginning to be complying with the request to delay appliance installation. When asked again if they would agree to be formally included, the builders consented. This increased the total of "participating" builders from the 10 agreeing from the outset to 12. These 12 builders accounted for about 35% of construction in Charlie One in 2000.

As an added measure, the builders also agreed to post decals, to be furnished by the CMPD, on doors announcing in English and Spanish that "Appliances are *not* in this house!" Cunius and Rost were to monitor the extent to which these "participating builders" complied with the agreed measures by making regular checks on houses nearing completion to see whether they contained appliances and displayed decals. These "compliance" checks would be made on all houses in the district, not merely those of the builders who agreed to participate in the experiment. This was decided because it was anticipated that some of the non-participating builders, constituting a control group of sorts, might decide to adopt the measures when they heard about them. Indeed, some of them might already have been delaying appliance installation. Without knowing which of the "controls" were doing so, it would be difficult to interpret the results of the experiment.

Houses were selected for checks as soon as they reached the "pre-completion" stage, i.e., kitchen cabinetry was installed and the houses had windows that could be secured and doors that could be locked. Appliances were rarely installed before this stage, which was reached three or four weeks before completion. The officers would walk around each house to check for decals and would attempt to enter it. If they found it properly secured and they could not enter, they would look through the windows of the kitchen (always on the ground floor) to see whether appliances were present. For each house, they would record whether (1) it was at "pre-completion" stage, (2) it was secured, (3) decals were posted and (4) "target" appliances were present (i.e., plug-in appliances and any appliances that were to be hardwired, but had not yet been installed, thereby making them easy targets for theft).

This task was made easier by a data entry program loaded on their laptop computers devised by the crime analyst (Ryan Jackson). This program not only sped up data entry, but also enabled reports of the results of each round of checks to be provided to each builder. This served to remind participating builders of their agreement and to alert them to possible reneging on the agreement by site supervisors. By the time that the experiment was completed on October 31, Cunius and Rost had completed 15 rounds of compliance checks involving a total of 8,050 separate checks on individual houses.

It quickly became apparent from the checks that some of the participating builders, who had agreed to post decals and delay appliance installation, were failing to comply. In fact, few of them made much use of the decals, and one large builder was found to have appliances present in about 80% of the checks made at the "pre-completion" stage. Constant reminders, in the form of the officers' statistical reports on their levels of compliance, and personal approaches by the officers, failed to correct this situation. As expected, some builders, not formally included in the experimental group, were also found to be delaying appliance installation (though they were not installing decals because these had not been supplied to them). In other words, the boundaries between the participating and non-participating builders had become blurred.

The final tally of checks is enumerated in the Appendix. Builders are listed according to the percent of checks at pre-completion in which no target appliance was found to be present (i.e., in order of their compliance with the recommended practice). Throughout the six months of the experiment, the average compliance was 78% for the 12 participating builders; the same computation was 43% for non-participating builders. Compliance did not improve much after the first few weeks of the project. Implementation of the preventive measures was therefore only partly successful. There were still many houses in which appliances were present at completion stage, even for participating builders. Of the houses completed in Charlie One during the six months of the experiment, about 41% (an estimated 745) contained target appliances during the vulnerable pre-completion stage. In other words, considerable opportunity remained for appliance thefts.

EVALUATING THE PREVENTIVE MEASURES

Given that so many houses in Charlie One were still at risk of appliance theft, although significantly fewer than before, one could expect only limited success from the experiment. Burglars would still be able to find appliances if they were prepared to search a little longer. At the same time, it could be expected that builders who delayed installation of appliances until occupancy (whether officially participating in the experiment or not) would reduce their rates of burglary. This preventive measure is a form of target removal, which has been found to be effective in numerous contexts (Clarke, 1997b). The best-known examples relate to cash reduction programs in convenience stores (Hunter and Jeffery, 1997), betting shops in Australia (Clarke and McGrath, 1990) and buses in the United States (Chaiken et al., 1974; Stanford Research Institute, 1970). In each case, target removal in the form of cash reduction resulted in substantial declines in robbery.

Accordingly, the evaluation of the experiment sought answers to three questions:

(1) Did builders, whether or not they agreed to participate in the experiment, who made it their practice to delay installation of appliances until occupancy, significantly reduce their risks of appliance burglaries?

(2) Did builders who made a formal commitment to delaying installation (participating builders), but did not always do so, have lower rates of appliance burglaries than the non-participating builders?

(3) Over all, did the experiment bring about a reduction of appliance burglaries in the Charlie One District?

(1) Relationship between Burglary Risk and Delayed Installation of Appliances

If builders never installed appliances before occupancy, they would obviously never lose these appliances to burglary while the house was under construction. Unfortunately, only a few small builders always followed this practice (accounting between them for a total of only 19 completed houses during the experiment — see Appendix). Given this fact, it became important to explore whether the risk of burglary was proportionate to the degree to which builders followed this practice (whether or not they had agreed to participate in the experiment). This question was examined by sorting the 59 builders covered by the compliance checks — irrespective of whether they had committed to the experiment — into three groups: 20 builders with low percentages of houses (<17%) in which targeted appliances were present at the pre-completion stage; 20 builders with medium percentages of houses (24-66%) with appliances present; and 19 builders with high percentages of houses with appliances present (>70%). The numbers of houses completed and appliance burglaries reported were obtained for the duration of the experiment for these groups of builders.

While numbers of burglaries are small,[6] the three groups differed according to expectation (see Table 1). For builders with low percentages of targeted appliances present, the burglary rate for these appliances (0.9 per 100 houses completed) was about one-quarter of the rate for the high group (3.9 per 100 houses completed).

The high burglary rate (2.7) for all appliances for the group of builders who most frequently delayed installation of targeted appliances supports the conclusion that delayed installation does protect builders from burglaries, since this rate includes hardwired appliances — the installation of which was not delayed.

Table 1: Appliance Burglary Rates for Three Groups of Builders with Varying Percentages of Targeted Appliances Present at the Pre-completion Stage

Charlie One District, May-October 2000

Houses with targeted appliances present at pre-completion	Number of builders	Houses completed*	Burglaries of targeted appliances		Burglaries of all appliances	
			No.	Rate per 100 houses	No.	Rate per 100 houses
Low % with appliances	20	560	5	0.9	15	2.7
Medium % with appliances	20	891	13	1.5	17	1.9
High % with appliances	19	311	12	3.9	13	4.2

*Excluding 58 houses not covered by compliance checks

(2) Differences in Burglary Rates between Participating and Non-participating Builders

Despite the disappointing rates of compliance for the participating builders, targeted appliances were found to be present in many fewer of their homes (about 22%) during compliance monitoring than for the other builders (appliances present in about 56% of checks). One might therefore expect that the participating builders would experience fewer burglaries. Contrary to expectation, however, the participating builders experienced virtually the same rates of burglaries of targeted appliances as the non-participating builders, and somewhat higher rates of burglary of all appliances (see Table 2).

Table 2: Appliance Burglary Rates for Participating and Non-participating Builders

Charlie One District, May-October 2000

	Houses completed*	Burglaries of targeted appliances		Burglaries of all appliances	
		No.	Rate per 100 houses	No.	Rate per 100 houses
Participating builders (n=12)	631	10	1.6	22	3.5
Non-participating builders (n=47)	1131	20	1.8	23	2.0
All builders (n=59)	1762	30	1.7	45	2.6

*Excluding 58 houses not covered by compliance checks

One possible explanation for this anomalous result is that the participating builders might have been more vulnerable to burglary because of the location or size of their sites. Even after the experiment was introduced, cruising burglars could find appliances even though many of the houses were compliant.[7] Greater prior vulnerability of the participating builders could help explain why they were willing to take part in the experiment. It would also be consistent with the fact that the real difference in burglary rates between them and other builders involved hardwired appliances, which were given no protection by the preventive measures.[8]

To check whether the participating builders were at greater risk before the experiment, the analysis in Table 2 was repeated for the two years before the experiment, 1998 and 1999. Once again, data were analyzed only for May to October in both years. Not all the participating builders completed houses in these years, and the mix of other builders in the two years was different from that in 2000. Nevertheless, the analysis did provide some support for the idea that the participating builders might previously have been at greater risk of burglary. As shown in Table 3, burglary rates for the participating builders were higher in 1998 and 1999 than for other builders; of the four comparisons possible, the burglary rates were higher in all but theft of target appliances in 1999 (though the difference was very small).

Table 3: Appliance Burglary Rates for Participating and Other Builders

Charlie One District, May-October 1998 and 1999

	Burglaries of targeted appliances		Burglaries of all appliances	
	Rate per 100		Rate per 100	
	1998	1999	1998	1999
Participating builders	5.8	4.0	6.3	5.7
Other builders	4.6	4.1	4.9	5.1

(3) Overall Impact of the Experiment on Burglary Rates in Charlie One

The last and perhaps most important question concerns the overall impact of the experiment on rates of burglary in the Charlie One district. This was assessed by comparing the rates of appliance burglary for May-October, 2000 (the period of the experiment) and those for the same time period in the two previous years. This analysis produced the most striking finding in the study. As can be seen in Table 4, the rate of appliance theft in the Charlie One district dropped more than 50% in 2000 compared with the previous two years.[9]

To check that these declines in burglary in Charlie One were not simply part of a wider fall in these crimes, rates of appliance burglary were calculated for the entire area covered by the CMPD. Comparisons of the rates for Charlie One and the remainder of the CMPD show that the drop in these burglaries is much greater in Charlie One (see Table 5).

Table 4: Appliance Burglary Rates, Charlie One District May-October, 1998-2000

	Houses completed	Numbers of burglaries		Rates of burglary (per 100 houses)	
		Targeted appliances	All appliances	Targeted appliances	All appliances
1998	1072	54	58	5.0	5.4
1999	1437	58	76	4.0	5.3
2000	1820	30	45	1.6	2.5

Table 5: Appliance Burglary for Charlie One and All Other Districts in CMPD: May-October, 1998-2000

	Charlie One	Other CMPD Districts
Houses completed:		
1998	1072	2212
1999	1437	2892
2000	1820	3343
Appliance burglaries (target):		
1998	54	56
1999	58	39
2000	30	60
Appliance burglaries (all):		
1998	58	66
1999	76	51
2000	45	73
Burglary rate (target appliances):		
1998	5.0	2.5
1999	4.0	1.3
2000	1.6	1.8
Burglary rate (all appliances):		
1998	5.4	3.0
1999	5.3	1.8
2000	2.5	2.2

Table 5 also provides little evidence of geographic displacement of the problem from Charlie One to the other districts served by the CMPD. Rates of appliance burglary did not increase markedly in these districts during 2000.

A second possible form of displacement involves the targets of theft. Was there evidence that reductions in appliance thefts from construction sites in Charlie One were accompanied by increases in thefts of other items? An analysis conducted by the crime analyst attached to the project in its evaluation phase (Michael Humphrey) found that, for May-October 1999, 93 other thefts were recorded for Charlie One construction sites, while 87 were recorded for the same period in 2000. These figures translate into theft rates of 6.5 per 100 completed houses in 1999 and 4.8 per 100 in 2000. Far from suggesting displacement of the problem to other thefts, these figures suggest that, as anticipated at the outset, the reduction in appliance thefts might have brought wider benefits through a reduction in other thefts.

Before summarizing the results of the experiment, the possibility should be discussed that the reduction in appliance burglaries was the result not of delayed installation, but of the constant presence on the sites of Cunius and Rost when making the compliance checks. Each round of compliance checks took 8-10 days to complete, involving one visit per construction site of about 30 minutes. This can hardly be described as a constant presence. Indeed, the officers believed that before the compliance checks, when they were on regular patrol duties, they spent more (not less) time in the construction sites. In addition, during the entire period of the experiment they never once saw another police patrol car in the construction sites. It therefore seems unlikely that police presence was the cause of the decline in appliance thefts.

Summary of the Results of the Experiment

Delaying installation of appliances until occupancy removes the opportunity for theft, and the evaluation shows that builders who tend to follow this practice are likely to reduce their risks of appliance burglary. Rates of these offenses were considerably lower for builders who delayed installation for a high proportion of their houses.

The evaluation also showed that, in the period of the experiment, there was a substantial overall reduction in the rate of all appliance theft in the Charlie One District. This is a little difficult to explain given that the burglary rates for participating builders were not lower than those of the other builders in the period of the experiment.

However, this could have been due to the greater prior vulnerability of the participating group, whose burglary rates before the experiment were higher than those of the other builders. The experiment succeeded in lowering their burglary rates as well, but not to the level of the non-participating group.

Also difficult to explain is why theft rates declined when there were still so many houses (40%) with appliances present at the pre-completion stage. This means that "cruising" burglars would still have been able to find appliances if they were prepared to search a bit longer. But they seemed unwilling to do so, which suggests that the preventive measures were perceived as more widespread than they were in reality — a phenomenon known as "diffusion of benefits" (Clarke and Weisburd, 1994). Thus, some of the burglars might have decided it was no longer worth the effort of driving out to Charlie One when they heard that the installation of appliances was being de-layed, when they found it more difficult to locate appliances, or when they began to encounter houses with the warning decals. Further-more, it seems that few of them displaced their attention to building sites outside Charlie One. Burglary rates did not increase in these building sites that, in any case, had never been as tempting as the ones in Charlie One.

The discussion below of the lessons to be drawn from this project concentrates on issues of wider significance, but we should not overlook the value that the new response has had for Charlie One and the CMPD. The district now has fewer thefts to which to respond, which saves time, money and resources. Moreover, the district is spared the frustration of being held accountable for the crime, but not really being able to do anything about it. Cunius and Rost are more content in their work because of their pride in having brought a more intelligent, more effective, and ultimately timesaving response to this particular problem.

FOLLOW-UP ACTION

At the conclusion of the experiment, Cunius and Rost met with each of the 12 "participating" builders to obtain views on the experi-ment. All 12 were certain that delaying installation of appliances had been effective in reducing thefts. Some believed that other thefts had also declined. All 12 said they would continue to delay installation as a matter of policy. Some said that it should be a countywide policy.

Some problems of coordinating delivery of appliances with closing dates were reported,[10] and several builders said that they had experi-enced difficulties in getting site supervisors to comply with the policy. Only a few reported objections from purchasers, who mostly accepted the need for the measures once the reasons were explained to them. Providing coupons for the delivery of free pizza to meet the immediate need for food pending installation of appliances (a precautionary measure suggested by early discussions with builders about the experiment) mollified the more vociferous complainants.

Three further rounds of compliance checks made by the two officers after the conclusion of the experiment (during January-March 2001) showed that the participating builders had maintained their levels of compliance. Indeed, the overall 81.5% compliance rate for the group was slightly higher than during the experiment (78%). Other builders were also delaying installation in an increased proportion of houses (51% during January-March 2001 compared with a little under 43% during the experiment). The officers believed that this increase was the result of site supervisors moving from employer to employer. In some cases, those previously employed by participating builders converted their new employers to the policy of delayed installation.

As part of a broader effort to "market" the practice of delaying appliance installation, Cunius and Rost continued their efforts to persuade other builders to adopt it. They also made presentations of the results to CMPD command staff, to local builders associations and to the problem-oriented policing conference held by the Police Executive Research Forum in December 2000. They held briefing meetings for officials in nearby cities and for the press, the latter resulting in a favorable article in the Charlotte *Observer* (the local newspaper). They were invited to draft short articles for publication by the Police Executive Research Forum and for the house journal of the state builders' association.

In another effort to extend the practice of delayed installation, Captain Johnson asked Cunius and Rost to "sell" the idea to builders who were embarking on the construction of apartment complexes in Charlie One — at the time of writing, this was becoming a full-time responsibility for one of the officers. Johnson also asked the officers to explore the possibility of delaying installation of dishwashers, which had been excluded from the experiment because they are generally "hardwired." The officers discovered that these units could be supplied as "plug-ins," though they would still have to be connected to the water supply. When undertaking a further round of compliance checks in March 2001, they established that dishwashers were installed at the pre-completion stage in 64% of the 388 checks they made. However, only one dishwasher was stolen in March from the total of 279 houses completed, a risk of less than 0.4 per 100 houses. This was thought not to justify the effort that would have been required for both manufacturers and builders to change their practices to allow for delayed installation of dishwashers.

At the time of writing, Captain Johnson had recommended two further actions to his superior officers, building on the work to date. The first involved instituting a department-wide policy of not investigating reported thefts of appliances by builders who had refused to delay installation until occupancy, and informing such builders that proven means were available by which, through an adjustment in their own practices, they could substantially reduce such thefts. This did not gain the approval of the CMPD's executive staff. The second recommendation, still under consideration, involved the adoption of a countywide ordinance requiring all builders to delay installation of appliances.

LESSONS OF THE CASE STUDY

As noted earlier, the case study served three purposes: (1) it met its original goals by providing a comprehensive example, within the CMPD, of what is involved in a concentrated, careful application of the full dimensions of problem-oriented policing; (2) it enabled the CMPD to address the problem of theft of appliances from construction sites by learning as much as possible about the problem, by testing the effectiveness of a new response, and by ultimately achieving a substantial reduction in such thefts; and (3), as an unanticipated bonus, it provided the authors, as a result of their involvement in the project, with new insights into the complexities of carrying out problem-oriented policing and enabled them to see more clearly what is needed to enable others to realize, more expeditiously, similar results. It is these lessons gleaned from the project that are summarized here.

As explained, the project began life as a conventional police operation — one in which, having decided to take a proactive stance, the two Charlie One officers, Cunius and Rost, planned to undertake an intensive patrol and investigative effort to identify, arrest and prosecute the criminals responsible for the construction site thefts. In fact, this enforcement effort continued long after the project had become an exercise in problem-oriented policing because of the time taken to complete the analysis and identify alternative responses. As a result, the two officers spent every available hour in 1999 patrolling the sites and working with detectives to build cases against anyone suspected of, or arrested for, construction site theft.

By one measure, this was a successful operation because cases were made against 20 individuals in 1999 compared with only two individuals in 1998. But when related to the number of such crimes reported, the intensified effort aimed at detection, arrest and prosecution was a failure. The number of appliance thefts in Charlie One actually increased in 1999 to 167 from 109 in 1998, and the rate of theft per 100 houses increased to 5.3 from 4.7. This early analysis led the police officers involved to conclude that, despite their efforts, conventional police work would not solve the problem. Not only had the officers' extraordinary efforts to identify, arrest and prosecute offenders made little impact; they had been unable to acquire information about where the appliances were being sold, which could have led to new and potentially more fruitful investigative efforts.[11]

If the Charlie One team had accepted defeat at this point, the project would have been merely one more example of the limited capacity of conventional policing to reduce many ordinary crimes. In fact, the project demonstrates that where conventional policing has failed, problem-oriented methods can succeed. Some earlier examples of similar failures followed by successes involved the efforts to control slug use in the London Underground ticket machines (Clarke et al., 1994), graffiti in the New York City subway (Sloan-Howitt and Kelling, 1990) and pay phone fraud in the Port Authority Bus Terminal in Manhattan (Bichler and Clarke, 1996). In all three cases, the police had tried and failed to deal with the problem through stakeouts, intensified patrols, surveillance, and the prosecution of arrested offenders. They arrested only a small proportion of the offenders, they found it difficult to prosecute successfully, and, even if successful, the sentences imposed by the courts seemed to have little deterrent effect. In New York, the newspapers regularly ran stories about police frustrations in dealing with the problems in the bus terminal, sometimes including photographs of police standing by as alleged offenders continued to make fraudulent use of the phones.

In all three cases, the problems were solved only when the managers of the facilities stepped in with preventive measures of their own. In the case of the London Underground, the ticket machines were modified to block slug-use and, in the Port Authority Bus Terminal, conventional pay phones were replaced with more advanced models programmed to make fraud impossible. In the case of the New York subway, the solution consisted of an intensive and sustained program of graffiti cleaning.

In Charlie One, the builders had no intention of taking ownership of the problem and finding solutions as in the above examples. It was easier for them to trust to luck and swallow any losses. The Charlie One team, however, was unwilling to give up without having achieved any positive results. By the time it was clear that conventional policing was not going to work, the problem-oriented analysis had begun to point the way to the solution eventually adopted. Cunius and Rost were eager to try this solution, and the district's captain, Johnson, who was convinced that further effort was justified, was enthusiastic in his support of them. Even though Johnson was working in a supportive management structure, this cannot have been an easy decision for him to make. After a disappointing period of failure in pursuing the first initiative, it required that he commit substantial resources, at a time of great competition for the limited personnel resources available to him, to a long and sustained effort, with no guarantee of success. But this points to one of the strongest general lessons of the project. If, based on the positive results derived from problem-oriented policing, it is to become a standard method of doing police business, the police (and those to whom they are accountable) will have to become accustomed to measuring the success of their efforts over a longer period of time, and will have to find ways to justify the use of the resources required to produce such positive results.

Furthermore, to obtain the maximum benefit from the project, police must not rest content with reductions in the local problem. With a commitment to improve the quality of policing more broadly, police, like the Charlie One team, must be prepared to invest additional effort in documenting and disseminating the results. In this way, local inquiry and action can have national benefits, and, reciprocally, studies conducted elsewhere can have local benefits. This is particularly important for a problem such as construction site theft, which, by its very nature, is likely to be troublesome in most places for only a relatively brief period of time. Once the volume of construction decreases, the problem will likely disappear. But somewhere else, where construction is just beginning, the problem will soon emerge. It is important to enable those affected in the new location to profit from the experience of dealing with the problem gained elsewhere.

This means that these wider benefits of local action should be included in any assessment of the costs and benefits of such action, which could radically affect any conclusions about the investment of resources. In Charlie One, the project, by conservative estimate, prevented over 100 thefts (i.e., about 6 per 100 houses completed) in 2000. The district commander characterized this, when compared to other allocations of resources, as a good return on the time invested by the two officers. However, if the practice of delaying appliance installation were adopted more widely — throughout the county, or in the entire region, the state and ultimately the nation — without the need for so heavy an initial investment of resources, but with similar benefits, the cost-effectiveness balance would be even more favorable.[12]

Seeking these wider policing benefits will require police administrators to act increasingly like the heads of local public health departments, whose professional commitment extends beyond their communities to building knowledge for their profession. Thus, while the principal duty of police administrators will still be to safeguard the communities in their care, they will also increasingly have to meet the important responsibility of alerting other communities to new hazards, to evaluating measures taken in response to these hazards and to disseminating the results achieved. This will require them to undertake a delicate political balancing act. They must act successfully to deal with the problem locally, while at the same time justifying the additional expenditure needed to benefit communities elsewhere in the region, the state, and the country. The desirability of encouraging police agencies to engage in such studies, and the benefits to be realized beyond the jurisdiction conducting the study, constitute strong arguments for a program of federal financial assistance for such efforts.

Few police departments currently possess the technical capacity to evaluate and disseminate the results of their operations. If the required knowledge and skills exist in any degree, they are most likely to be found in departmental crime analysis units — and frequently not even there. This brings us to another important lesson of the project, which concerns the vital role of crime analysts in problem-oriented policing, and how their work relates to the role of police officers — on which much more attention has focused.

As originally conceived, problem-oriented policing anticipated the heavy involvement of individuals trained in analysis (Goldstein, 1979, 1990). But as problem-oriented policing has developed, most of the emphasis has been placed on the potential contribution of those who are depended on to carry out the daily, challenging work of policing — line police officers — but who also are at the lowest level in the police hierarchy. The Charlie One project leaned heavily on the contribution of the two officers, Cunius and Rost, and, by any measure, their contribution — especially to the analysis — was far beyond what could normally be expected of line officers. They spent days sorting through and re-classifying theft reports relating to construction site theft. They repeatedly interviewed builders to collect data about their security practices and theft experiences. They constructed databases that made it possible to calculate the rates of theft for individual builders, first by number of building permits issued and later by certificates of occupancy. They prepared graphs and tables setting out the results of these calculations so that relatively unsophisticated audiences could understand them. Above all they spent countless hours, in all kinds of weather, making and recording the results of thousands of compliance checks. Along the way, they absorbed many lessons about analyzing a problem, developed their own analytical skills, and grew in their capacity to present the findings in a coherent, persuasive manner.

However, even with the support and guidance they received, the officers would readily acknowledge that they could not have undertaken much of the work that was carried out by the crime analysts, who created computer maps of the construction site thefts, obtained and processed data on building permits and certificates of occupancy, and designed the computerized data collection systems for the compliance checks.

The crime analysis unit in the CMPD — in its size, the abilities of its staff, and its highly developed use of computerized databases, including advanced mapping — is among the strongest such units to be found in a police agency. It was possible, through the involvement of Clarke and Goldstein in this project, to build on those strengths — giving the analysts the additional knowledge and skills needed to carry out problem-oriented policing. Drawing on their experience, Clarke and Goldstein provided the theoretical background needed for guiding the project. They elaborated on the action research methodology of problem-oriented policing, which is too often simplistically captured in the four stages of the SARA (Scanning, Analysis, Response and Assessment) model. And they demonstrated how this would play out in dealing with the problem of construction site theft. Sensitive to the traditional perimeters of crime analysis and drawing on their experiences in other contexts, Clarke and Goldstein were in a unique position to contribute further by drawing attention to the importance of:

(1) having realistic expectations about the results of enforcement efforts;

(2) focusing the project on a highly specific problem, or form of crime, i.e., appliance theft;

(3) supplementing the most common form of "hot spot" mapping with carefully developed information about the environment being mapped (e.g., the stage of construction reached and the identity of the different builders operating in the various subdivisions);

(4) relating the absolute numbers of appliance thefts to the number of vulnerable homes, thereby producing suitable measures of risk before reaching conclusions about trends or patterns in these thefts;

(5) using acquired data to compare security practices and risk of thefts among builders, and to engage builders in assuming some responsibility for solving the problem;

(6) assuring that, in the language of routine activity theory, there are capable guardians of vulnerable targets;
(7) being alert to the possibility of diffusion of benefits and not being deterred from preventive action by the threat of displacement;
(8) monitoring closely the process of implementation; and
(9) utilizing an evaluation design that would permit definitive conclusions about the value of the response.

Police officers charged with undertaking a problem-oriented project and crime analysts who have limited themselves to the traditional forms of crime analysis cannot be expected to have an intuitive grasp of these points, and they will need to call upon others for advice. We believe that the repository of the research skills required in problem-oriented policing, at least for the larger police departments, should be the crime analysis unit. This does not diminish in any way the contribution that police officers — both line and management — can make in addressing problems. As Cunius and Rost demonstrated, in an exceptional example, their contribution is vital and they can be drawn more fully into the process. Police agencies should continue to encourage all of their personnel to think about their work in terms of the problems they handle and their effectiveness in dealing with them. But officer involvement, by itself, absent some special analytical and research skills, will not be sufficient to realize the full potential in problem-oriented policing.

Judged by the CMPD, crime analysts have the necessary background to profit from the appropriate level of training in problem-oriented policing, which should also include components on environmental criminology and program evaluation. Unfortunately, training courses of this kind are not readily available, and providing them will be a considerable challenge for police leaders and others, such as municipal governments, federal agencies, and universities that support advances in policing.

More is needed than training, however, to turn crime analysts into effective resources for problem-oriented policing. Equally important is that they be brought more directly into the management of a police agency; that, to the extent they become involved in in-depth analysis of the effectiveness of their agency in dealing with specific problems, they be recognized as the equivalent of product researchers in the private sector. Chief executives in the business world lean heavily on those who are equipped to analyze the quality of their end product. Properly trained crime analysts, engaged in the systematic study of problems that the police handle, as contemplated in problem-oriented policing, should have direct access to the top police administrator; should be involved in management meetings; and should be routinely consulted for guidance on how to improve the effectiveness of police efforts. Fully developed, their unique contribution could go a long way toward increasing the effectiveness of the police and, as a consequence, the professional status of the police in the community.

CONCLUSION

In reflecting on this project, a reader might be inclined to ask several basic questions. Why was so much attention given to such a discrete and, in relative terms, low volume crime? Why should it have taken more than two years and substantial resources to explore and address the problem? Was the involvement of the two authors and the backgrounds they were able to bring to the project warranted, and did their senior status distort the results of the "experiment?" Would the research methods utilized meet the tests of scientific inquiry? Didn't much of what was explored simply constitute common sense? Wasn't the solution implemented almost embarrassingly simple? Why make so much both of the experiment in addressing the theft of appliances and of the process by which it was carried out?

The answers to these questions are to be found in the current state of policing — in the United States and elsewhere. Despite the enormous investment made in policing, we know little about the problems police handle on a daily basis. The people affected — citizens, businesses, industries — also know little about them. And our knowledge about the most effective and economical ways in which to address these problems is very limited, and often primitive. While some progress has been realized in recent years, we are only at the beginning in testing the value of specific strategies for dealing with specific problems. We have not developed, within policing, a protocol, a staff, a methodology, and, most importantly, a way of thinking that leads to the systematic study of problems and the relative merit of different strategies for dealing with them. The body of research that is available, usually conducted outside police agencies, is often inaccessible to the police. So, given the primitive state of affairs, getting going requires a great deal of trial and error. It is not a neat process. Indeed, it is a rather messy process. It requires getting one's hands dirty. It requires digging for data and often making do with less than what one would want. It requires correcting and often supplementing existing data. It exposes difficulties that were unanticipated; phenomena that cannot easily be measured; findings and results that become blurred. It requires being ready to retreat or change course, and start all over again.

These are among the reasons the project took as much time, resources, and coaching as it did. And these are the reasons why we saw merit in recording all of the details of this relatively modest exploration. Through publication, others can build on these efforts — and thereby ultimately contribute to the critical need to build a strong commitment within policing to gain new insights into the problems the police are expected to handle, and to develop a sophisticated capacity within policing to conduct such inquiries.

Address correspondence to: Ronald Clarke, School of Criminal Justice, Rutgers University, 123 Washington Street, Newark, NJ 07102.

Acknowledgments: This project was completed under a grant (970CWX0060) made to the Charlotte-Mecklenburg Police Department by the Office of Community Oriented Policing, U.S. Department of Justice.
   Most of the work on this project was carried out by Officers Daniel Cunius and G. Eric Rost of the CMPD. They identified the problem of theft from construction sites as warranting attention in the course of their routine patrol work. They subsequently nominated it for more intensive examination and, when the study was approved, compiled much of the needed data, acquired information from builders, participated in all stages of the analysis, monitored implementation of the agreed-upon response, and prepared and presented the findings of the study. Throughout all stages of the project, they were strongly supported by their captain, E. Charles "Chuck" Johnson, who also participated in all stages of the analysis, in engaging the builders, and in presenting the findings of the study. Technical assistance in the compilation and mapping of the data was, initially, provided by Carl Walter, who also acquired and integrated data from other county agencies. Ryan Jackson, who succeeded him as the crime analyst assigned to the Charlie One district, acquired and integrated the data on "certificates of occupancy" and developed the computer program for recording compliance. Michael Humphrey provided the technical support for the final stages of the project. Steve Ward, senior assistant district attorney assigned to work full-time in the CMPD, took a close interest in the project and attended many of the project meetings. The write-up of the project was greatly facilitated by the detailed notes taken on several of the early project meetings by Officer Lisa Carriker.
   Dennis Nowicki, the former chief of police of the CMPD, initially encouraged taking on this project as a case study in problem-oriented policing. In its final stages, the project has received strong support from the

new and current chief of the CMPD, Darrel Stephens. The former Director of Research and Planning, Dr. Richard Lumb, was generous in his arrangements for allocation and scheduling of staff time, as was Acting Director, John Couchell. Finally, James LeBeau of Southern Illinois University provided us with valuable statistical advice.

REFERENCES

Bichler, G. and R.V. Clarke (1996). "Eliminating Pay Phone Toll Fraud at the Port Authority Bus Terminal in Manhattan." In: R.V. Clarke (ed.), *Preventing Mass Transit Crime.* (Crime Prevention Studies, vol. 6.) Monsey, NY: Criminal Justice Press.

Chaiken, J.M., M.W. Lawless and K.A. Stevenson (1974). *The Impact of Police Activity on Crime: Robberies on the New York City Subway System.* New York, NY: The New York City Rand Institute.

Clarke, R.V. (1999). *Hot Products. Understanding, Anticipating and Reducing the Demand for Stolen Goods.* (Police Research Series, Paper No. 112.) London, UK: Home Office.

—— (1998). "Defining Police Strategies: Problem Solving, Problem-Oriented Policing and Community-Oriented Policing." In: *Problem-Oriented Policing: Crime-Specific Problems and Critical Issues and Making POP Work,* vol. 1. Washington, DC: Police Executive Research Forum.

—— (1997a). "Problem-Oriented Policing and the Potential Contribution of Criminology." Unpublished Report to the U.S. National Institute of Justice (Grant # 95-IJ-CX-0021).

—— (ed.) (1997b). *Situational Crime Prevention: Successful Case Studies* (2nd ed.). Albany, NY: Harrow and Heston.

—— R.P. Cody and M. Natarajan (1994). "Subway Slugs: Tracking Displacement on the London Underground." *British Journal of Criminology* 34:122-38.

—— and D. Weisburd (1994). "Diffusion of Crime Control Benefits: Observations on the Reverse of Displacement." In: R.V. Clarke (ed.), *Crime Prevention Studies,* vol. 2. Monsey, NY: Criminal Justice Press.

—— and G. McGrath (1990). "Cash Reduction and Robbery Prevention in Australian Betting Shops." *Security Journal* 1:160-163.

Constructor (1999). "A Billion Here and a Billion There. A Guide to Theft and Vandalism Control." *Constructor* (November) LXXXI(11):1-4. Alexandria, VA: The Associated General Contractors (AGC) of America.

Dayton, J. (1993). "Construction Theft Takes Sharp Rise." *The Business Journal Serving Greater Sacramento.* February, 22, Volume 9 (48):1-7.

Eck, J.E. and W. Spelman (1988). *Problem-Solving. Problem-Oriented Policing in Newport News.* Police Executive Research Forum/National Institute of Justice. Washington, DC: Police Executive Research Forum.

Farrington, D.P. and P.A. Langan (1998). *Crime and Justice in the United States and in England and Wales, 1981-96.* Washington, DC: U.S. Department of Justice.

Felson, M. (1998). *Crime and Everyday Life* (2nd ed.). Thousand Oaks, CA: Pine Forge Press.

Goldman, M.D. (1999) "Cure Can Cost More than Construction Site Theft." *Washington Business Journal* June 14:1-3.

Goldstein, H. (1996a). *Problem-Oriented Policing: The Rationale, the Concept, and Reflections on Its Implementation.* London, UK: Police Research Group, Home Office.

—— (1996b). "Problem-Oriented Policing." An Address to the Summer Conference of the Association of Chief Police Officers, Manchester, England, July 3, 1996.

—— (1994a). "Examining the Current Status of Problem-Oriented Policing and Thinking Through an Agenda for Research and Technical Support for the Concept." Unpublished memorandum addressed to Craig Uchida, Office of Community Oriented Policing Services in the United States Department of Justice, July 11, 1994.

—— (1994b). "Suggestions for Inclusion in the National Institute of Justice Research Agenda Relating to the Police." Unpublished memorandum addressed to Jeremy Travis, Director of the U.S. National Institute of Justice, September 29, 1994.

—— (1979). "Improving Policing: A Problem-Oriented Approach." *Crime & Delinquency* (April):234–58.

—— (1990). *Problem-Oriented Policing.* New York, NY: McGraw Hill.

Hunter, R. and C.R. Jeffery (1997). "Preventing Convenience Store Robbery through Environmental Design." In: R.V. Clarke (ed.), *Situational Crime Prevention: Successful Case Studies* (2nd ed.). Albany, NY: Harrow and Heston.

Laycock G. and N. Tilley (1995). "Implementing Crime Prevention." In: M. Tonry and D.P. Farrington (eds.), *Building a Safer Society: Approaches to Crime Prevention.* (Crime and Justice: A Review of Research, vol.19.) Chicago, IL: University of Chicago Press.

McGreevy, S.L. (1999) "Theft and Vandalism: How To Protect Yourself" *CONTRACTOR.mag.com,* The Newsmagazine of Mechanical Contracting 11/99:1-4.

Read, T. and N. Tilley (2000). *Not Rocket Science? Problem-Solving and Crime Reduction.* (Crime Reduction Research Series, Paper No. 6.) London, UK: Home Office, Police Research Group.

Scott, M.S. (2000). *Problem-Oriented Policing: Reflections on the First 20 Years.* Washington, DC: U.S. Department of Justice, Office of Community Oriented Policing Services.

—— and R.V. Clarke (2000). "A Review of Submissions for the Herman Goldstein Award for Excellence in Problem-oriented Policing." In: C. Sole Brito and E.E. Gatto (eds.), *Problem-oriented Policing: Crime-specific Problems, Critical Issues and Making POP Work,* vol. 3. Washington, DC: Police Executive Research Forum.

Sloan-Howitt, M. and G.L. Kelling (1997). "Subway Graffiti in New York City: 'Gettin Up' vs. 'Meanin It and Cleanin It.'" In: R.V. Clarke (ed.), *Situational Crime Prevention: Successful Case Studies* (2nd ed.). Albany, NY: Harrow and Heston.

Snyder, R.G. (2000). "Construction Theft: What You Can Do To Prevent It." *NC Builder Magazine* December, 1-2.

Stanford Research Institute (1970). *Reduction of Robbery and Assault of Bus Driver. Vol. III. Technological and Operational Methods.* Stanford, CA: author.

Stewart, L. (2000). "Firms Discount Equipment Lost To Crime." *Construction Equipment* (April), 101(4):66-72.

—— (1998). "Simple and Sophisticated Strategies to Thwart Thieves." *Construction Equipment* (August), 98(2):60-70.

APPENDIX

Builder Compliance Rates and Burglaries
Charlie One, May-October, 2000

BUILDER	Compliance Checks[1]	Target appliance present[2]	Appliance Compliance[3]	Homes completed[4]	Burglary of target appliance[5]	Burglary of any appliance[6]
1	23	0	100.0%	2	0	0
2	121	0	100.0%	0	0	0
3	1	0	100.0%	0	0	0
4	13	0	100.0%	3	0	0
5	6	0	100.0%	2	0	0
6	1	0	100.0%	0	0	0
7(H)	23	0	100.0%	10	0	0
8(H)	2	0	100.0%	2	0	0
9	27	1	96.3%	1	0	0
10	295	17	94.2%	56	0	0
11	377	25	93.4%	111	0	2
12	130	9	93.1%	14	0	0
13	21	2	90.5%	3	0	0
14	1122	131	88.3%	108	3	9
15	87	11	87.4%	58	0	0
16	123	16	87.0%	25	0	0
17	23	3	87.0%	20	0	0

BUILDER	Compliance Checks[1]	Target appliance present[2]	Appliance Compliance[3]	Homes completed[4]	Burglary of target appliance[5]	Burglary of any appliance[6]
18	668	102	84.7%	117	2	4
19(H)	6	1	83.3%	4	0	0
20	24	4	83.3%	24	0	0
21	487	118	75.8%	84	1	1
22	58	17	70.7%	8	0	0
23	137	48	65.0%	15	1	1
24	583	207	64.5%	218	1	1
25	120	51	57.5%	64	0	0
26	18	8	55.6%	2	0	0
27	17	8	52.9%	14	0	0
28	222	112	49.5%	57	1	5
29	100	51	49.0%	14	0	0
30	141	73	48.2%	41	5	5
31	43	26	39.5%	5	0	0
32	33	20	39.4%	17	0	0
33	319	196	38.6%	106	1	1
34	96	59	38.5%	49	0	0
35	186	116	37.6%	67	0	0
36	164	104	36.6%	40	2	2
37	118	75	36.4%	34	0	0
38	105	69	34.3%	33	0	0
39	62	41	33.9%	16	1	1

BUILDER	Compliance Checks[1]	Target appliance present[2]	Appliance Compliance[3]	Homes completed[4]	Burglary of target appliance[5]	Burglary of any appliance[6]
40[H]	3	2	33.3%	7	0	0
41	133	93	30.1%	16	0	0
42	68	48	29.4%	17	0	1
43	502	362	27.9%	108	2	2
44	59	44	25.4%	55	0	0
45	75	58	22.7%	11	2	2
46	72	57	20.8%	15	0	0
47	143	114	20.3%	28	2	2
48	45	37	17.8%	12	0	0
49	28	24	14.3%	6	0	0
50	15	13	13.3%	0	0	0
51	109	98	10.1%	6	0	0
52	30	27	10.0%	2	1	1
53	162	151	6.8%	13	3	3
54	244	230	5.7%	18	2	2
55	155	150	3.2%	2	0	0
56	62	62	0.0%	0	0	0
57	4	4	0.0%	0	0	0
58	1	1	0.0%	1	0	0
59	38	38	0.0%	1	0	0
	8050	3334	58.60%	1762	30	45

Notes to Appendix:
(1) Number of checks made to determine if target appliances were present in a house. These are appliances that plug into an electrical outlet or any appliance that is scheduled to be hardwired, but have not yet been installed and are, therefore, like a plug-in appliance easily stolen.

(2) Number of times a target appliance was found present during a compliance check.

(3) The percentage of compliance checks when target appliances were not present within the home.

(4) A completed home is a home that has passed all inspections required by the building code and qualifies for a Certificate of Occupancy.

(5) Number of burglaries resulting in the theft of one or more targeted appliances.

(6) Number of burglaries resulting in the theft of one or more appliances, including hardwired appliances.

(H) indicates the builder uses hardwiring exclusively in installing all appliances.

NOTES

1. Burglary of a home under construction is classified, until it is occupied, as commercial.

2. No one among the team was aware at first that these data existed, and, moreover, could be obtained in a usable form. In undertaking problem-oriented and situational prevention projects, it is often found (by asking the right questions, and by probing and pressing) that needed data are kept by other agencies and that these will be released (although pressure may have to be applied).

3. This exemplifies the need for an iterative relationship between analysis and response. As soon as a promising response is identified, its costs and benefits need to be further analyzed. The alternative of comprehensively exploring all available response options runs the risk of losing momentum.

4. Some of those unwilling to participate were large national builders. This suggests that the "buy-in" of outside interests in a problem-oriented project would depend on several identifiable factors: (1) whether the interest (or business) has local roots or is from outside the city — with corresponding degrees of commitment to the welfare (i.e., level of crime) in the local community; (2) whether local operations are customized or represent a cookie-cutter approach developed by a national corporation to maximize efficiency and, therefore, profits; and (3) possibly the size of the

private enterprise. Regarding the latter, a small contractor might not find it as easy to absorb the cost of losses as does the large contractor.

5. It is awkward and somewhat intimidating for police to approach contractors (and other business) people — to get them to take steps that will reduce crime. They fear being told that reducing crime is their job and that they should go about doing it. Asking others to act requires exposing the limited capacity of the police — and that is awkward for a "macho" type operation. Moreover, police are supposed to be apolitical, and sensitive to their use of coercion in their work. Pressing to engage others, from their perspective, draws them into activities some see as improper. The project demonstrates the power of data in equipping the police to engage others. The police often put themselves in the position of complaining that groups or individuals are shirking their responsibilities. But these complaints don't get them anywhere and can put the police in an embarrassing light. The opportunity to present rigorously developed data should be seen as a major new "weapon."

6. These small numbers account for the lack of statistical significance in the differences between groups.

7. The burglars' search for appliances might even have been narrowed by the decals telling them which houses had no appliances and thus which ones to avoid.

8. Another force might also have been at work. Burglars might have been returning to a familiar, favorite hole (as in fishing) — one in which they previously found in abundance what they were looking for — but now were faced with the need to search more intensively.

9. One-way Chi square tests found significant differences between observed and expected numbers of targeted and all appliance thefts across the three years.

10. The contractors split their deliveries, arranging for hard-wired appliances to be delivered at one time, followed by immediate installation, and for the "plug-ins" to be delivered as homes were occupied. Apparently they incurred minimal costs in adopting this practice.

11. Cunius and Rost ended up being enthusiastic about the project — and its potential — and are now effective spokesmen in challenging the deeply ingrained commitment to always reverting to the use of the criminal process (i.e., investigation, arrest, prosecution, etc.). This was evident during a presentation they made on the project at the annual problem-oriented policing conference in San Diego in December 2000, where they

strongly rebutted suggestions made by some in the audience that a more vigorous patrol and investigative effort would have brought results. It is also evident in a report made by the two officers in April 2000 to the COPS office. This opens with the following paragraph: "In May 1998, we thought we knew about problem solving. We worked third shift and we were concerned about the construction site thefts in our district. We approached our captain with a plan to reduce thefts. The plan was thought out over a shift and was comprehensive. The plan was not a band-aid method but was made to target the three elements which make up a crime (suspect, victim and opportunity). We were to work with the burglary detectives to help identify the suspects. Once the suspect was arrested, we were going to petition the courts to get them the maximum prison sentence. As for the victim builders, we wanted to get after hour contact numbers in case suspects were apprehended in their neighborhoods. We were also going to exchange crime prevention ideas with the builders in order to improve and increase the builder's use of crime prevention techniques. As for the opportunity element, we wanted to alter our methods of patrolling the neighborhoods under construction. We planned on staking-out neighborhoods, using marked and unmarked patrols as well as altering the days and times we patrolled. We thought this plan would reduce the construction site thefts. Within six months our plan was barely intact. The site managers we contacted were either reassigned or had left the company. This made the after hour contact list and distribution of crime prevention information worthless. We did not identify any suspects and our directed patrols did not reduce the reported crimes. We had thought through our plan, but left out one major aspect, analyzing the problem."

12. The amount of time devoted to the project by Cunius and Rost should not be taken as an indication of what a similar effort would require in other circumstances and in working under a more restricted time frame. The officers were periodically involved in other police activities; they were involved in the investigation of crimes and the prosecution of offenders; they spent considerable time learning new techniques of analysis and presentation; and they had the luxury, in this first-time project, of engaging in some wide-ranging explorations that, while productive, would not be required in a replication.

FROM THE SOURCE TO THE MAINSTREAM IS UPHILL: The Challenge of Transferring Knowledge of Crime Prevention Through Replication, Innovation and Anticipation

by

Paul Ekblom

Research, Development and
Statistics Directorate,
U.K. Home Office

Abstract: Knowledge, in combination with pragmatic, cultural, organisational and conceptual factors, determines the performance of practitioners such as police, local government community safety officers and product designers. This paper addresses the serious and widespread obstacles to the transfer and application of knowledge generated by professional criminological research, development and evaluation, to the mainstream of practice in the overlapping fields of crime prevention and problem-oriented policing. The emphasis is on those obstacles inherent in the nature and form of knowledge itself. It therefore relates content-free concepts of knowledge management to content-rich considerations of the particular qualities of crime prevention knowledge and how it is applied in practice. It covers key issues of replication, innovation, and anticipation through, for example, foresight activities. It draws on ideas from design, evolutionary epistemology, memetics, more conventional anthropological views of cultural transmission and evolution, and organisational research on diffusion of innovation. The aim is to open up new ways of thinking centring on "genotypic" principles of prevention that apply across contexts and across time — which can provide the foundations for practical suggestions for training, guidance and design of knowledge bases. So many, and diverse, connections emerge to the works of one renowned social scientist that this paper seems almost an exercise in following the Donald Campbell trail.

TRANSFER AND APPLICATION OF KNOWLEDGE: THE PROBLEM OF MAINSTREAMING

The fundamental approaches to crime prevention are known. We are beginning to establish what is effective and cost-effective in broad terms, and work continues to develop a reliable and systematic evidence base. Building on major assessments of what works in crime prevention and reduction for the U.S. Congress (Sherman et al., 1997) and the U.K. government (Goldblatt and Lewis, 1998; Ekblom et al., 2001 in press), the U.K. Home Office is midway through a £400m Crime Reduction Programme which aims both to be evidence-based and to generate more such evidence through rigorous evaluation and assessment of cost-effectiveness (e.g., U.K. Home Office, 1999). On the academic side, a "Campbell Collaboration" for crime and justice[1] has now been inaugurated whose primary purpose is to generate high-quality reviews of evidence of effectiveness and cost-effectiveness of crime prevention (see Farrington and Petrosino, 2001). Building a rigorous knowledge base of what works, and is cost-effective, is a challenging task (and, as will be seen, one that we can never aspire to finish). Equally challenging to the strategic delivery of crime prevention policy and practice is the *transfer* of the knowledge we have acquired, from its source — often in intensively nurtured and well-funded demonstration projects involving top-level, practically-oriented academics working with advanced and committed practitioners under controlled conditions — to *application* in the mainstream by police, local community safety staff, designers, architects and others. For a number of fundamental reasons to be discussed below, moving crime prevention knowledge from source to mainstream encounters so many obstacles that it seems like an exercise in struggling uphill. The aim of this paper is to look closely at this important task, and draw on understandings from a range of fields to help do it in a smarter and more effective way.

Attempts to apply the results of successful demonstration projects, and of research and evaluated good practice more generally, have regularly encountered difficulties in delivering mainstream activity that performs nearly so well — even allowing for the more complex and less favourable conditions often found in the mainstream. Evidence for this is found, for example, in assessments of England's Safer Cities Programme (Sutton, 1996; Knox et al., 2000); research accompanying "Thematic Inspections" of crime reduction in the police forces of England and Wales by Her Majesty's Inspectorate of Constabulary (Hough and Tilley, 1998; Read and Tilley, 2000); a U.K. Audit Commission review of local crime prevention (U.K. Audit Commission, 1999); research on problem-oriented policing in both the U.K. and U.S. (see Leigh et al., 1998; Eck, 2001; Scott, 2001); and assessment of early experience of the Burglary Reduction and Targeted Policing Initiatives of the U.K'.s Crime Reduction Programme (Tilley et al., 1999; Bullock et al., in press).

Three common symptoms are of central relevance here:

(1) Shortcomings of analysing crime problems.

(2) Shortcomings of devising solutions that are both customised to these problems and their causes, and that are also innovative.

(3) Shortcomings of implementing the solutions.

Some important but fairly mundane and tractable factors account for some of these limitations of performance, such as lack of project planning and management skills, and pragmatic constraints of timing, funding, securing agreement, etc. Beyond these is a range of challenging fundamental causes, which together form a pernicious and resilient web across the path of good practice:

(1) In the police, particularly but not exclusively, cultural and organisational change to accommodate the preventive, problem-oriented approach is slow. There is the familiar over-concentration on catching criminals rather than tackling wider causes of crime.

(2) Compartmentalised, method-oriented thinking still predominates, alongside a myopic emphasis on problems internal to the organisation rather than out there (Eck, 2001; Scott, 2001; Read and Tilley, 2000; U.K. Her Majesty's Inspectorate of Constabulary, 2000); analytic thinking, and the risk-taking inherent in innovation, do not follow naturally from the organisation's style of working and are not rewarded. Certain kinds of organisational structures and processes — for example, top-down implementation of detailed guidelines and protocols and imposition of detailed objectives and targets — impede, or foster, attention to problem-solving, use of evidence and learning as part of day to day practice (Nutley and Davies, 2000). In this respect, changing the thinking of individual practitioners through education and training may have only limited impact if they are pressured into recidivism the mo-

ment they return to routine work: *organisational development* is needed to change the whole organisation simultaneously, including the way it learns (Argyris and Schon, 1996).

(3) But organisations, too, do not exist in isolation. The wider environment of public expectation and media criticism which the police and local government inhabit is not conducive to problem-orientation and innovation. Nor are the rules governing public accountability and the way money can be spent, and stifling and over-detailed central control in general (Nutley and Davies, 2000; Faulkner, 2001:288-289). Key Performance Indicators in principle are valuable "levers" for encouraging practitioners to act on research such as repeat victimisation (Tilley and Laycock, 2000), but their narrow and superficial use ("my Chief requires me to find five hot-spots per month") can be part of the problem.

(4) Additional difficulties occur where crime problems, causes and solutions span major divisions of labour in society (Ekblom, 1986; Ekblom, 2001a), and partner organisations must find ways to pool their resources of time, money, knowledge and technology, and link their diverse approaches and priorities to deliver prevention. In extreme cases there may not even be a starting-point of consensus about the extent, existence or definition of particular crime and community safety problems, let alone what to do about them. The working culture of any one institution may comprise a distinct blend of explicit knowledge, hidden assumptions or beliefs, motives and values that are hard to tease apart and rationally link up to partner institutions or individuals.

(5) Practitioners' understanding and choice of interventions is similarly hampered by fragmentation. There are still significant occupational divides between enforcement-oriented and civil approaches, and, within the latter, between situational and offender-oriented prevention (Ekblom, 2000a). Solutions are thus compartmentalised and restricted in scope when experience suggests the benefits of synergy. "Natural history" classifications that are based on familiar, face-value categories (particularly "sweeping" ones such as "physical security," "social" or "community prevention") have immediate appeal but are too vague and inconsistent to help when it comes to detailed capture and storage of "what works" information, and selection and planning of action by the user. Better frameworks do exist (for example, Clarke's (1997) "16 techniques" of

situational prevention), but they are partial, not comprehensive, and may be insufficiently analytical.

(6) There are limitations to the depth and quality of practitioners' understanding of the causes of crime and thus their interpretation of the specific crime problems they analyse. In part this can be attributed to the predominance of the narrow "blame-the-offender" cultural focus, which precludes wider and more dispassionate causal analysis. But there is also a lack of time for analysis, reflection and learning, and lack of provision for teaching. A tradition of "oral transmission" of knowledge (Scott, 2001) imparts limited and perhaps inaccurate information, and constantly draws practitioners back into their own occupational culture. Career development traditions of generalism and "moving on" among police and local government mean that individuals acquire only limited practical expertise, invest limited time in education and training for any one job and are rarely in a position to learn how to apply it, nor to teach or coach new staff for long, or to give feedback to educators about the longer-term benefits and limitations of their courses.

(7) That training which is available is often superficial. Modular formats are convenient and helpful for keeping up with changing knowledge. But they are insufficient as a substitute for more intense foundation courses, and inadequate if put together without the necessary underpinning of a needs assessment, an aim and a set of learning outcomes.

(8) Education, training, briefing and mass media are not the only deficient knowledge transfer mechanisms. Laycock (2000, 2001), and Tilley and Laycock (2000) emphasise the lack of contact and cultural common ground between researchers and practitioners, which prevents each from understanding, and communicating with, the other's world. Sherman (1998) makes similar observations. More generally still, there is growing understanding that traditional, centralised or top-down knowledge-diffusion mechanisms are not universally applicable, especially to circumstances where localised solutions are appropriate (Nutley and Davies, 2000).

(9) Whether knowledge is imparted through training and education, mass media, or by live, hands-on advice and collaboration between practitioners and researchers, and whether diffusion is centralised or decentralised, an even more fundamental difficulty lies with the nature, scope and quality of that

knowledge itself. The state of criminological knowledge is incomplete and fragmentary. Although criminologists are moving gradually in the direction of integrated models of the causation of crime (see Wikström et al., 1995; Ekblom, 1994, 2000a), there is still far to go.

(10)The terminology in use to describe causes of, and interventions in, crime is often vague and inconsistent. This hinders thinking, communication and collaboration. This is a particular problem with international knowledge bases, where translation and inexperienced interpretation add a further layer. And no lexicon will help if the underlying concepts themselves are loosely defined. As the report of a current European debate put it (Ministère délégué à la Ville, 2001:4), "Making the information exchanged comprehensible, going beyond [mere considerations of] translation the vocabulary and the concepts of crime prevention vary from one country to another and are vehicles of misinterpretation and misunderstanding." The consequences of a lack of a conceptual framework (Ekblom, 2000a, 2001b) go beyond communication and thinking — they underlie the fragmentary nature of crime prevention knowledge, and contribute to the failure of theory to inform practice (Laycock, 2001) and practical interventions to inform theory (Farrington, 2000).

Ultimately the improvement of performance in crime prevention must rest on a combination of remedies to all these constraints — establishing a problem-oriented and innovative culture receptive to research evidence, designing organisations and their management procedures to be conducive to this culture, and establishing a wider supportive climate for those organisations in their turn; improving training and building bridges between practitioners and researchers; and improving the quantity, quality, form, conceptual basis and organisation of crime prevention knowledge itself. This paper focuses on the last, knowledge, although links to the other issues are made where appropriate.

There is growing awareness that knowledge does not flow naturally from source to mainstream, but has to be actively moved uphill. There is no "gravity feed" mechanism: passive dissemination is not enough to ensure implementation of research findings and the adoption of an evidence-based approach (Nutley and Davies, 2000). Consequently, alongside efforts to generate knowledge through research, development, evaluation and high-quality evaluation reviews such as in the Campbell Collaboration, explicit efforts to transfer that knowledge are being stepped up. At the time of writing there is much activity involving a mix of climate-setting, education and training, practitioner networks, guidance material and the establishment of knowledge bases:

(1) Detailed "what works" and "how to do it" material is being assembled in the form of "toolkits" for the U.K. government-supported Crime Reduction website (www.crimereduction. gov.uk, which also provides for practitioner discussion groups to share experience horizontally). Toolkits aim to supply a strategic and tactical framework for understanding local crime problems and contexts, and how to identify, implement and evaluate solutions.

(2) The new European Crime Prevention Network has interests in sharing knowledge and training, and is accompanied by a new European Union (EU) funding stream, Hippokrates, to this end.

(3) Europol is seeking to develop knowledge bases (Browne et al., 2001) and centres of excellence (Kerkhof, 2000) for organised crime prevention practice.

(4) The International Centre for the Prevention of Crime maintains a "digest of good practice" directory (www.crime-prevention-intl.org).

(5) The Council of Europe has a range of action projects and reports which aim to transfer knowledge and know-how to Eastern European and CIS countries (e.g. Alexandersson et al., 1999).

(6) On the more traditional education and training side, analysis of the needs for education and training formed an important aspect of the guidance material put out by the Home Office to accompany the Crime and Disorder Act 1998 (www. homeoffice.gov.uk/cdact/actgch6.htm), which established a statutory duty on local authorities and the police, with other key agencies and the community, to work together at district level to develop and implement strategies for reducing crime and disorder in the area. At the time of writing, another major training review is taking place.

(7) The U.K. now has:

- a "Community Justice" National Training Organisation (www.communityjusticento.co.uk), which promotes training, development and education for practitioners in a wide range of relevant fields;

- a Crime Reduction College;
- and various charitable organisations, foremost among them Crime Concern (www.crimeconcern.org.uk) and NACRO (www.nacro.org.uk), which have an important national training role.

(8) The new Regional Crime Directors structure of the Home Office in England and Wales is developing a target-setting, support and quality assurance role, in which it is currently planned that criminological researchers with practical experience will coach, and hand-hold, local practitioners.

(9) Within the design-against-crime field, a current U.K. government-funded project (www.designagainstcrime.org), managed by the Design Council, aims to transfer knowledge (and also to alert and motivate designers and design decision makers) by assembling a list of exemplars, producing materials for teaching design against crime from school to graduate levels, and developing a national scheme on information and training.

By the time this paper is published many of these developments may of course have progressed further or been overtaken by events, but the trend towards actively organising the transfer of knowledge is likely to grow. When designing any knowledge base or setting out any training curriculum, however, we have to be very clear why we are doing it and what exactly we are hoping to transfer. To rush into construction is to court serious risks of expense and effort on the part of the designers and compilers and confusion and wasted opportunity for practitioners.

Help is at hand from one direction: a set of approaches known as "knowledge management" appears to have emerged as a discipline almost overnight, to cater generically for transfer in an increasingly knowledge-driven society. Knowledge management (see, for example, Macintosh [1999] for one description of the field) requires investment in the capture of knowledge, sharing of that knowledge, ensuring it flows effectively; and promoting its application. In effect it aims to embed within an organisation or a network an entire knowledge-culture and set of supporting systems (even to the extent of "knowledge proofing" all other processes and facilities).

However, this approach, while very useful, is not sufficient because it is content-free. In this paper I seek to put some of that content back, by dealing with knowledge in fairly generic terms but attuned to what we know about crime prevention. More specifically, my aim is to help to improve the process of moving crime prevention knowledge uphill from source to mainstream by discussing: the purpose and nature of that knowledge from a practical, task-performance perspective; how the form of useful knowledge is determined by the particular qualities of prevention; the implications this has for the collection of crime prevention knowledge through research, impact and process evaluation; and the organisation of that knowledge so it may be readily shared, retrieved and applied to tackle current, emergent and anticipated crime problems.

In the course of all this I first cover knowledge in terms of day-to-day practice, and then revisit some of the issues from the perspective of the race to innovate between preventers and offenders, which involves anticipation as well as quick adaptation, and places greater requirements on us to speed up and deliberately direct the development of knowledge. This involves drawing on a range of unfamiliar ideas from the fields of biological and cultural evolution and a wider understanding of (occupational) culture. Finally, I make particular reference to the need for the organisation and transfer of knowledge to be based on a common conceptual framework to link practical methods and theoretical principles and mechanisms of prevention, much as medical science does for medicine. As well as taking us through some intellectually interesting territory, all this has practical implications for the design of crime prevention knowledge bases and other media of transfer.

Henceforward, in referring to *the* Knowledge Base I mean the body of crime prevention knowledge however it is conveyed — not merely the transfer medium of *a* particular computerised knowledge- or database.

THE PURPOSE OF KNOWLEDGE:
Improving, Extending, and Sustaining Performance

Prevention can happen as an entirely incidental function of human activity, as when a passer-by deters a burglar merely by walking down the street at the right moment. But my present focus is purposeful "crime preventer" roles. A wide variety of people and institutions, private, public and commercial, act as purposeful crime preventers. They are involved in carrying out tasks which deliver, or support, crime prevention interventions. These can range from self-protection and informal social control, to job-related surveillance and site management (as in railway platform staff), to dedicated private security services, to design of products and environments against crime, to formal and professional policing, probation and punishment and rehabilitation of offenders.

Purposeful performance is about transforming inputs into desired outcomes. Improvements in the performance of crime prevention practitioner roles, through better judgements, decisions and actions, aspire to several things:

(1) Better *responsiveness* to crime problems — *targeting* on the needs of the victim and wider society, and on the causes of crime, and *prioritisation* of prevention.

(2) Greater *cost-effectiveness* of prevention.

(3) Greater legitimacy/ acceptability of actions.

(4) More complete *coverage* on the ground, in terms of the proportion of crimes that need tackling which actually receive the appropriate action.

(5) Wider *scope,* in terms of the range of crime problems preventers are willing and able to tackle.

Such improvements in performance can be delivered by professional crime prevention practitioners, when directly implementing the intervention themselves. Alternatively, professionals can *insert* prevention in the community — *mobilising* other people and institutions to take on responsibility for various "crime preventer" roles. Mobilisation can be described as an algorithm under the acronym CLAMED (Ekblom, 2001c; Ekblom and Pease, 2001):

(1) *Clarifying* the preventive goals to be achieved and tasks to be done in tackling a particular crime problem — whether these involve implementing the interventions themselves or helping and motivating others to implement.

(2) *Locating* the preventers — identifying institutions and individuals with the potential to own the goals and take responsibility for carrying out the crime prevention tasks — and qualified to do so because of their resources, acceptability for the role and the alignment of their interests.

(3) *Alerting* them (if they don't know already) that there are particular tasks to be done, or raising expectations that may lead them to apply pressure on others to do the tasks (as with consumer pressure on car manufacturers to raise security).

(4) *Motivating* them to do it (for example by legislation to impose duties, regulation, incentives and persuasion — reviewed in Laycock and Webb, 2000 and discussed in Ekblom and Pease, 2001).

(5) *Empowering* them to undertake the tasks and achieve the goals.

(6) *Directing* them towards specific crime prevention roles and goals, and away from possible negative side effects and excesses of interventions, such as stigmatisation, loss of privacy or even vigilantism.

Empowerment in particular can be delivered by supplying practitioners and the organisations in which they work with a range of *resources*. These include *raw materials*, such as funds and basic information, and a *capacity* to use those materials to the desired end. In an education, training and support context, this capacity is characterised as human resources with a set of *competencies* or practical skills and know-how, which are underpinned by (more cognitive) *knowledge*. (This is reflected in the "core competencies" approach to crime prevention education and training adopted, for example, in the U.K.'s Crime Reduction College and advocated by the "Community Justice" National Training Organisation. See for example Home Office (1997). Competencies are complemented by various kinds of *equipment* to make them more effective, such as closed circuit television (CCTV) (and the know-how to use that). They may also acquire certain *legal powers* or wider moral *legitimacy* to render what they do acceptable (and to place limits on that).

Individual practitioners and professional organisations acquire these various kinds of empowerment through a range of *capacity-building* processes and facilities: *legislation* to bestow powers; *education and training;* "off-the-shelf" supply of *guidance and operational information* from an infrastructure; transmission, transfer or sharing from *networks*; and *partnership*. The main rationale of the last is the pooling of complementary resources to tackle problems like crime, whose symptoms, causes and/or solutions span the normal division of labour in society (Ekblom, 2001a). Organisations with the power and the legal obligation to act, such as the police, may not always be the ones with the know-how or the scope to influence the opportunities and incentives for crime (Laycock and Webb, 2000).

In this wider context, raw materials and basic human resources are the major enablers, and awareness and motivation major drivers, combined in an organisational and network *culture* and a wider *climate* of support. However, neither money, staff nor will are much use without reliable knowledge and know-how. Appropriately applied, these are the key to performance in reducing crime. They are not merely distinct and detachable components, of course, but bind the whole together and provide the core substance. Without them, all the organisational procedures, structures and task management frameworks in the world are just hollow shells (which, sadly, does not stop these being continually invented).

CRIME PREVENTION AND WHAT WE CAN KNOW ABOUT IT

Moving beyond the rather limited and abstract concepts of competency and underpinning knowledge into a more content-rich zone, we can actually identify *five* distinct types of crime prevention knowledge:

(1) *Know-about* — knowledge about crime problems and their costs and wider consequences for victims and society, offenders' *modus operandi*, legal definitions of offences, patterns and trends in criminality, empirical risk and protective factors and theories of causation.

(2) *Know-what* — knowledge of which causes of crime are manipulable — what preventive methods work, against what crime problem, in what context, by what intervention mechanism/s, with what side-effects and what cost-effectiveness, for whose cost and benefit.

(3) *Know-how* — knowledge and skills (competencies) of implementation and other practical processes, operation of equipment, extent and limits of legal powers, instruments and duties to intervene, research, measurement and evaluation methodologies.

(4) *Know-who* — knowledge of contacts for ideas, advice, potential collaborators and partners, service providers, suppliers of funds, equipment and other specific resources, and wider support.

(5) *Know-why* — knowledge of the symbolic, emotional, ethical, cultural and value-laden meanings of crime and preventive action.

Doing practical, operational crime prevention involves gaining, and applying, all five Ks. But know-how, and in particular its *process* aspect, brings it all together. This paper focuses on know-what and know-how, with some reference to know-about; and know-why makes a brief but important appearance.

A familiar way of organising descriptions of know-how for local crime prevention schemes is the "*preventive process*" (Ekblom, 1988, 2000a; Laycock and Webb, 2000) equivalent to "SARA" (Scanning,

Analysis, Response and Assessment) in problem-oriented policing terms (Hough and Tilley, 1998; Leigh et al., 1998). This involves:

(1) Identification of crime *problem* and setting of *objectives* for reduction.

(2) *Diagnosis* of causes of crime problem.

(3) Selection of specific *interventions,* and creation of practical, cost-effective and acceptable operational *solutions.*

(4) *Implementation* and *"insertion"* (mobilising other individuals and institutions to implement specific interventions — Ekblom, 2000a; Ekblom and Pease, 2001).

(5) Evaluation, feedback and adjustment.

Dutch experience (van Soomeren, 2001) has centred round a more general project planning and management/ quality assurance methodology such as ISO 9001. Since the preventive process or its equivalent is a cycle, in a training context it has sometimes proved more fruitful to engage with the police culture by inaugurating the process at the "doing" stage, after which evaluation allows for analysis and (re)consideration of the problem.

A more detailed version of the preventive process is in Alexandersson et al. (1999) and Ekblom (2001a). Variations on this process centre, for example, on approaches that identify indicators of risk some distance causally upstream of crime rather than waiting for crime patterns to become established — for example the *"risk and protective factors"* perspective of Farrington (2001), or *crime impact assessment. Design against crime* works through a range of processes including:

(1) Remedial design to existing items post-manufacture or -construction (fitting an add-on security product, such as a crooklock to a car; or making a modification, such as building an entrance porch onto a housing block).

(2) Adjustment or upgrading of successive versions of an existing product (e.g., a more secure generation of mobile phones).

(3) Creating something more or less entirely new (and untried and untested by criminals) — such as a new shopping centre, a new personal organiser or a new financial system.

All these design models involve repeated cycles of generation, testing, selecting among alternatives and adjusting the chosen design. And the whole family of variations on the preventive process each involve some balance between replication of what has been done before, and innovation. We now turn to these.

Know-What: Replication, Innovation and Outcome Evaluation

Replication of successful crime prevention methods is an obvious aim of transferring practice knowledge. But even where we have good-quality, relevant and reliable "what works" information for tackling a specific crime problem, replication is a lot harder than we may at first think. Tilley (1993a) studied a number of attempted replications, in the Safer Cities programme, of the highly successful Kirkholt burglary prevention project (Forrester et al., 1988, 1990). The replications strikingly failed to deliver such good results. This suggested a paradoxical quality of crime prevention replication itself. In practical terms what, exactly, can be replicated if apparently close, literal, high-fidelity copies are likely to be less effective than the original?

Mechanisms, Contexts and Theories

Tilley's own answer is to define replication in a less literal, and more abstract, way. The Scientific Realist approach he adopts focuses on how causal intervention *mechanisms* — the way the preventive method works — interact with necessary features of the *context* to trigger the desired preventive *outcome* (Pawson and Tilley, 1997). The unsuccessful Kirkholt replications may have attempted to trigger a preventive effect in the new locations by means that insufficiently fit the specific crime problem there (burglary of *terrace* houses with *back alleys*) or its wider causal context (offenders motivated by *drugs;* neighbours with irremediably *hostile or indifferent relations*).

Practical replication, from this perspective, is not about mere cookbook copying of superficial features of interventions, and then hoping they will work like crop dusting uniformly gets rid of pests; or even a matter of looking for vaguely similar circumstances in which to implement the interventions. Rather, it is about getting the right mechanism to trigger the desired causal process of intervention in the right context, to deliver the desired outcome. Significantly, many of the studies of mainstreaming listed at the start of this paper noted the practitioners' *lack* of attention to preventive mechanisms. They were unclear about how, exactly, the intervention was supposed to work.

It is worth looking more closely at the concepts of mechanism and context. A *mechanism* is a dynamic process of causation, leading up to a particular event or set of events. That event can be the crime itself, and the mechanism describes the causation of that crime. Alternatively, the event can be the *non*-occurrence of an expected crime. In this case the mechanism can describe the intervention, a new and distinct causal influence which interrupts, diverts or weakens the *existing* mechanism — the causes that would have led to the criminal event.

Now for the *context*. Interventions do not act in a causal vacuum — as just described, they work by changing the balance of causal mechanisms that are active, undermining some old ones and/or introducing others that are new (Tilley and Laycock, 2000). Causation always involves some interaction between entities in which there is an exchange of energy, matter, information or influence. While we often think of contexts as an out-of-focus, taken-for-granted background, they are not a kind of optional "add-on" feature to understanding how an intervention works — they are central. Matches which set alight dry newspaper may nonetheless fail to ignite damp firewood. The causal mechanism for the bonfire lies not merely in the capacity of the matches to set things alight in the right conditions of dryness, but inseparably in the capacity of the paper to be set alight, and in the absence of rain. Likewise, a whole conjunction of causal conditions has to be present for a particular crime to occur — as described in Cohen and Felson's (1979) Routine Activities Theory, where a "likely offender has to meet a suitable target in the absence of capable guardians." (A much-elaborated version of this forms the Conjunction of Criminal Opportunity, described below.) The causal capacity of the offender to be provoked into defacing posters has to be matched by the capacity of a particular poster to provoke. And on the intervention side, a particular treatment may prevent recidivism only for offenders with a particular personality capable of being influenced by that treatment, in a wider family and employment context supportive of the process. Neighbourhood Watch may only work where good neighbourly relations already exist or are capable of being established, and neighbours can physically see and hear each other's homes.

Transferrable knowledge has to be based on *regularities* of some kind, patterns of events or observations which can be predicted to apply if certain conditions are present. Conventional (social) science regularities take the form of *theories* — highly compressed and generic causal abstractions applicable across many contexts that can be used to explain, predict and manipulate events. From the Realistic Evaluation perspective, descriptions of how crime preventive interventions *work* are abstracted regularities of a more localised and particular kind. They take the form of "Context-Mechanism-Outcome configurations" (Pawson and Tilley, 1997), which are a kind of self-contained packet of explanation and prediction for a specific kind of non-event (that is, a criminal event otherwise expected to happen in the absence of the intervention). Theories tend to focus on very narrow aspects of causation. A theory of prevention (in this case deterrence) might, for example, describe and explain how, in general, perceived *risk* of the offender getting caught is a more potent preventive cause than perceived *cost* of getting caught. In contrast, a Context-Mechanism-Outcome configuration (CMO) would aim to describe a wider and more complete web of causation — spelling out all the essential influences, including those characterised by theories, that come together to make a set of related criminal events fail to happen. A CMO might explain how a CCTV camera acts to reduce crime in a *particular* car park, how some rather more abstracted regularity acts across certain *types* of car park, or even, if enough research has been done and enough knowledge synthesised — across car parks or enclosures *in general.*

As CMO configurations become more generalised and abstract they more closely resemble conventional theoretical explanations, albeit integrated rather than single-factor ones. Both mechanisms and theories are *generative* — that is, they can explain, or generate predictions of, an open-ended set of observations or pattern of results given that we also have other information on context. Like theories, too, CMO explanations are highly *conjectural* — hypotheses to be tested and if necessary falsified.

In testing theory, it is usual to look for evidence which exclusively shows one alternative explanation to be true. In the case of mechanisms, by contrast, it is likely that several are operating simultaneously — several of the hypothesised processes may be true and, moreover, a number may be active in any given situation. In fact, in one set of car park contexts, Tilley (1993b) identified nine possible mechanisms behind a possible CCTV effect, and used detailed information, in exploratory fashion, to try to identify which were active. To illustrate just two, the cameras could have acted by literally facilitating surveillance and arrest; or by especially attracting to the car park those drivers who were security-minded anyway, and thus who would be sure to conceal valuables and lock doors. This multiple causation is not really surprising, though, because the immediate causal precursors of criminal events involve actors in a number of roles (offenders, preventers, promoters — see Ekblom, 2000a, 2001c, and below) all in close interaction, perceiving and anticipating one another's moves against each other and against the crime target, in front of a complex environmental backdrop. The "combinatorial" nature of the mechanisms that act through these causal precursors means that we can develop a kind of language for generating quite systematic and rigorous descriptions of causes (including theories where available), and of interventions.

Implications of a Mechanism Approach for Evaluation, Knowledge and its Application

Mechanisms certainly complicate the task of evaluators. Crime prevention initiatives often involve implementing a whole package of methods, and evaluators have to try to identify which method or combination of methods from that package actually worked and are worth replicating (Ekblom and Pease, 1995; Farrington 2000). Now they are being asked to look additionally within each method to see which mechanisms worked in which contexts. However, a focus on micro-detail of mechanisms and evidence for their operation (as advocated by Pawson and Tilley, 1997 under the label "Realistic Evaluation"), and the related approaches of "Theories of Change" and "Rival Explanations" (reviewed and compared from a crime prevention perspective in Laycock, 2000), do have advantages. It may help to unravel "package" impacts where conventional evaluation designs that neglect this extra level of theorising and data exploration may not. As Pawson and Tilley (1997) note, too, sensitivity to contextual interactions can often resolve apparently conflicting evaluation findings — a serious problem for the practitioner seeking authoritative advice. So methodological improvements in internal validity of evaluations (attributing cause and effect), straightening out conflicting findings and improved capacity for context-sensitive replication should outweigh the extra effort of looking for mechanisms and CMO configurations. Finally, Farrington (2000) urges that evaluations of interventions should wherever possible be used to test theories. If we strive to link our mechanisms and CMO configurations to theories, or complexes of theories, this purpose can still be served.

Turning now to the results of evaluations — i.e., knowledge of what works — the causal significance of context has implications here, too. At the very least, there is a major generalisation problem. Not even the best-stocked and highest-quality store of "what works" information is sufficient to guarantee that knowledge gleaned in one context can successfully deliver when simply applied without significant adjustment to others. And one can never hope to conduct enough properly-evaluated replications to give coverage to the full range of contexts likely to be encountered.

Given all that has been said in this section so far, the proper approach to replication here would be to *assemble generic principles of intervention and then apply them alone or in combination as appropriate to specific circumstances* — fitting theories and/or abstract distillations of preventive mechanisms to particular problems and contexts. From this perspective a "true replication" of one distinctive feature of the Kirkholt project could be identified as the whole Repeat Victimisation approach (Tilley and Laycock, 2000; Laycock, 2001). (Interestingly, this approach relied not only on "pure" knowledge products comprising a "programme theory" and a set of "articulated tactics," as these authors put it, but on an entire system of transfer and support implemented and developed over some years.)

In terms of application there is an obvious trade-off in the utility of the extremes of specific and generic knowledge. Specific CMO configurations are more easily envisaged and implemented because they spell out relatively complete descriptions of causation; but, being localised or "situated," they cover only limited ranges of problem and context. Theories, describing one or two very abstract causal processes, apply over a wider range of crime problems and crime contexts, and hence are more transferrable; but they may be challenging to convert to specific practical interventions, and there is greater risk of interference from unmeasured or uncontrolled intervening variables on the way.

In practice, though, such "intervening variables" should not be considered as some extraneous nuisance, as they would be if a researcher was seeking a convenient way of testing a particular theory. In real-world implementation they are part of the game. This means knowledge based much more on a wide range of theoretical principles; and in CMO terms, configurations that are more generalised, structured and synthesised — a huge and jumbled pile of situation-specific configurations would be unusable.

Such structure and synthesis will at the very least involve "branching contingencies." *If* neighbour relations are good, *then* the following mechanisms may work (given further contextual specifications). *If not*, then other mechanisms may work and other interventions may be appropriate. (Such a synthesis of some Neighbourhood Watch findings is in Tilley and Laycock, 1995.) Interestingly, our knowledge of "what works" in the remedial treatment of convicted offenders has also begun to evolve in this interactional direction, treatment being contingent on the type of individuals to receive it and whether they have reached the right state of readiness to benefit (Vennard and Hedderman, 1998; Andrews et al., 1990). And, of course, the same applies in medical science, where contemporary gene-specific treatments are the culmination of a process of customising treatments to patients.

From Abstract Principles and Mechanisms to Real-World Intervention Methods

Generic intervention *principles* (such as "discouragement through increased effort") and spelled-out, context-specific intervention *mechanisms* (such as "blocking offender access to target enclosure in terraced houses") are both regularities, and, one hopes, evidence- and theory-based. They are invisible abstractions that are generative of patterns of outcomes. But to realise any intervention we have to implement real-world *methods* (such as a specific course of literacy skills for offenders, or the addition of a concierge) or *designs* (e.g., the most appropriate design of alley gate — ten bars, galvanised, slam-locking or whatever). This is equally valuable know-what information. However, the decision to deploy particular methods and designs should be subordinated to the choice of principles and mechanisms, and the details of their realisation should reflect these too. (For brevity, "methods" are henceforth taken to include practical designs.) But note that one person's intervention method is another person's implementation principle — someone has to have expert knowledge of how best to galvanise the gates or the best employment terms for concierges.

We have already seen, with the car park CCTV example, how one intervention method can trigger and act through several possible mechanisms. This means that any knowledge base of interventions would have to articulate between real-world *methods* of prevention — the several spelled-out *mechanisms* by which those methods are conjectured to work in particular contingent contexts — and the generic *principles* which, singly or in combination, underlie the mechanisms. In terms of knowledge base design, a structure is needed which promotes "flipping" between these three perspectives. In practical terms this could well involve a relational database, with its one-to-many and many-to-many relations (Ekblom, 2000c; Ekblom and Tilley, 1998).

The problem-oriented approach subordinates choice of method to the nature of the crime problem and the causes to be tackled. So when good, professional practitioners design a real-world intervention method or select and adapt an existing one to a particular context, they need to draw on, and bring together, a whole range of generic principles and mechanisms, and an equally wide range of specific methods to realise them. (This is not only to get the best out of past experience, but to avoid making matters worse. Fitting a communal entrance porch to a medium-rise building to block unwelcome access and facilitate surveillance needs to be checked to ensure it doesn't offer a foothold for burglars to reach first-floor windows, as once reputedly happened when such a fixed recipe was being followed.) This is often facilitated by taking the offender's perspective, or "thinking thief" (Ekblom, 2001d, 2001e). More broadly put, practitioners have to be helped to think more like *expert consultants*, innovating and reconfiguring their diagnoses and solutions on the fly, and less like *technicians* slotting in a simple prepackaged remedy to one of a limited set of fault diagnoses, like a washing machine service engineer. Bodies of "what works" knowledge therefore need to be designed in such a way as to help practitioners to consider the *whole* interacting picture of causes of crime and the *whole* range of possible intervention principles, mechanisms and methods as they apply to a problem *in situ*, and then work up customised proposals.

Feedback

There is, though, a further step in the application of knowledge. Good first-guesses can be made about what combination of generic principles and what realised methods are likely to work in the new context, particularly as we begin to find out more about context/mechanism interactions. But in most cases there is an element of launching into the unknown. A stage of *feedback and adjustment* is therefore required to get the intervention right. (Of course, persistent failure to get one approach working should lead to its abandonment in favour of another.) The classic project management "plan-do-review" cycle should be shortened and repeated so that clues to misalignment and failure are picked up and acted upon quickly rather than held back till the very end when adjustment is difficult.

This all resembles the creative trading-off of diverse requirements, simulation, prototyping, laboratory attack testing and field testing that goes into the process of designing a material product from first principles. It suggests that crime prevention practitioners of all kinds could learn a lot from the thought processes and techniques of product designers. From a broader perspective, the emphasis on transfer of generic intervention principles and local realisation and adjustment enables the resolution of a long-standing quality-assurance dilemma in evidence-based crime prevention — how to ensure interventions are designed simultaneously to reflect expert, reliable, evidence-based knowledge, from the *centre*, of what works, without stifling innovation and adaptation to *local* context. Nutley and Davies (2000) discuss this with particular reference to the Repeat Victimisation strategy described by Laycock (2001) — seeing it as a useful hybrid of centralised and decentralised approaches to diffusion of innovation. The Communities That Care approach (summarised in Farrington, 2000) promotes a similar blend.

In view of what was said above about the existence of multiple mechanisms behind a crime reduction effect, one important task during the trial-feedback-adjustment cycle should be to determine which of the conjectured preventive mechanisms are in fact operating in the particular context. Feedback is a useful way of identifying which causes are active, and the knowledge gained helps the practitioner to tweak the right controls next time round. It is also of more technical use in evaluation: what better way to know that you have caught hold of a cause by its tail, than when you can move it up and down, and see the preventive effect switch on and off in step? This happened with Poyner and Woodall's (1987) installation and removal of anti-shoplifting equipment in a London store. Medical research abounds with examples of similar Scientific Realist approaches — adding neurotransmitter chemicals, blocking receptor molecules etc., to unpick causes by manipulation. However, this ideal may only apply to crime prevention under limited circumstances — namely, when there is a ready ability to control conditions and manipulate the causes, and a sufficient flow rate of criminal events for changes in frequency to be rapidly and reliably observed. In many cases, sadly, this is as unrealistic as the aspiration to the universal application of random controlled trials in project-type work. Feedback is, however, easier to apply in more routine, case-type activity, like the handling of domestic assaults. Sherman (1998) argues for the routine collection of feedback on outcomes of patrol attendance at various kinds of incident to improve performance of practitioners.

Information on conjectured mechanisms and theories — not only those that appear to have operated, but also those which were ruled out — is of more lasting value than the important but ephemeral role it can play in feedback. It can contribute to the assembly of *comparative and representative* knowledge of how important or unimportant these mechanisms were in general. (Phillips [1999] attempts to do this in her review of CCTV evaluations and the mechanisms that underlie the pattern of impacts and non-impacts observed.) And a mechanism that failed to work in one context may well work in another and is worth recording for that alone.

The wider significance of the feedback requirement elaborated in this section is that, in practice, there is no sharp divide between *replication* (involving adaptation of existing preventive methods to tackle the same crime problems in new contexts) and *innovation* (generating distinctively novel methods and/or tackling new crime problems). The performance processes involved are on a continuum from "try something that has always been shown to work against all such problems, and in all such contexts" to "try something entirely new to cope with entirely new problems and entirely new contexts" (see also Osborne's [1998] typology of evidence-based innovations, also summarised in Nutley and Davies [2000]).

We will return to all these know-what issues when we adopt an evolutionary perspective.

Collecting Know-How — A Key Role of Process Evaluation

The replication-innovation issue connects closely to another facet of Tilley's (1993a) study of replications. Practitioners attempted a too-literal copying of the specific interventions devised for Kirkholt, when they should have been more intelligently following the steps of the preventive process to home in on the specific local problems in the new locations, and customise solutions which may or may not resemble the original.

This once more illustrates that know-what alone is insufficient for good performance. Successful prevention requires knowing how to deliver the right interventions to the right causes of a crime problem, properly attune them to the context, and adjust through feedback; and do all this in an efficient, effective, sustainable and acceptable way. Replicating crime prevention interventions therefore needs the Knowledge Base to capture the key ingredients of know-how. As with interventions, these regularities of knowledge can take the form of *generic* implementation principles (such as "always consider testing situational intervention methods on elderly users"), or *specific* elements that have to be attended to for particular intervention methods to succeed (such as "check in advance whether alley gates require cat-flaps" [Johnson and Loxley, 2001]). Wider difficulties of implementation, relating for example to joint decision-making issues, have been well-described by Hope and Murphy (1983) in the U.K., and

Pressman and Wildavsky (1984) in the U.S., and many of the lessons have long been incorporated in practitioner guidance materials. The steps of the preventive process provide a self-evident framework for specifying and organising know-how (including how the other types of knowledge are to be obtained and used as the process unfolds). They therefore also define the key questions of a process evaluation to capture this information from particular crime prevention projects or programmes (see Sutton, 1996, for an example). Under "collecting information on crime problems," for example, the Knowledge Base can assemble novel and useful (or useless) features of crime surveys developed and employed in an initiative.

It is also useful to capture and improve on practical know-how of the means of obtaining feedback itself. As already said, feedback in crime prevention may be too slow, unreliable or expensive if it relies on waiting for sufficient numbers of potential crimes to fail to happen. It therefore becomes important to specify *intermediate* outcomes, and to develop rough and ready indicators of these to give quicker and cheaper knowledge of results. Knowledge of detailed intervention mechanisms can guide this process.

As the Campbell Collaboration emphasises, it is important to know what *doesn't* work in particular contexts, or at all — practitioners do not want to waste effort and opportunity in using or reinventing the flat tyre. But this applies to know-how as much as to know-what. A good understanding of the generic causes of failure at a number of levels is vital to salvage constructive knowledge from unsuccessful schemes. (Rosenbaum's [1986] "theory failure, program or implementation failure, and measurement failure" are a good start, but can be developed further as will be seen below.) A learning culture supports this approach; and an innovative culture accepts an element of unpredictability, extemporisation (rather than rigid management plans) and failure as a risk inherent in pioneering work, provided that strategic goals are adhered to, lessons are learned and mistakes are not replicated.

All these proposed requirements for acquiring know-how and know-what information on implementation, intervention, context and outcomes of success or failure can be costly of time and effort — often in short supply in a practical situation where bidding for, and spending, money has to be done within a set timeframe. But the potential collective benefit of such information, in terms of improved performance over a much wider set of activities and a longer time frame, means that it is worth devoting a "tithe" to evaluation (Ekblom and Pease, 1995). Such evaluation becomes easier and more routine at the point of conduct, the more the *infrastructure* for "evaluability" is put in place in advance (Ekblom, 1996b).

NEW PERSPECTIVES ON THE CRIME PREVENTION ARMS RACE — BIOLOGICAL AND CULTURAL EVOLUTION

The here-and-now operational view of knowledge, adopted so far, is not the whole story: knowledge itself must evolve, and the knowledge-gathering, synthesis and transfer processes must be designed to help it evolve efficiently. In earlier papers (Ekblom, 1997, 1999) I described crime prevention as an arms race between preventers and offenders, with move and adaptive countermove played out over shifting ground as social and technological change constantly create new opportunities for offending — new targets, new environments, new business models, new information sources. There are strong similarities with military arms races, biological coevolution of predator and prey, and other "evolutionary struggles."

In this analysis, individual elements of crime prevention knowledge — particularly know-what — become wasting assets. (A Knowledge Base containing what used to work is worse than useless — ask any ammonite!) And new crime problems emerge which we don't immediately know how to tackle. (In an interesting equivalence between the Campbell collaboration and Cochrane, its medical counterpart, this is equivalent to the arrival of new occupational diseases and the evolution of antibiotic-resistant pathogens.) Sustaining and extending crime preventive performance therefore becomes a race to innovate and to disseminate that innovation — a race to acquire, share and apply new knowledge faster than offenders and wider aspects of social and technological change can invalidate it.

This new perspective requires us to extend the criteria for improved performance that we set out when discussing the purpose of knowledge. For improvement to be significant, and sustained, it involves more than just building of the capacity of practitioners by transferring to them what we know already, or even developing that capacity by incrementally pushing forward the frontiers of evaluated knowledge. It requires gearing up in an entirely new way.

To gear up we must go beyond the management and expansion of existing knowledge assets and jump to a higher level where we deliberately improve the overall process of knowledge management itself — capturing, organising, storing, maintaining, updating and transferring the knowledge more quickly and more effectively. Part of this is deliberately bootstrapping our own self-awareness of what knowledge is, the better to improve it. But there is more: if crime prevention, and hence crime prevention knowledge, is now in an evolutionary game, it should itself adopt evolutionary tricks to keep up (Ekblom, 1997, 1999; Cohen et al., 1995). Mainstream Knowledge Management institutions (e.g., Macintosh, 1999) have acknowledged the same evolutionary need, and hence the same concern with improving *processes* that act on knowledge assets. The evolutionary pressure here is not, however, that of the arms race between predator and prey, but the commercial pressure of competition.

At this point, therefore, it is worth pausing to introduce some developments in evolutionary and cultural anthropological thinking which may not be familiar to those in the crime prevention field. These developments cover both the nature of knowledge and how it evolves. The aim is partly to generate immediate practical suggestions, but partly also to open up a different way of thinking which might help academics and practitioners alike to produce new ideas in the future — and to explore some fascinating connections on the way. This will mean revisiting some topics already covered, but from a fresh angle.

New Developments in Evolutionary and Cultural Thinking

Conventional biological evolution is no longer the whole story. Donald Campbell — he of the Collaboration, in fact — also had something else named after him: Campbell's rule (Durham, 1991). According to this rule (Campbell, 1960, 1965, summarised in Blackmore, 1999:17), biological evolution, creative thought (at the heart of innovation, of course) and cultural evolution resemble each other. They do so because all are evolving systems where there is blind variation among the replicating units and selective retention of some units at the expense of others. The analogy with cultural accumulations is not from biological evolution *per se*, but from a general model of evolutionary change for which biological evolution is but one instance. This kind of thinking was developed in tandem with the philosopher of science, Karl Popper (e.g., Popper, 1972; Tilley, 1982).

Knowledge as social scientists usually understand it is perhaps a subset of culture, but Plotkin (1993) explicitly defines knowledge in "universal Darwinist" terms, which relate more deeply to all the kinds of evolution on Campbell's list. Following Campbell (1974) himself, Plotkin calls this approach to understanding the universals of the acquisition and application of knowledge "evolutionary epistemology." The approach applies whether that knowledge was genetically inherited from its parents or psychologically learned during an organism's lifetime. *Inherited* means obtained by "genetic learning" across generations over evolutionary timescales, where adaptations such as the permeability of a reptile's skin reflect knowledge of the mean and range of the humidity of the environment. The knowledge is acquired through the trial and error process of variation; natural selection of the fittest (weeding out of the less fit by predation and competition for finite resources); and high-fidelity replication in the next generation. *Learned* means obtained by a single animal during its lifetime through trial and error generation of behaviours, and retention of successful ones — those that led to reward. (Throughout this discussion of learning the more sophisticated cognitive learning mechanisms of humans, and the wider range of goals than mere survival and reproduction, are set aside for simplicity of exposition.)

Inherited knowledge reflects things about the world which are constant or only very slow to change in relation to the time span between successive generations of animal. Learning is a specific adaptation which evolved to gain knowledge of the much faster changes that occur *between* generations — within an individual animal's lifetime — which inheritance mechanisms cannot track. With both learned and inherited knowledge, the ultimate purpose of the knowledge is survival and reproduction of the animal — or at the genetic level, the successful transmission to future generations of the particular genes encoding the adaptations. This evolutionary epistemology relates rather closely to the performance framework adopted in this article — knowledge in a biological context is "for" adaptation and practical problem-solving that leads to survival and replication, whether of organisms in their lifetime or of genes across generations.

With animals, learning usually dies with the individual that acquired it during its lifetime. The kind of learning most animals are capable of (such as some equivalent of "the best food in winter is under *that* log") relates to the unique, and changeable, circumstances of those particular individuals' habitats. From the "selfish gene's" perspective (Dawkins, 1976), in which organisms are mere "vehicles" for reproducing genes, this knowledge is as disposable as the individuals that accumulate it. There is neither any survival benefit, nor any mechanism, to write this knowledge into the genes and transfer it to the next generation. In the special case of humans, however, learning also means cultural transmission of knowledge, across and between generations, of the fruits of learning by others.

Certain cultural/social anthropologists have long proposed "diffusion" models to explain, for example, how particular tools and techniques spread within or between cultures — whether this concerns traditions of pottery design or new methods of crime prevention. (These models are related to organisational/industrial science views on innovation summarised in Nutley and Davies, (2000) although the two approaches do not seem to have joined up.) There is now emerging a Darwinian approach to the transmission of culture, known as "memetics." This term is modelled on "genetics" and coined — as "meme" equivalent to "gene" — by Dawkins (1976).

Memes are ideas, patterns of behaviour, plans, beliefs, religions or advertising jingles, that are transferred from one human mind to another. As they transfer — replicate — they are copied more or less accurately. Successive copying errors allow them to evolve. As any shopper for soap powder knows, or any reader of e-mails, there is intense competition for brain-space. From the meme's eye view, those variants which get into the next generation of the transfer process by copying and reproduction, and by their appeal or utility to the human host, survive to compete another day; those which do not, die out. Hence memes can vary (mutate), differentially survive and replicate — in the same way as genes do in biological evolution. They can be said to have a selfish life of their own, albeit one that is totally dependent on the existence of humans, their speech and their information and communications technology to store, reproduce and transmit them. Biological viruses are entirely dependent on living cells in the same way.

Darwin based his model of *natural* selection on the *artificial* genetic selection of livestock. Advertisers and evangelists alike are accomplished craftspeople of artificial memetic selection and transfer; but now we may see a practical science emerging, which we should usefully watch for its potential impact on professional education, training and on-the-job guidance. From the human host's perspective, in traditional societies most transfer of memes is vertical — parents/extended family to children. In modern societies, an increasing proportion is horizontal — with children and adults picking up knowledge, values etc., from each other, from books and from mass media including the Internet. As the rate of social change accelerates, the younger generation in particular may judge the older generation a less useful source of ideas to copy, and place more weight on information from their contemporaries (Laland and Odling-Smee, 2000). In training terms, this means less of an emphasis on formal once-and-for-all learning of everything at the start of a career, and more on continuing professional development, on-line guidance and networking.

A recent, readable exposition of memetics is in Blackmore (1999). Hull (2000) further explores the concept. Debate in this still very contentious and rapidly-developing area continues (see the articles edited by Aunger, 2000, and referred to individually at points below). Key issues centre on the nature of memes, how they are replicated from one human mind to the next, and even the validity and utility of the concept altogether. These qualifications apart, I believe there is enough to be gained from applying biological and cultural models of evolution and transmission to crime prevention knowledge, provided that concepts like memes are used with due awareness of contention.

Replication and Innovation from Evolutionary and Cultural Perspectives

Replication and innovation in crime prevention are both ways of generating new responses to crime based on past knowledge. Replication relies on this knowledge to a greater and more literal extent; innovation to a lesser but broader-ranging extent. As discussed, they are surprisingly close in crime prevention practice. Translating the ideas developed in the previous section into evolutionary terminology suggests further approaches to getting know-what and know-how in the most appropriate format for transfer, particularly for handling the future. It also provides a more convenient language for articulating concepts of transfer, replication and innovation.

Know-What Translated: from Generic to Genotypic

With biological replication, Dawkins (1976) identifies three key features for making it work: fidelity (accurate copying), fecundity (potential of fast, efficient copying) and longevity (the gene to be copied stays around long enough for the copying to be achieved). Blackmore (1999) applies these features to memes. In crime prevention terms, this covers the replication of individual crime prevention methods or designs. It also relates more strategically to the issue of *programme integrity* — the faithful replication of a programme's favoured intervention methods, ability to sustain the implementation and teach it to a stream of new staff, and avoidance of "mission drift." An interesting attempt to manage this process explicitly, in an offender-oriented crime prevention context, is the *Communities That Care* programme (Farrington, 2000).

Fidelity has to be qualified. As we have already seen in the earlier discussion on mechanisms and contexts, extremes of literal fidelity in replication, if they can be achieved, are much less likely to work than people had assumed. From the evolutionary perspective they are fixed, "inherited" responses that assume that the when and the where of the new context don't matter. To a significant extent, genetic transmission relies on the *environment* to carry fixed and predictable information to the next generation — which is why humans have "forgotten" the gene for synthesising Vitamin C, and normally rely perfectly well on finding it in the natural diet. This goes wrong, of course, when our environment, and our diet, change. Implicit knowledge of crime prevention, too, is only revealed when the context changes, and what once worked now fails. We therefore have to find ways of excavating the hidden contextual ingredients.

This may not always be possible. What kind of knowledge of "what works," then, can be transferred with fidelity across successive generations of practice, and between different contemporary contexts — but which is capable of evolution in the longer term and adaptive learning in the shorter? Some concepts in biological development can help here: know-what could usefully take a form closer to the *genotype* than to the *phenotype*. The genotype is the information in an organism's genes that describe how to make it. The genotype has the potential to develop in different ways according to the environment in which it is deployed, adjusting and unfolding through processes of maturation/ learning/ feedback. The phenotype, the completed adult organism, is one specific realisation of the genotype having undergone one specific life-trajectory of development. In the terms of the earlier discussion of replication and innovation, genotypic know-what in crime prevention is equivalent to the transfer of generic *principles* of intervention (and implementation) with the potential to be realised in different ways in different contexts. In the short-term at least, alongside such principles we must transfer highly specific, phenotypic, crime prevention *methods* that are known to work in various combinations in the here and now, such as a particular design of lock.

Know-How Translated: from Replication to Reconstruction

The debate about memes and cultural transmission connects replication to another significant and related issue. There is a powerful case to be made that cultural replication is not simply some kind of "photocopier" process, but that each new "copy" of some meme involves the recipient in *reconstructing* it from limited information (to demonstrate this, try recalling a recently-heard joke sufficiently well to re-tell it, or whistling a newly-heard tune) (Bloch, 2000; Boyd and Richerson, 2000). In the biological world, genotypes lead to phenotypes through the process of embryological development, maturation and learning, a succession of reconstructive stages in which the unfolding organism interacts with, and takes in material and successively more complex information from its environment. Each stage, itself the product of an earlier interaction, then acts as a component of the next interaction — a process known as *epigenesis* (Plotkin, 1998).

In practical crime prevention terms, such reconstruction is self-evidently important. With the preventive process, and in particular the stages of insertion in the community, implementation and intervention of preventive action, we can even make out a kind of epigenetic sequence where more and more information is gathered and incorporated in the unfolding plan of action. We can therefore note the importance of both having the right *descriptive information* and having an orderly *scaffolding* for efficient and accurate reconstruction of the action, stage by stage, from descriptions of schemes stored in a knowledge base. Contrast this to Scott's (2001) account of the inadequacy of orally-transmitted knowledge in policing, where much information is lost and distorted; and contrast it, even, with the paucity of the descriptions of many crime prevention projects that one finds in management information systems or best practice guides.

Another part of the same reconstructive picture has already been introduced, but the message of replicating Kirkholt and other success stories is more clearly articulated in genetic or memetic terms. Fidelity of replication is greater in a *functional* sense when practitioners try to copy *instructions* — intelligently following a process which involves taking in information on the problem and context, applying appropriate principles and generating a customised solution — rather than reverse-engineering from end-*products* (Blackmore, 1999; Hull, 2000). The products in question could be a commercial rival's secure car design or a successful burglary reduction scheme. A specific example of instructions is the performance standard approach to design, discussed under the "future" heading below. Effective instructions require not just information and structure, but the communication of an organised set of goals or objectives. (Sperber [2000] underlines the contribution of "intentionality" in understanding fidelity in cultural transmission.) Toolkits for creating effective sets of instructions via plans, flowcharts, checklists, decision trees and feedback recognise this (see, for example Hough and Tilley, 1998; and the toolkits at www.crimereduction.gov.uk).

One message from consideration of replication as innovation and reconstruction is that the academic concepts of external validity and generalisability, while remaining important considerations in evaluations and Campbell-type evaluation reviews, are too narrow to depict what must underlie high-fidelity replication of principles in new circumstances. In fact, the kind of replicability required is more proactive, covering conditions that must be present — or if not naturally present, actively established. (In this, it is more like the "method' section in accounts of chemistry experiments: "...care was taken to keep the temperature and pressure constant..." etc.). Thus, for example, if a certain intervention needs, to make it work, the context of good community structure in terms of mutually-supportive relations between neighbours, then part of the groundwork of any replication would involve trying to establish these conditions, for example, by setting up residents' associations.

To guide future reconstruction of successful schemes in potentially different contexts, key aspects of the preventive process therefore need to be recovered during process evaluation and recording for a knowledge base. One step of that process worth mentioning here is when proposed intervention mechanisms are converted into real-world crime prevention methods. *Troublesome tradeoffs* (Ekblom, 2001d, 2001e) centre on the need to design these methods so they serve their purpose without excessive cost, or unacceptably interfering with other goals such as convenience, aesthetics, environmental concerns, reliability, safety or privacy. The particular tradeoffs that were in play in a given attempt to design a preventive method, and the pros and cons of rejected, alternative solutions with different balances of those tradeoffs, could be useful for practitioners reconstructing in different contexts. For example, a solution that was too expensive to use in a context where offenders were amateurs, could yet be useful elsewhere against professionals. The experience is thus not wasted.

All of this gives us clues about how best to design knowledge bases supportive of reconstruction, where the action-descriptions they contain have a fighting chance of being replicated successfully and systematically. To build on recommendations listed previously, each entry for a traditional "*case study*"-type knowledge base of crime prevention schemes must centre on clear instructions for applying combinations of accurately described generic principles and specific methods. Principles and methods alike must not only cover interventions, but also describe the activities of implementation and insertion. For each of these "three I's" should be listed distinctive "points to watch during reconstruction" such as tradeoffs and feedback/adjustment issues. The whole should be presented in a structured sequence of stages embedded in the Preventive Process, which effectively offers a pathway for "recapitulating" the development of the scheme. Preliminary attempts to follow some of these maxims were developed by Ekblom and Tilley (1998) and Ekblom (2000c). Case studies may not, however, be the most efficient way of organising what-works knowledge, although they are undoubtedly necessary for illustrative purposes. The synthesised, distilled, approach based on *toolkits,* and containing contingent choices and instructions, may well be better. (For an equally preliminary attempt to specify something along these lines see Ekblom, 2000b.) The end result may take the form of a branching flowchart or algorithm rather than a linear set of instructions, and would be more suited to interactive media than paper.

Knowing and Coping with the Future

Gearing Up is about catching up with existing crime problems we can't yet handle, tackling new, emergent, problems and preparing for the unknown ones that the future will throw at us. Biological evolution can only teach us about adaptation to problems in the here and now — the "blind watchmaker" (Dawkins, 1986) cannot look ahead — it simply collides with the future. (If it were so capable, then the evolution of resistance to malaria would not have bequeathed many of African origin the agonies of sickle-cell disease. This was a "quick-fix" that conferred immediate advantage without thought of longer-term consequences.) But even blind evolution has ways of coping with the unknowable future, beyond this "level zero," which we can build on in our smarter, culturally and scientifically-mediated ways. We can distinguish several higher levels of perception and response to the future.

Level 1 — Spare Capacity

The first level of coping is simply being ready to respond with "plain" replication or "more of the same." An example is spare capacity to handle a wave of car crime that involves familiar *modus operandi.* But maintaining spare capacity is expensive, although some savings can be made with greater efficiency.

Subsequent levels involve coping innovatively. Innovation is *desirable* for its ability to deliver greater cost-effectiveness of existing types of solution. But it is *vital* when old problems demand new solutions by virtue of their numbers going out of control, and even more so when new problems emerge. As Campbell's rule acknowledged, at some point in the creative process, variation — the generation of ideas — has to be blind, irrespective of whether it concerns evolution of a new type of armoured skin for a reptile or design of a new crime-resistant wrapping for a CD box. But the creative process can be *prepared*, ready to swing into action in several ways, involving the detection and prediction of problems and the subsequent response to them. Various kinds of knowledge are needed for each approach, and the knowledge itself must be organised for deployment.

Level 2 — Scanning and Innovative Capacity

The next simplest approach is being prepared for the future by looking out for emergent crime problems. The medical world invests considerable effort in *scanning* for outbreaks of new diseases, or old ones returning with new virulence. We can do the same with new crimes and new *modus operandi* (Ekblom and Pease, 2001), shortening the cybernetic "control loop" of "change→detect-and-respond" as much as we can. Specific threats coming over the horizon can then be assessed and responded to, whether by doing nothing, further monitoring, or acting to develop and deploy preventive measures.

Purely on the response side, we can invest in *developing and building innovative capacity*: familiarising designers with crime and how to prevent it, for example, as is currently happening with the U.K. Design Council's Design Against Crime initiative (www.design council.org.uk; www.designagainstcrime.org). As with adapting to the problems of the present, it is the richness of the repertoire of generic principles and methods of know-what and know-how which enables large numbers of potentially good ideas to be generated to meet predicted threats. In this connection, the U.K.'s Foresight Crime Prevention Panel (U.K. Department of Trade and Industry, 2000) argued for a hard science base for crime prevention and a wider design against crime capability. Another aspect of preparing for innovation is improving the retrievability of the repertoire through organisation of the Knowledge Base. A third aspect is the deliberate establishment and cultivation of networks of influential innovators — who can both transfer knowledge to their fellows, take in knowledge from the centre, and return new or amended knowledge to the centre.

The significance of this last aspect is insufficiently recognised: for the centre to be able to dispense knowledge, it has first to obtain it. Reliance on centrally-initiated development and evaluation studies is insufficient. Encouraging innovation out there among practitioners rather than stifling it with over-management, can feed the centre with new and sometimes unexpected knowledge in the form of new practical or even, occasionally, theoretical principles. If the knowledge-harvesting mechanisms are there, doing can lead to thinking. Such benefits are more likely to flow if the practitioners themselves are already well versed in generic knowledge of intervention *principles* so they have a strong and evidence-based repertoire from which to create new ideas (and if they are committed to selective commissioning of high quality evaluations). However, simply loading them down with detailed knowledge of concrete intervention *methods* is another form of asphyxiation. Such information should therefore not be dominant in guidance material. But it should be readily retrievable when wanted, particularly because (as Petroski [1992] notes in a kind of countervailing principle) much progress in design comes from trying to resolve faults and flaws in existing products, a point related to the obsolescence issue discussed below.

Level 3 — Future-Proofing

Beyond building, and liberating, innovative capacity in a generalised way, the next level involves specific actions to *future-proof* individual crime prevention methods and designs, and to future-proof the whole armoury. Situational crime prevention in particular requires this treatment because it has to face the extremes of the arms race. However, it is worth pointing out that offender-oriented interventions (whether enforcement tactics and technologies, or treatment) also face resistance from criminal individuals, organisations and subcultures. Moreover, the validity of their analysis of causes, and efficacy of their interventions, depends just as much on the changing social and cultural background.

To future-proof our armoury of interventions they must be made as *adaptable* to social and technological change and to offenders' countermoves, and hence become as *sustainable* as possible. It is also necessary to *monitor for obsolescence* and *weed out* those practices which no longer work and have run the course of modifications to keep them going. Here, a "pipeline" of new security systems can be maintained (as with satellite TV, banknotes and credit cards), so that old methods can immediately be replaced as they become defunct. We also have to make situational interventions *varied* — so the offender can't quickly "crack one, crack them all'; and *unpredictable* through the richness and subtlety of interventions that we can design.

Design against crime, as a subset of situational prevention (Ekblom, 2001d, 2001e), faces an even more intense innovative requirement for adaptation and sustainability. Paradoxically, although design embodies cultural evolution, its individual products, once they leave the factory or are erected on a building site, are largely fixed — like the anatomy of mature organisms. As such, it is only a matter of time before criminals find ways round them or social and technological change pass them by. We can resolve this paradox by noting that the design concept resembles the genotype, the manufactured design realisations the phenotype.

Adaptability of the manufactured or built *phenotype* can be achieved most simply by designing products into a wider *secure system* that involves humans or at least intelligent, decision-making software able to react by making instant countermoves to offenders, summoning assistance and so on. (This has echoes of Dawkins' [1982] "extended phenotype," in which for example, a beaver's dam is as much an expression of the beaver's genetic plan as are its teeth and tail.) A neat example of such adaptability appeared as a prize-winning entry in the Royal Society of Arts' 2001 Student Design Awards (www.rsa-sda.net/sda_oe_2001/htm/br/br_14.htm): a "gypsy"-style ring, with diamonds embedded in the circumference, was fitted with a platinum housing that the wearer could slide neatly over the gemstones when out and about in risky areas. (One could almost imagine her saying to herself "This looks like a three-diamond situation, I'd better shift the cover round a bit.") The more general issue of designing products for use by real people in real situations means that any security system that relies on, or has to mesh with, human actions must be very well-researched. For example, designers of goods that cease to function when removed from their familiar home, or when an unauthorised user (with different fingerprints, say) tries to operate them, must identify and cope with all the contingencies of legitimate use — servicing in a dusty workshop, coping with resetting after a power-cut, lending to one's son or daughter, etc. This represents a huge amount of practical know-about knowledge concerning legitimate *modus operandi* that matches the information designers need to know about the criminal equivalent.

Alternatively, the products themselves can be made *upgradeable* in some way. This is normally the field of remedial design, but it is possible to anticipate and facilitate such remedy in advance. The Amsterdamse Poort shopping mall was designed to take security shutters, but these were not to be installed unless the crime problem became too large and security staff proved unable to cope; security addons are made for cars (pre-designed options being better than poorly-integrated after-purchases); and software patches can be downloaded for defending computer facilities against new attacks by viruses or fraudsters. In effect, these feedback strategies are the equivalent of *learning* in the world of artifacts (one book and television series was even entitled "How Buildings Learn" — Brand, 1997). Enhancements of adaptability such as these are a good way of coping with the uncertainty of the design process. Designers, and design decision-makers in marketing or the company boardroom, may understandably hesitate to take the risk of incurring additional cost in their products if the risk of crime is uncertain (Ekblom, 1997; 2001d, 2001e). Upgradeability allows the manufacturing and sales costs, if not the design costs, to be fine-tuned according to emergent or anticipated need.

The innovative capacity that supports the general approach of Level 2, and the specific strategies of *adaptability, variety* and *unpredictability* of Level 3, require, at base, a fount of *creativity*. Here, we return to generic, or genotypic, principles. These cover far broader sets of circumstances — present and future — than piecemeal specific elements of realised design. They are also less prone to being left behind in the arms race. Our professional crime prevention consultants must be armed with a whole battery of these principles, which they can mix and blend in combination to generate new designs to apply to new contexts and the changing "fitness landscape" (Dennett, 1995) of what works.

A diverse range of ideas (discussed in Ekblom, 1997, 1999) can be drawn on to flesh out this view. In biological evolution, some theories of the survival value of sexual reproduction centre on the ability it confers to shuffle genes for disease resistance. This enables sexual organisms to keep ahead of pathogens — in effect, constantly changing the locks. (On the other side of the contest, malaria parasites apply exactly the same principle — they have huge numbers of genes which they shuffle to alter their biochemical disguises and repeatedly confuse the host's immune system.) A related vision comes from engineering science (Hapgood, 1993), where the evolutionary pressure stems from industrial competition. Here, innovation comes from being equipped with sound theory- and evidence-based principles capable of being applied combinatorially to many problems rather than fixed expertise in any one field of technology that could sooner or later be bypassed by commercial rivals. Another, more abstract, link is with linguistic competence in the Chomskian sense (e.g., Pinker, 1994). The concept of *generative grammar* contrasts with the classical view of language as merely a scaling-up of "simple" learning or imitation. It envisages the capacity to produce infinite numbers of new grammatical utterances from a rich, but finite, supply of grammatical principles and combinatorial elements (words). (All these links exemplify the fundamental "generative" view of causality espoused by Scientific Realists like Tilley.)

One important way of releasing creativity is the *design freedom* that comes from guidance and regulations based on *performance standards* rather than fixed specifications. An example could be "door to withstand attack by currently available tools for 3 minutes," rather than "door to be made of 5mm manganese steel." The performance standards must of course reflect our knowledge-about crime risks in general, and "take in" local and current information on the resources offenders are able to bring to bear in overcoming crime resistance (Ekblom and Tilley, 2000), whether this is a blow from a boot, a thermic lance or an elaborate confidence trick. They are an ideal embodiment of genotypic principles that can be "programmed" with contextually-specific knowledge. They are a good example, too, of "copy the instructions rather than copy the product." The U.K. Loss Prevention Division of the Building Research Establishment adopts performance standards for housing construction, safes etc. which acknowledge current methods of attack. The European standards system CEN, at least applied to housing and crime (van Soomeren, 2000), takes the wider process-oriented approach even further.

Level 4 — Empirical Anticipation

Evolution is blind to the future and the genotype cannot itself anticipate specific changes in the environment to which it must adapt. If clairvoyance were possible, over the aeons of evolutionary time some animal would have evolved to exploit its tremendous adaptive potential. In fact, nearly all animals have. Biological evolution has managed to equip individual animals with a limited phenotypic capacity to *anticipate* in the short-term — through the widespread and repeated evolution of *eyesight*. Although not widely-appreciated, we already live partly in the future because the speed of the light we perceive is dramatically faster than the movement of matter. We can see the lion coming and make ready, rather than waiting till it jumps on us to try to fight back. In effect, the aim is not just to shorten the control loop by scanning, but to turn it into a mesh (in cybernetic terms), where we see the problem coming and respond before it happens. Any gazelle equipped with the natural equivalent of today's simplistic, "wait till it happens" burglar alarms would not last long (Ekblom, 1997). And organisms can learn, and predict, cyclic trends in the environment, like the seasons, longer-term dry spells or perhaps shorter-term cataclysms like earthquakes and eruptions provided these are accompanied by reliable advance indicators.

In the human context, it is *know-about* which supports this predictive facility. Empirical knowledge of crime trends and cycles, and statistical techniques for filtering out chance fluctuations and incidental background influences, leads to *atheoretical predictions* — crime forecasts — which can be quite powerful (Pease, 1997). Leading indicators can also be used, such as commodity prices (the elevated cost of computer chips post-Kobe earthquake was apocryphally responsible for driving theft of computer components) or predictions of artificially-imposed scarcity (as with the ivory trade, or trade in endangered animals — apparently even tortoises in the UK are trading for £200 as opposed to £10 a generation ago, leading to theft).

Level 5 — Theoretical Anticipation

But it is wider knowledge of processes and indicators of social and technological change, linked to generic *theories* and principles, that help crime preventers to anticipate properly in an open-ended manner that ranges beyond simple projection. Such knowledge enables us to predict the qualitatively new crime problems which may appear over the next few years. We may be able to spot the likely targets of familiar crimes like theft (Clarke's [1997] concept of "hot products" — those which are Concealable, Removable, Available, Valuable, Enjoyable, Disposable). At the very least, we can use these concepts to refine our leading indicators — for example, covering what's newly fashionable among 17-year-olds. But we can take it into the specifics of product design. This could involve making those items which look set to become valuable, harder to remove in one piece and hence harder to dispose of. By doing this we can hope to avoid or mitigate some of the sorry episodes of the control loop of "naïve design leading to crime harvest and retrofit solution" (Pease, 1997; Ekblom and Pease, 2001), documented for mobile phones by Clarke et al. (2001). Ideally we again replace the loop or reaction with a "mesh" of anticipation. In this respect, designers have a uniquely advantaged position to control crime risks, because unlike most professional crime preventers, they have one potential cause of crime under their own control from its conception — their own product. Of particular importance is the ability to predict the new *resources* (Ekblom and Tilley, 2000) that offenders may deploy to exploit opportunities, such as overcoming the crime resistance of targets with a new cutting tool or hindering more conventional attempts to enforce the law. Using knowledge of offenders' resources to anticipate their likely *countermoves* (Ekblom, 1997, 1999), including displacement, is vital for the design of preventive methods that are *sustainable*. Beyond specific resources we can develop a higher-level understanding, and hence a predictive capacity, of the way offenders innovate, and disseminate those innovations among themselves. Finally, on the positive side of anticipation, we may even spot potential new technologies to *support* preventive applications and make them happen.

The first round of the U.K. government's Foresight Programme (1993-97) did not explicitly or systematically cover crime (Rogerson et al., 2000). But it did produce a good example of efforts to anticipate, and respond, to the problems of fraud and identity theft. The Management of Information programme (www.dti-mi.org.uk) explicitly set out to correct known market failures in making the knowledge (and the knowledge-based technology, applications and services) come about. Round two of Foresight (1999-2002) contained a Crime Prevention Panel (U.K. Department of Trade and Industry, 2000) which aimed to do just this more systematically.

Organising our knowledge bases of know-about and know-how can help us to make such predictions more routinely and systematically, and spread the capacity for accurate prediction to a wider range of crime preventers. For an example of an embryonic crime risk and crime impact assessment guide for product designers/manufacturers, which is also intended to help identify new crime prevention opportunities, see Ekblom (2000d). A similar approach could be developed for local practitioners.

Handling the Challenges of Prediction

But we must not get too optimistic about the capabilities of prediction — it remains a difficult game. We cannot be certain even of such apparently tight predictions as hot products. False positive and false negative errors are likely. "Set-top boxes," to convert televisions to receive digital signals, were predicted as a new hot product; but at a stroke this risk was removed when the television companies decided to give the boxes away free and recoup their money instead from service charges. Investment in developing and manufacturing security in the boxes would have been wasted. Inevitably, too, there will be some obscure technology in an unlikely field for which we have failed to make the connection with crime. Rogerson (e.g., Rogerson et al., 2000) notes this with reference to the first round of Foresight.

Unreliability of prediction can be coped with in two ways. Again, the biological equivalent is instructive. Short lifespan creatures such as insects die before they can learn much, so haven't found it worthwhile to invest in neurological structures capable of much learning. Investing their resources in a high reproduction rate is their strategy for coping with the many unpredictables and consequent performance failures the species consequently encounters — some genes always get through to the next generation. In ecological terms, this opportunist approach is known as an "r" strategy (Colinvaux, 1980). With long lifespan animals the environment is more likely to change over their lifetime. They therefore have a greater requirement to adapt more closely to their environment by learning; and a greater opportunity to do so. They make greater investment in staying alive, and in supporting the fewer offspring they produce (the "K" strategy). Back to crime prevention: with long-lived products such as houses, town centres or cars, the phenotype — the existing exemplars of the product — should be designed to be upgradeable as described above. With short-lived products — perhaps this even includes mobile phones — the product phenotypes can be written off, and most design against crime effort spent improving the security of the genotype — expressed in future models. There are however limits to this strategy. In complex products like cars, the effort and cost of trying to squeeze in a previously-neglected security function once a model has been finalised or is being revised for the next version, is considerable. Even software solutions in complex systems need an immense amount of testing if they are not to have unpredictable and undesirable interactions. It is far cheaper to incorporate security when the fundamental architecture is being determined, and leave it lying dormant until and unless required.

There are more advanced approaches to improving practical predictions and minimising the harmful consequences of acting on the wrong ones. They stem from the quality and subtlety of the process which produces ideas and rejects unlikely prospects before we waste resources and opportunity in building them, or worse, mainstreaming them. Dennett's (1995) concept of the "Tower of Generate and Test" supplies the fundamental idea here (see also Blackmore, 1999). This is an imaginary tower in which each floor has creatures that are able to find better and smarter moves, and find them more quickly and efficiently. In other words, the individual creatures are successively more intelligent; and creativity is increasingly amplified, but concentrated and chanelled. Note that all these processes use or contribute to evolutionary processes one way or another.

(1) Darwinian creatures, on the ground floor, rely only on inherited knowledge, and die when this fails to predict or avoid trouble in their environment. The faulty knowledge thus fails to be passed on.

(2) Skinnerians on the next floor are less likely to die, but with simple trial and error learning kill off *behaviour* that doesn't work, and preserve behaviour that does.

(3) Popperian creatures on the next floor can imagine outcomes in their heads and solve problems by thinking about them. In Popper's words (1972:244), this ability "permits our hypotheses to die in our stead." Evolutionary pressure is not halted, but temporarily taken off-line from the real world and re-cast in acts ranging from intuitive imagination to research and development. In crime prevention terms, "rational design" comes at this level. Like "engineering science" (Hapgood, 1993) it involves seeking to get first attempts at solutions right, through a thorough knowledge of intervention principles and practical real-world fixes, simulation, and simulated attack testing, even before the first physical *prototype* is tried out (it thus combines know-about, know-what and know-how). But we can become smart from failure too. The knowledge of what didn't work during its lifetime would die with the individual Darwinian animal — although the gene pool of its species is less likely to produce that strategy in future. The Skinnerian animal knows only what is a waste of time attempting in the future. But the Popperian designer can learn much more from what designs did not work and how crime resistance was overcome. Interestingly, systematic failure mode analysis was pioneered by the late Leslie Wilkins to understand and prevent wartime air crashes, as part of a systems approach he then successfully applied to crime causation (Wilkins, 1997). This was one of the intellectual roots of situational prevention.

(4) The final level, the Gregorian, is named after the psychologist Richard Gregory, who first pointed out (1981) that cultural artifacts not only require intelligence to produce them, but also enhance their owner's intelligence (and in the terms of

this paper, performance). Such artifacts can include tangible things such as scissors, calculators, virtual reality design simulators or other tools; but as Dennett (1995) notes, they also include "mind tools." With these, Gregorian creatures (including crime preventers) can find good moves and evolve new behaviours much faster. One general-purpose mind tool for helping crime preventers is discussed in the next section. But before that, we will consider the wider set of mind tools needed for understanding, prediction and manipulation of crime — science and social science — and their limitations.

Wider Limits to a Purely Scientific Approach — How Much Smarter Can We Get?

Much of the cultural knowledge transferred between people serves the obvious practical purpose of aiding survival in the physical world. This perspective has been emphasised particularly in American conceptions of culture. In contrast, some European approaches have focused on the more "spiritual" aspects of culture in terms of identity, meaning and values (see, for example, Kuper, 2000). This is, however, an artificial dichotomy, because humans create their own niches for living to a remarkable degree (Laland and Odling-Smee, 2000). Those niches are not only material (such as cities) but intensely social and highly-differentiated (hence the significance of context in determining whether preventive methods will work and how they should be adjusted). To be a competent actor and survive and prosper (and perhaps reproduce our bodies and disseminate our ideas) in our own, socially-constructed world, individual members of a culture need to know an enormous amount. In materialist terms most of this is "trivial pursuits" material — fashions, football teams, the rules of etiquette and so on. But it is not so much the specific content as the identity, solidarity and conformity that matters. As such, the content is free to drift. So the validity of what we can know in this social world is in important respects confined to specific times and places (Popper, 1972; Gergen, 1973; Tilley, 1982). Technologically-driven change makes this equally true in the material world. And with crime, as already stated, both technological and social change are further compounded by the deliberate counter-adaptations of offenders.

But despite this ephemerality, some elements of knowledge are of much more durable and transferable value — they are intended to remain applicable over long spans of time and across diverse contexts. This comprises the knowledge and evidentiary methods of *science*. Paradoxically, science itself rests on *cultural* values of objectivity and rules of evidence and is an invented evolutionary process of generating knowledge that relies on competition between theories and selection through falsification (Popper, 1972; Hull, 1988; Plotkin, 1993) and parsimony.

The Knowledge Base of crime prevention aims to be scientific, and thus by default aspires to the durability just described. From this perspective, on the know-about side, criminologists of course seek to build and test theories of the causation of crime. On the know-what "engineering" side, knowledge is built up through scientifically rigorous evaluation that involves applying explicit fitness tests to filter those interventions that work from those that don't. (Ideally, the two forms of knowledge should come together: where interventions are firmly based on theories, evaluation can test these too [Farrington, 2000].) Here, fittest is deliberately defined as "evidence-based, cost-effective, sustainable and acceptable" etc., rather than "eye-catching or fashionable." In another curious coincidence, many of the methodological fitness tests which scientific evaluation applies were developed and codified by none other than Donald Campbell (e.g., Cook and Campbell, 1979) — who therefore occupies a prominent position on the top, Gregorian, floor of the Tower of Generate and Test.

It is important to acknowledge the limits to the criminologists' aspiration to science and technology, in terms of the peculiarities of *social* science. Not only do criminologists have to track the "here and now" aspects of knowledge just discussed; they have to do so in a world with a strong intersubjective content dealing in shared social judgments, meanings, beliefs and perceptions. Filtering all this out in the name of a spurious universality, permanence and objectivity would leave precious little to work on! Criminology and crime prevention must also work with higher-level emergent entities such as niches, markets for stolen goods and social climate, which may well have significant causal power and practical significance (Ekblom, 2001f), but which are of course far more open to debate than the relatively rock-solid hierarchies like "atoms-molecules-cells-tissues" in the hard sciences.

But this contrast should not be taken too far. Even the *harder* sciences such as biology have to extract information on enduring processes from a historical and local pattern of evolution (and mind-bogglingly, so might physicists and cosmologists — see Smolin, 1997). The nature of a biological gene or a species is debated every bit as intensively as that of a cultural meme. And particular technologies, of course, nowadays have only a relatively brief usable life-span in terms of support through availability of spare parts, expertise of service engineers, even retrievability and decodability of stored information. (Do you still own a record player for those old 45s from the Sixties? Contrast this with the durability of the various flint-tool technologies of the stone age, which sometimes lasted tens of thousands of years essentially unchanged.)

What can be drawn from this discussion for practical knowledge management? Basically, any attempt to develop a cumulative knowledge base must accommodate the social-research paradox of trying to build a science that can handle varied, complex and reflexive human perceptions and beliefs. It must further reconcile the evolutionary paradox of trying to be enduring whilst coping with social and technical change. Somehow, it may help resolve both paradoxes if we strive constantly to keep aware of working simultaneously from the two perspectives of generic or genotypic *principles*, and specific, phenotypic or real-world *methods*. It may also help if we ensure practitioners are empowered with *processes* and ways of thinking, because these endure and can act on whatever know-what material is currently valid.

The content of the subculture of crime prevention practice is evolving all the time. But many of the evolutionary pressures on the memes that make it up derive from fashion, market interest, ideology or untutored common sense. *All* of these may help a meme to survive and proliferate; but *none* of these guarantee progress towards greater and more sustainable effectiveness. Only those elements of practice which are constantly exposed to the fitness pressures of scientific methods will evolve in the direction we want, whether these pressures act through the testing of theory, the evaluation of what works, the generation of evidence-based interventions targeted on carefully identified causes and risk factors, and the use of feedback to select and attune specific interventions to context. This is where evolution and science meet — squaring the circle of Donald Campbell's contributions.

THE ORGANISATION OF KNOWLEDGE: CONCEPTUAL FRAMEWORK NEEDED

I began this paper by referring to the important issue of knowledge acquisition. I then moved on to identify a whole range of issues concerning the transfer of knowledge to, and its application by, practitioners. The aim was to improve their performance in detecting, anticipating and tackling current, emergent and future crime problems. Throughout, I have aimed to put the distinct features of crime prevention content back into some fairly abstract models of performance and knowledge management. But now it is time to consider the state of crime prevention knowledge as a whole, which brings together issues of its acquisition and organisation that have emerged at various points.

Transfer mechanisms are not the whole story in the conveyance and application of knowledge: what is at the receiving end also counts. Anthropologists such as Bloch (2000) note that much of the efficiency of replication depends on there already being in the mind of the receiving party a substantial cognitive *schema*, or conceptual framework, primed to decode, interpret and assimilate the message. This suggests a further strategy for knowledge transfer in which an early, relatively protracted, "foundation" training imparts the schema, and specific parcels of knowledge are then subsequently integrated with it — from knowledge bases, guidance updates, continuing professional development, and live collaboration with researchers possessed of the knowledge. Because the fundamentals of the message are already in place, the burden on the practitioners in ingesting this new information is minimised — they don't have to take it all in at once. This of course poses the question of what the schema should contain and how it should be structured. We can illustrate the wider significance of a schema by studying the transfer system in medicine, which centres on a know-what knowledge base like that to which the Campbell Collaboration aspires, but which goes far wider.

Lessons from Medical Knowledge — From Cochrane to Campbell

The Campbell Collaboration aims to be the lead international focus for the acquisition of reliable know-what knowledge of crime prevention. But from the various points raised in this paper, it is pretty clear that high-quality systematic reviews of impact evaluation and cost-effectiveness, although entirely necessary and a high priority, are far from sufficient to get that knowledge transferred and applied in mainstream practice. It is evident from their writings (e.g., Farrington and Petrosino, 2001) that the leading lights in the Crime and Justice group of Campbell are aware of this, but developing the necessary approach is no small task. It is not merely a matter of finding the right connecting cable of content-free knowledge management and transfer media such as training, to plug into a convenient socket already installed on the Knowledge Base. We have to build the socket, wire it up to the Knowledge Base, and reconfigure the content and structure of the Knowledge Base itself, so it is assembled, integrated, and structured ready for transfer.

Campbell's intellectual roots are in the Cochrane Collaboration, set up to document well-specified and -evaluated medical interventions. A closer look at medicine and medical science can indicate what else is required to make a whole system of knowledge acquisition and transfer work. (The medical model is however far from perfect. Sherman [1998] and Laycock [2000a] discuss some of the difficulties of applying the medical approach to evidence and evaluation in crime prevention — the former in terms of medicine as a "battleground between research and practice," where an evidence-based approach is far from well-established; and the latter in terms of the kinds of evaluation methods that best apply.)

(1) The Cochrane collaboration rests on a well-developed *process* model of medical diagnosis, prevention and treatment (which information is incorporated within the evaluations of medical trials).

(2) Cochrane also has in the background a schema or conceptual framework that is highly-developed, in the form of medical science. This gives it a common, well-defined, consistent and internationally-translatable terminology, clear analytical concepts, an understanding of levels of explanation (biochemical, cellular, tissue, organ, whole organism, etc.), and rich, well-tested and well-integrated theory deriving from the interplay between practice and fundamental scientific research. The frontiers apart, most knowledge fits on well-constructed scaffolding.

(3) The framework is organised so well that medical training empowers practitioners with a complete map of causes and interventions, which they can tap into at a level of sophistication appropriate to their job (consultant surgeon or paramedic). Onto the schema they can place, and through it assimilate, new items of knowledge as they come in throughout their working life.

(4) The medical science framework also supports storage and retrieval in any number of specific knowledge bases that are all recognisably part of the same schema, and can provide information in a form suited to replication and accurate reconstruction of procedures ranging from preventive medicine to drug treatments to open-heart surgery, combining formal

teaching and with structured apprenticeship and supporting manuals. In the U.K., it was found necessary to establish a mediating organisation to transfer the results of Cochrane reviews to medical practitioners — the National Institute for Clinical Excellence (www.doh.gov.uk/mounice.htm).

(5) There are well-established (although still imperfect) know-about systems for disease epidemiology, including scanning for accident prevention and emergent diseases (and even anticipation of outbreaks for example, of new strains of influenza). There are also know-what feedback systems for routinely monitoring the effectiveness and side-effects of treatments in use (see Sherman, [1998] for proposed application of this to police case work).

(6) Systematic mapping of knowledge supports gap analyses.

(7) Many of the more recent advances in medicine and medical science are now coming from a deep theoretical understanding of how the body works, what causes disease and how interventions might interfere with those diseases. Rational approaches to problems enable the more rapid and self-aware design and simulation-testing of large numbers of potential drugs — which is vital, because medicine is in its own arms races with antibiotic-resistant bacteria (Ekblom, 1999) or mutating lineages of cancer cells.

Cochrane — know-what — is thus embedded in a wide, and deep, complex of know-about and know-how, that is integrated through a common schema or framework.

The Campbell collaboration on crime and justice in some ways faces greater challenges than Cochrane. Whereas most people respond predictably most of the time to most of the common medical treatments, as discussed above every replication of crime preventive action in fresh contexts is far more of an innovation. And we have not yet developed a body of knowledge and theories which enable us to predict the interactive effects of different contexts, like the contra-indications on the side of medication containers. What does the Campbell collaboration, and crime prevention more generally, have that can fulfill the process and conceptual roles supplied for Cochrane by wider medical science?

We do at least have some fairly well-developed practice *processes*, including the Preventive Process and others documented above — although the occupational culture and climate are far from conducive to applying these processes in a full blown problem-oriented way. But we have no universally-adopted *conceptual* equivalent to Cochrane's medical science to support reviews and syntheses of what-works evidence, let alone the wider connections to practice, except in isolated areas. Laycock and Tilley (1995) make a useful start in their strategic analysis of Neighbourhood Watch options. Phillips (1999) uses a Scientific Realist mechanism approach to integrate diverse findings from CCTV evaluations. Laycock (2001) describes a synthesis of context-sensitive knowledge on repeat victimisation, worked up from empirical beginnings into an entire strategic approach to targeting of preventive action, including multimedia approaches to transfer, and performance indicators to help and require the transfer to embed in practice. However, these are all separate "rafts" of organisation rather than regions of a common framework that builds out from generics to specifics. Beyond the broad overview level described at the very beginning of this paper, detailed knowledge remains limited on all fronts, and that which we have is fragmented — a flotsam of free-floating items described in inconsistent and often vague terms. No wonder it is an uphill struggle to transfer this knowledge and apply it in the mainstream!

A Possible Solution — The Conjunction of Criminal Opportunity Framework

For some while I have been developing a framework for crime prevention as a whole which aspires to organise and synthesise knowledge. The *Conjunction of Criminal Opportunity* framework (Ekblom, 2000a; Ekblom, 2001b, 2001c) was in fact first published in this series under the less user-friendly label of "Proximal Circumstances" (Ekblom, 1994). The framework (CCO for short) had its origins in attempting rigorously, yet faithfully, to describe and classify some 2,000 diverse crime prevention schemes implemented under the Safer Cities programme, a requirement which ensured its robustness.

CCO is based on a definition of crime prevention as intervention in the causes of criminal events to reduce the risk of their occurrence and the potential seriousness of their consequences. This is deliberately theory-oriented, but not attached to any one theory; nor to any particular method of prevention. In its detail it is fundamentally an expansion and a filling-out of the Routine Activities nexus of Cohen and Felson (1979), covering 11 generic kinds of immediate causal precursors of criminal events ranging from offender-centred (such as offender's criminal predisposition) to situational (such as the target enclosure). Each precursor is matched by equally generic intervention principles. The exhaustive mapping of immediate causes of criminal events and non-events supports a Scientific Realist articulation of context and mechanism, although it is not confined to that approach. In fact, it has the potential to express any criminological theory in the same, consistent, molecular terms. The current version is briefly summarised in the Annex.

The aim of CCO has moved far beyond its origins as a structured classification and knowledge base (Ekblom, 1994), towards supporting the wider evolution of crime prevention as a professional discipline (Ekblom, 1996a, 1998). In fact, from the present perspective it could be considered as a Gregorian "mind tool" of the universal, "Swiss army knife" kind. By linking it to the Preventive Process, the aspiration became one of addressing the problems of transferring and applying crime prevention knowledge to practice described at the beginning of this paper. In effect, this means helping crime science and crime prevention move towards something resembling medical science and the practice of medicine — or at least the idealised view of this portrayed above.

CCO can endow practitioners with an instrument that gives them wide-angle views of the generic causes of crime (Figure 1, Annex 2), and the full repertoire of preventive interventions in those causes (Figure 3, Annex 2). From this systematic coverage they are able to zoom in for a precision focus on specific interventions in specific contexts. CCO can equip practitioners undergoing training with a ready-made framework or schema which primes them to efficiently receive, and assimilate, individual items of knowledge transferred in the same terms at later points in their career.

More generally CCO aims to support practitioner performance in the shape of intelligent, principle-driven replication, reconstruction and innovation to cover both familiar, novel and anticipated crime problems and contexts. It fosters a "consultant'-like, rather than a "technician-like" approach, and organises knowledge and knowledge retrieval to support creativity rather than strangle it. It can flip perspectives between analytic intervention principles on the one hand — theories and mechanisms — and real-world preventive methods on the other. This "many-to-many" relationship can be visualised as a tree (principles) and a spider's web (methods); the webs themselves may be further cross-linked into synergistic packages of methods (Figure 4, Annex 2). Although fundamentally analytical, CCO is not reductionist. From its criminal event perspective it can work outwards to more complex and remote causes. It supports a view of a holistic "causal system" of intensely interacting components as the conjunction comes together in particular Context-Mechanism-

Outcome configurations. The causal components it describes can support a "combinatorial" approach to generating diagnoses and interventions.

On the knowledge-acquisition side the aim is to support the cultivation, accumulation and maintenance of further knowledge. By setting out a "universal story of preventive action" (Figure 2, Annex 2), it supplies a scaffolding for management information systems linked to quality assurance of implementation, and for capturing know-how information in evaluation, feedback and adjustment, and failure mode analysis. This last can build on Rosenbaum's (1986) characterisation, diagnosing intervention failure (ranging from generic theory to specific mechanism), insertion failure (failure to mobilise and hand over responsibility and direction for a crime prevention task, using the detailed CLAMED analysis described at the beginning of this paper), and implementation failure. It can be linked up with the rigorous cost-effectiveness language of the U.K.'s Crime Reduction Programme (see Figure 5, Annex 2, and Dhiri, 1999).

CCO provides a language for partner professionals and practitioners in different countries to use for rigorous and explicit communication of crime prevention knowledge, for common understanding of diagnoses, and for collaboration on preventive action. In this, it connects with conventional knowledge management views (Macintosh, 1999) that an enterprise-wide vocabulary is necessary to ensure that knowledge is correctly understood.

CCO is well-placed to identify gaps in knowledge of causes and interventions. For example, during the development of the CCO framework the significance of offenders' resources became apparent. (Tools, weapons, information, MOs, courage etc are a generic consideration in the creation and restriction of criminal opportunities [Ekblom and Tilley, 2000].) CCO can also be used to support explicit predictive tools such as crime impact assessment and foresight (Ekblom, 2000d).

CCO has been taken further in practical ways, mainly in an education, training and support context, in collaboration with a range of professions. It now appears in the U.K. Crime Reduction website as a supporting guide to "toolkits" of good practice (Ekblom, 2001c); and its use is currently being explored in several contexts. One example is in scoping an international knowledge base for the prevention of organised crime (Ekblom, 2001f). Here, efforts are under way to extend the framework by identifying higher-level causal entities beyond the "molecular" ones leading to the immediate criminal event — such as networks, markets and niches. Attempts are also under way to develop it as the framework for a computerised knowledge base to describe individual preventive schemes in explicit, reconstructable and principled ways (Ekblom and Tilley, 1998; Ekblom, 2000). Finally, there are plans under way to apply it in the preparation of guidance for those who design against crime (www.designagainstcrime. org).

CCO is deliberately positioned as a "high-investment-in-training, high-yield-in-performance" approach. The framework is not based on simple "aide-memoire"-type structures like the "Problem Analysis Triangle" (Hough and Tilley, 1998). No other profession (public health, architecture, for example) would send its practitioners into the field and expect them to deliver with such limited conceptual resources! But the contest between simple and sophisticated frameworks is ultimately a question to be resolved by constructive criticism and practical development and evaluation work, trying simultaneously to maximise user-friendliness and added-value in improved performance.

Whether CCO has the potential to become *the* framework for synthesising crime prevention knowledge and the practice process, and facilitating replication and innovation, must of course remain an open question. (The answer to this, as with other successful universals like the VHS video cassette format, will turn not just on utility but on marketing.) But currently it seems the most coherent option, and one, moreover, which is capable of further evolution.

The Practical Importance of "Know-Why"

The rational-spiritual distinction made by anthropologists is also important in a more immediately practical way. Freiberg (2001) makes the point that an entirely rational, scientific and technological enterprise of crime prevention will not work. This is not an attack on the science itself; more an acknowledgement that humans, and human society, have emotional, symbolic and communitarian needs when it comes to dealing with crime — blame, justice, revenge, condemnation of violation of norms, sympathy to victims, etc. Failure to cater for these needs may leave "civil" and causally-based approaches to prevention in a sidetrack every bit as limiting as that of the purely ritual side of criminal justice, which seeks to meet such emotional requirements sometimes without delivering much that is materially effective against crime. Gilling (1997) argues more broadly that it is pointless to seek to introduce greater rationality into what is an intensely political, fashion-driven and gesture-prone field, through frameworks such as CCO. Rationalists can make the strong rejoinder that it is precisely because of the lack of conceptual clarity, hard evidence and good theory synthesised into a sound knowledge base that crime prevention is especially prone to these features. When swimming in these waters without such aids, professionals are left struggling to make their case for particular courses of action to lay colleagues. Nevertheless, this does not let us entirely off the hook. Some kind of deliberate, systematic accommodation is needed between the rational "social engineering" world of causation and intervention, and the world of meaning, blame and value.

Freiberg makes interesting recommendations about how modern prevention could extend into this dimension of emotion and symbolic meaning and gain cultural acceptability — one of the key aspects of improvement of performance identified at the beginning of this paper — *without* sacrificing its rationality. This is the reason I mysteriously included *know-why* among the K's of knowledge. Know-why would cover knowing what the symbolic and emotional requirements of preventive action are; knowing the means of satisfying them; and knowing how to make the rational and the symbolic work together by ensuring the problem-solving approach attends to the *value-* and *ethics-* dimensions of fairness, justice and deservingness, community involvement and participation. Freiberg offers restorative justice as a model (which can be said to have preventive dimensions as well as retrospective ones). Crime prevention can learn from the well developed field of medical ethics. This reacts to, or sometimes anticipates, issues such as human cloning, which require the development of new know-why ideas and norms; and proactively launches public debate to constantly redefine the link between the effective and the acceptable.

The move to extend links to the judicial side of prevention is also indicated in notions of "community prosecution" (Scott, 2001) — where local prosecutors' offices take on the function of helping to solve local crime problems as well as prosecuting individual cases in isolation. In the former Soviet Union, too, courts not only denounced and sentenced the convicted criminal, but made recommendations for prevention. At the very least, awareness of the symbolic side should avoid the outrage often engendered by naïve rationalist schemes which appear to blame the victims, excuse offending or treat the offender to "undeserved" sailing trips or the like for perfectly rational character-building purposes.

At a more strategic level, such knowledge would include *climate-setting* by attempting to change social norms relating, for example, to the acceptability of drink-driving or to the civil responsibility of manufacturers or designers for looking to the security of their products and environments (Ekblom and Pease, 2001). (Perhaps such climate-setting could also eventually extend to acceptance of "sailing trip" type action, provided this was effective — but that is a matter for debate.) We also need to find ways of making detached, causal analyses less vulnerable to the charge that we are merely "making excuses" for misbehaviour when, for example, we attribute it to tempting opportunity or early childhood experiences. Somehow we need blame and causation to articulate better; and we need to spread this understanding as widely as medical ethics people carry *their* debate and understanding to the media and the wider public. (If successful this may do more than help rationalist crime preventers avoid scathing newspaper headlines — it might actually get the public and the media, and hence politicians, more interested in civil approaches to prevention. At present, in the English-speaking world at least, there is almost exclusive focus on judicial approaches.)

A final point to note on the know-why subject is that scientists and detached administrators are not the only ones to risk ignoring the symbolic side of prevention. Commercial institutions are often seen as taking an entirely "rational" approach to crime by staff or customers — reporting and responding to it only if it is in their calculated interests to do so. This stance sometimes collides, with serious consequences, with the image they wish to portray.

GENERAL CONCLUSION

The transfer, reception and application of crime prevention knowledge from the source, in research and development, to the mainstream of practice, centre on several key ingredients. These are: a rigorous yet practical conceptual framework for prevention; a problem-oriented, innovative and risk-taking occupational culture of practitioners well-connected to a network of practically-oriented researchers, appropriate organisational structures and processes; well-developed, multi-media training; and a well-structured and wide-ranging Knowledge Base itself. The Knowledge Base should be of high quality and reliability, and should draw on general principles of knowledge management. But it should also be attuned to the distinctive nature of crime prevention. It should contain information of the right kind and in the right form to reconstruct and adapt successful interventions from generic principles attuned to specific crime problems in specific contexts, and to invent entirely new ones. It should be capable of evolving to accommodate new research, the shifting background of technological and social change, and the adaptive offender. Much of this Knowledge Base should be communicated to practitioners in a "foundation" course which represents a "high-investment, high-yield" strategy that primes them to receive details and updates throughout their professional career.

We must complement this knowledge by establishing a climate where managers and sponsors of practitioners, in their turn, accept the risk and loss of total control that goes with innovation, and support the collective interest in evaluation, including learning from failure. And more broadly, we must try to establish a wider common ground of understanding and belief about causes and cures of crime, and find ways to connect this with collective values on blame and fairness so that rational attempts to intervene do not clash unproductively with popular expectation.

Knowledge transfer is not simply about cognitive, technical considerations and a conducive climate. As with all attempts to change culture, there is a political dimension in which we must actively recognise and accommodate diverse interests in how information is shared and knowledge defined (Guba and Lincoln, 1989; Bellamy, 2001). This is not, however, to advocate relaxed acceptance of cultural relativism in crime prevention practice — we are in the game of evangelism, but we must win it by making practitioners *want* the knowledge we produce, and want the quality of intervention that comes with principles that stem from tested theory, a what-works knowledge base and application of feedback. To achieve this we need convincing arguments, demonstration of mutual advantage, joint ownership of the knowledge collection and transfer tasks with practitioners and other stakeholders, and joint design of solutions. We must also understand sources of resistance to change and work transparently to motivate practitioners, and to alleviate practical and managerial constraints on the application of knowledge. We must also strive to develop and maintain cultural and collaborative links between practitioners and researchers.

These are not easy requirements to meet. But if we — practice-oriented academics and researchers — are serious about making crime prevention work on the ground there is no alternative but to try to re-engineer the Knowledge Base, the systems of transfer that convey it to practitioners, and the wider set of working relationships and climate. In this way the mainstream of practice *does* come to lie downhill from the source in research and evaluation. Surely that is smarter than struggling against the current?

Address correspondence to: Paul Ekblom, Policing and Reducing Crime Unit, Research, Development and Statistics Directorate, U.K. Home Office, 50 Queen Anne's Gate, London SW1H 9AT. E-mail: <paul.ekblom@homeoffice.gsi.gov.uk>.

Acknowledgments: I am grateful for their helpful comments and encouragement to Susan Blackmore, Alan Brown, Rachel Cooper, David Farrington, Janet Foster, Martin Gill, Peter Homel, Gloria Laycock, Christine Lehman, Lawrence Singer, Stephen Sizmur, Paul van Soomeren, Mike Sutton, Nick Tilley, and Steve Trimmins.

REFERENCES

Alexandersson, L, T. Bersee, P. Ekblom, F. van Gelderen and A. Kohl (1999). *Assessment Report of the Experts Working in L'viv, Ukraine.* Council of Europe Project on Urban Insecurity and its Prevention in the CIS. Strasbourg, FR: Council of Europe.

Andrews, D., I. Zinger, R. Hoge, J. Bonta, P. Gendreau and F. Cullen (1990). "Does Correctional Treatment Work? A Clinically Relevant and Psychologically Informed Meta-Analysis." *Criminology* 28:369-404.

Argyris, C. and D. Schon (1996). *Organizational Learning II.* Reading, MA: Addison-Wesley.

Aunger, R. (ed.) (2000). *Darwinizing Culture. The Status of Memetics as a Science.* Oxford, UK: Oxford University Press.

Bellamy, C. (2001). Personal communication to P. Homel.

Blackmore, S. (1999). *The Meme Machine.* Oxford, UK: Oxford University Press.

Bloch, M. (2000). "A Well-Disposed Social Anthropologist's Problems with Memes." In: R. Aunger (ed.), *Darwinizing Culture. The Status of Memetics as a Science.* Oxford, UK: Oxford University Press.

Boyd, R. and P. Richerson (2000). "Memes: Universal Acid or a Better Mousetrap?" In: R. Aunger (ed.), *Darwinizing Culture. The Status of Memetics as a Science.* Oxford, UK: Oxford University Press.

Brand, S. (1997). *How Buildings Learn: What Happens after They're Built.* London, UK: Phoenix Illustrated.

Brown, P. (1996). "How the Parasite Learned to Kill." *New Scientist,* 16 November:32-36.

Browne, D., B. Dekker, P. Ekblom, L. Korsell, M. Levi, M. Maguire, M. Sutton and D. Oldfield (2001). *The Identification, Development and Exchange of Good Practice for Reducing Organised Crime.* Report to Falcone Fund, European Commission.

Bullock, K., G. Farrell, and N. Tilley (in press). *Funding and Implementing Crime Reduction Projects: Lessons from the Crime Reduction Programme.* (Crime Reduction Series Paper.) London, UK: Home Office.

Campbell, D.T. (1974). "Evolutionary Epistemology." In: P.A. Schlipp (ed.), *The Philosophy of Karl Popper,* vol. 1. La Salle, IL: Open Court Publishing.

—— (1965). "Variation and Selective Retention in Sociocultural Evolution." In: H. Barringer, G. Blanksten and R. Mack (eds.), *Social Change in Developing Areas: A Reinterpretation of Evolutionary Theory.* Cambridge, MA: Schenkman.

—— (1960). "Blind Variation and Selective Retention in Creative Thought as in Other Knowledge Processes." *Psychological Review* 67:380-400.

Clarke, R. (1999). *Hot Products: Understanding, Anticipating and Reducing Demand for Stolen Goods.* (Police Research Series, Paper No. 112.) London, UK: Home Office.

—— (1997). *Situational Crime Prevention: Successful Case Studies* (2nd ed.). New York: Harrow and Heston.

—— R. Kemper and L. Wyckoff (2001). "Controlling Cell Phone Fraud in the US: Lessons for the UK 'Foresight' Prevention Initiative." *Security Journal* 14:7-22.

Cohen, L. and M. Felson (1979). "Social Change and Crime Rate Changes: A Routine Activities Approach." *American Sociological Review* 44:588-608.

—— B. Vila and. R. Machalek (1995). "Expropriative Crime and Crime Policy: An Evolutionary Ecological Analysis." *Studies on Crime and Crime Prevention* 4:197-219.

Colinvaux, P. (1980). *Why Big Fierce Animals are Rare.* Harmondsworth, UK: Penguin.

Cook, T. and D. Campbell (1979). *Quasi-Experimentation.* Chicago, IL: Rand McNally.

Cornish, D. (1994). "The Procedural Analysis of Offending and its Relevance for Situational Prevention." In: *Crime Prevention Studies,* vol. 3. Monsey, NY: Criminal Justice Press.

Dawkins, R. (1986). *The Blind Watchmaker.* Harlow, Essex, UK: Longman.

—— (1982). *The Extended Phenotype.* Oxford, UK: Freeman.

—— (1976). *The Selfish Gene.* Oxford, UK: Oxford University Press.

Dennett, D. (1995). *Darwin's Dangerous Idea.* London, UK: Penguin.

Dhiri, S. (1999). *Analysis of Costs and Benefits: Guidance for Evaluators.* (Crime Reduction Programme Guidance, Note 1.) London, UK: Home Office.

Durham, W.H. (1991). *Coevolution: Genes, Culture and Human Diversity.* Stanford, CA: Stanford University Press.

Eck, J. (2001). "Improving Problem Analysis." Presentation at UK Problem-Oriented Policing Conference, Hinckley, UK, September.

Ekblom, P. (2001a). *Partnership: Definitions, Structures and Processes.* Working Paper for Council of Europe Committee of Experts on Partnership in Crime Prevention. Available from author.

—— (2001b, in press). "How to Think About Crime and its Reduction — Rigorously, Systematically and Inclusively." In: P. Ekblom, C. Lehman and K. Pease (eds.), *Reducing Offending II: An Updated Assessment of Research Evidence on Ways of Dealing with Offending Behaviour.* (Home Office Research Study.) London, UK: Home Office.

—— (2001c). "The Conjunction of Criminal Opportunity: A Framework for Crime Reduction Toolkits." Downloadable from UK Crime Reduction website (www.crimereduction.gov.uk/toolkits/ www.crime reduction.gove.uk/cco.htm).

—— (2001d). "Less Crime, by Design." Illustrated website version of paper presented at Royal Society of Arts, London, October 2000 (www.e-doca.net/Resources/Lectures/Less%20Crime%20by%20Design.htm).

—— (2001e, in press). "Less Crime, by Design." In: P. Ekblom, C. Lehman and K. Pease (eds.), *Reducing Offending II: An Updated Assessment of Research Evidence on Ways of Dealing with Offending Behaviour.* (Home Office Research Study.) London, UK: Home Office.

—— (2001f). "Organised Crime and the Conjunction of Criminal Opportunity Framework." In: D. Browne, B. Dekker, P. Ekblom, L. Korsell, M. Levi, M. Maguire, M. Sutton and D. Oldfield. *The Identification,*

Development and Exchange of Good Practice for Reducing Organised Crime. Report to Falcone Fund, European Commission.

—— (2000a). "The Conjunction of Criminal Opportunity — A Tool for Clear, 'Joined-up' Thinking about Community Safety and Crime Reduction. In: S. Ballintyne, K. Pease and V. McLaren (eds.), *Secure Foundations: Key Issues in Crime Prevention, Crime Reduction and Community Safety.* London, UK: Institute for Public Policy Research.

—— (2000b). "Crime Reduction Toolkits: A Contents Guide." Unpublished paper available from author.

—— (2000c). "A Formal and Systematic Description of a Preventive Scheme and its Components." Unpublished paper available from author.

—— (2000d). "Future Crime Prevention — A 'Mindset Kit' for the Seriously Foresighted." In: *Crime 2020* — CD-Rom with U.K. Department of Trade and Industry [2000] Report of Foresight Programme's Crime Prevention Panel. London, UK: (www.foresight.gov.uk/servlet /DocViewer/doc=1003).

—— (1999). "Can We Make Crime Prevention Adaptive by Learning from Other Evolutionary Struggles?" *Studies on Crime and Crime Prevention* 8(1):27-51. (www.bra.se/web/english; click on "Studies on Crime and Crime Prevention" and then the pdf button.)

—— (1998). *Community Safety and the Reduction and Prevention of Crime — a Conceptual Framework for Training and the Development of a Professional Discipline.* Paper on Home Office website under The Crime and Disorder Act: Guidance on Statutory Crime and Disorder Partnerships (www.homeoffice.gov.uk/cdact/cstrng5.htm).

—— (1997). "Gearing up against Crime: A Dynamic Framework to Help Designers Keep up with the Adaptive Criminal in a Changing World." *International Journal of Risk, Security and Crime Prevention* 214:249-265 (www.homeoffice.gov.uk/rds/pdfs/risk.pdf).

—— (1996a). "Towards a Discipline of Crime Prevention: A Systematic Approach to its Nature, Range and Concepts." In: T. Bennett (ed.), *Preventing Crime and Disorder: Targeting Strategies and Responsibilities.* (Cambridge Cropwood Series.) Cambridge, UK: Institute of Criminology, University of Cambridge.

—— (1996b). "Impact Evaluation for Practitioners: Making it Easier *and* Better." Paper presented at International Centre for the Prevention of Crime conference "Towards World Change," Vancouver.

—— (1994). "Proximal Circumstances: A Mechanism-Based Classification of Crime Prevention." *Crime Prevention Studies,* vol. 2. Monsey, NY: Criminal Justice Press.

—— (1990). "Evaluating Crime Prevention: The Management of Uncertainty." In: C. Kemp (ed.), *Current Issues in Criminological Research.* Bristol, UK: Bristol Centre for Criminal Justice.

—— (1988). *Getting the Best out of Crime Analysis.* (Home Office Crime Prevention Unit, Paper No. 10.) London, UK: Home Office.

—— (1986) "Community Policing: Obstacles and Issues." In: A. Walker, P. Ekblom and N. Deakin (P. Willmott, ed.), *The Debate About Community: Papers from a Seminar on Community in Social Policy.* (PSI Discussion Paper No. 13.) London, UK: Policy Studies Institute.

—— C. Lehman and K. Pease (eds.) (2001, in press). *Reducing Offending II: An Updated Assessment of Research Evidence on Ways of Dealing with Offending Behaviour.* (Home Office Research Study.) London, UK: Home Office.

—— and K. Pease (2001, in press). "Changing the Context of Crime Prevention." In: P. Ekblom, C. Lehman and K. Pease (eds.). *Reducing Offending II: An Updated Assessment of Research Evidence on Ways of Dealing with Offending Behaviour.* London, UK: Home Office Research Study.

—— and N. Tilley (2000). "Going Equipped: Criminology, Situational Crime Prevention and the Resourceful Offender." *British Journal of Criminology* 40:376-398.

—— and N. Tilley (1998). "'What Works' Database for Community Safety/Crime Reduction Practitioners: Towards a Specification for an Ideal Template." Unpublished paper available from author.

—— and K. Pease (1995). "Evaluating Crime Prevention." In: M. Tonry and D. Farrington (eds.), *Building a Safer Society: Strategic Approaches to Crime Prevention.* (Crime and Justice, vol. 19.) Chicago, IL: University of Chicago Press.

Farrington, D. (2001, in press). "Risk-Focussed Prevention and Integrated Approaches." In: P. Ekblom, C. Lehman and K. Pease (eds.), *Reducing Offending II: An Updated Assessment of Research Evidence on Ways of Dealing with Offending Behaviour.* London, UK: Home Office Research Study [ ].

—— (2000). "Explaining and Preventing Crime: The Globalization of Knowledge — the American Society of Criminology 1999 Presidential Address." *Criminology* 38:801-824.

—— and A. Petrosino (2001). "The Campbell Collaboration Crime and Justice Group." *Annals of the American Academy of Political and Social Science* 578:35-49.

Faulkner, D. (2001). *Crime State and Citizen: A Field Full of Folk.* Winchester, UK: Waterside Press.

Forrester, D., M. Chatterton and K. Pease (1988). *The Kirkholt Burglary Prevention Project, Rochdale.* (Crime Prevention Unit Paper No. 13.) London, UK: Home Office.

Forrester, D., S. Frenz, M. O'Connell and K. Pease (1990). *The Kirkholt Burglary Prevention Project, Phase 2.* (Crime Prevention Unit Paper No. 23.) London, UK: Home Office.

Freiberg, A. (2001). "Affective versus Effective Justice." *Punishment and Society* 3:265-277.

Gergen, K. (1973). "Social Psychology as History." *Journal of Personality and Social Psychology* 26:309-320.

Gilling, D. (1997). *Crime Prevention: Theory, Policy and Politics.* London, UK: UCL Press.

Goldblatt, P. and C. Lewis (eds.) (1998). *Reducing Offending: an Assessment of Research Evidence on Ways of Dealing with Offending Behaviour.* (Home Office Research Study No. 187.) London, UK: Home Office.

Gregory, R. (1981). *Mind in Science: A History of Explanations in Psychology and Physics.* London, UK: Weidenfeld and Nicholson.

Guba, Y. and E. Lincoln (1989). *Fourth Generation Evaluation.* London, UK: Sage.

Hapgood, F. (1993). *Up the Infinite Corridor. MIT and the Technical Imagination.* Reading, MA: Addison-Wesley.

Hope, T. and D. Murphy (1983). "Problems of Implementing Crime Prevention: The Experience of a Demonstration Project." *Howard Journal of Criminal Justice* 22:38-50.

Hough, M. and N. Tilley (1998). *Getting the Grease to the Squeak: Research Lessons for Crime Prevention.* (Crime Prevention and Detection Series Paper No. 85.) London, UK: Home Office.

Hull, D. (2000). "Taking Memetics Seriously: Memetics Will Be What We Make It." In: R. Aunger (ed.), (2000). *Darwinizing Culture. The Status of Memetics as a Science.* Oxford, UK: Oxford University Press.

—— (1988). "A Mechanism and its Metaphysic: An Evolutionary Account of the Social and Conceptual Development of Science." *Biology and Philosophy* 3:123-155.

Johnson, S. and C. Loxley (2001). *Installing Alley-Gates: Practical Lessons from Burglary Prevention Projects.* (Policing and Reducing Crime Unit Briefing Note 2/01.) London, UK: Home Office.

Kerkhof, G. (2000). *Directory of Excellence. A European Infrastructure for the Prevention and/or Reduction of Organised Crime.* Unpublished report to Europol.

Knox, J., A. Pemberton and P. Wiles (2000). *Partnerships in Community Safety. An Evaluation of Phase 2 of the Safer Cities Programme.* (DETR Regeneration Series.) London, UK: DETR (now Department for Transport, Local Government and the Regions).

Kuper, A. (2000). "If Memes are the Answer, What is the Question?" In: R. Aunger (ed.), *Darwinizing Culture. The Status of Memetics as a Science.* Oxford, UK: Oxford University Press.

Laland, K. and J. Odling-Smee (2000). "The Evolution of the Meme." In: R. Aunger (ed.), *Darwinizing Culture. The Status of Memetics as a Science.* Oxford, UK: Oxford University Press.

Laycock, G. (2001). "Hypothesis-Based Research: The Repeat Victimisation Story." *Criminal Justice* (London: Sage) 1(1):59-82.

—— (2000). *Social Research: Getting it Right for Practitioners and Policy Makers.* Draft Final Report to U.S. National Institute of Justice.

—— and B. Webb (2000). "Making It All Happen." In: S. Ballintyne, K. Pease and V. McLaren (eds.), *Secure Foundations: Key Issues in Crime Prevention, Crime Reduction and Community Safety.* London, UK: Institute for Public Policy Research.

—— and N. Tilley (1995). *Policing and Neighbourhood Watch: Strategic Issues.* (Crime Prevention and Detection Series, Paper No. 60.) London, UK: Home Office.

Leigh, A., T. Read and N. Tilley (1998). *Brit Pop II: Problem-oriented policing in Practice.* (Police Research Series, Paper No. 93.) London, UK: Home Office.

Macintosh, A. (1999). *Knowledge Management.* University of Edinburgh (www.aiai.ed.ac.uk/~alm/kamlnks.html).

Ministère délégué à la Ville (2001). "Summary of the Debates at the Seminar in Paris on January 22nd 2001 Concerning the European Crime Prevention Network." Unpublished report.

Nutley, S. and H. Davies (2000). "Making a Reality of Evidence-Based Practice: Some Lessons from the Diffusion of Innovations." *Public Money and Management* Oct-Dec: 35-42. London, UK: Chartered Institute of Public Finance and Accountancy.

Osborne, S. (1998). "'Naming the Beast': Defining and Classifying Service Innovations in Social Policy." *Human Relations* 30:1133-1154.

Pawson, R. and N. Tilley (1997). *Realistic Evaluation*. London, UK: Sage.

Pease, K. (1997). "Predicting the Future: the Roles of Routine Activity and Rational Choice Theory." In: G. Newman, R.V. Clarke and S.G. Shoham (eds.), *Rational Choice and Situational Crime Prevention: Theoretical Foundations*. Aldershot, UK: Dartmouth.

Petroski, H. (1992). *The Evolution of Useful Things*. New York, NY: Alfred A. Knopf.

Phillips, C. (1999). "A Review of CCTV Evaluations: Crime Reduction Effects and Attitudes toward its Use." In: K. Painter and N. Tilley (eds.), *Surveillance and Crime Prevention*. (Crime Prevention Studies, vol. 10.) Monsey, NY: Criminal Justice Press.

Pinker, S. (1994). *The Language Instinct*. New York, NY: Morrow.

Plotkin, H. (2000). "Culture and Psychological Mechanisms." In: R. Aunger (ed.), *Darwinizing Culture. The Status of Memetics as a Science*. Oxford, UK: Oxford University Press.

—— (1998). *Evolution in Mind. An Introduction to Evolutionary Psychology*. Cambridge, MA: Harvard University Press.

—— (1993). *Darwin Machines and the Nature of Knowledge*. London, UK: Penguin.

Popper, K. (1972). *Objective Knowledge*. Oxford, UK: Oxford University Press.

Poyner, B. and R. Woodall (1987). *Preventing Shoplifting: A Study in Oxford Street*. London, UK: Police Foundation.

Pressman, J. and A. Wildavsky (1984). *Implementation*. Berkeley, CA: University of California Press.

Read, T. and N. Tilley (2000). *Not Rocket Science? Problem-Solving and Crime Reduction*. (Crime Reduction Series, Paper No. 6.) London, UK: Home Office.

Rogerson, M, P. Ekblom and K. Pease (2000). "Crime Reduction and the Benefit of Foresight." In: S. Ballintyne, K. Pease and V. McLaren (eds.), *Secure Foundations: Key Issues in Crime Prevention, Crime Reduction and Community Safety*. London, UK: Institute for Public Policy Research.

Rosenbaum, D. (ed.) (1986). *Community Crime Prevention: Does it Work?*. Beverly Hills, CA: Sage.

Scott, M. (2001). *Problem-Oriented Policing: Reflections on the First 20 Years*. Washington, DC: U.S. Department of Justice Community Oriented Policing Services (www.usdoj.gov/cops/cp_resources/pubs_ppse/default.htm#Problem_Oriented_Policing).

Sherman, L. (1998). *Evidence-Based Policing.* Washington, DC: Police Foundation (www.policefoundation.org/pdf/Sherman.pdf).

—— D. Gottfredson, D. Mackenzie, J. Eck, P. Reuter and S. Bushway (1997). *Preventing Crime: What Works, What Doesn't and What's Promising. A Report to the United States Congress.* Washington, DC: U.S. Department of Justice.

Smolin, L. (1997). *The Life of the Cosmos.* London, UK: Weidenfeld and Nicholson.

Sperber, D. (2000). "An Objection to the Memetic Approach to Culture." In: R. Aunger (ed.), *Darwinizing Culture. The Status of Memetics as a Science.* Oxford, UK: Oxford University Press.

Sutton, M. (1996). *Implementing Crime Prevention Schemes in a Multi-Agency Setting: Aspects of Process in the Safer Cities Programme.* (Home Office Research Study No. 160.) London, UK: Home Office.

Tilley, N. (1993a). *After Kirkholt: Theory, Methods and Results of Replication Evaluations.* (Crime Prevention Unit Paper No. 47.) London, UK: Home Office.

—— (1993b). *Understanding Car Parks, Crime and CCTV: Evaluation Lessons from Safer Cities.* (Crime Prevention Unit Paper No. 42.) London, UK: Home Office.

—— (1982). "Popper, Historicism and Emergence." *Philosophy of the Social Sciences* 12:59-67.

—— and G. Laycock (2000). "Joining up Research, Policy and Practice about Crime." *Policy Studies* 21:213-227.

—— K. Pease, M. Hough and R. Brown (1999). *Burglary Lessons from the Crime Reduction Programme.* (Crime Reduction Research Series, #1.) London, UK: Home Office.

U.K. Audit Commission (1999). *Safety in Numbers: Promoting Community Safety.* London, UK: author.

U.K. Department of Trade and Industry (2000). *Turning the Corner.* (Report of Foresight Programme's Crime Prevention Panel.) London, UK: author. (Downloadable from www.foresight.gov.uk.)

U.K. Her Majesty's Inspectorate of Constabulary (2000). *Calling Time on Crime.* (Thematic Inspection on Crime and Disorder by Her Majesty's Inspectorate of Constabulary.) London, UK: Home Office.

U.K. Home Office (1999). *Reducing Crime and Tackling its Causes — a Briefing Note on the Crime Reduction Programme.* London, UK: Home Office.

—— (1997). *Core Competences for Crime Prevention Staff Employed within the Police Service.* York, UK: Home Office Crime Prevention (now Reduction) College.

van Soomeren, P. (2001). Personal communication to the author.

—— (2000). "Crime Prevention Solutions for Europe: Designing out Crime." Paper presented at conference on the Relationship Between the Physical Environment and Crime Reduction and Prevention, Szczecin, Poland (www.e-doca.net/Resources/Conference%20Papers/Szczecin/Designing_Out_Crime.pdf).

Vennard, J. and C. Hedderman (1998). "Effective Interventions with Offenders." In: P. Goldblatt and C. Lewis (eds.), *Reducing Offending: an Assessment of Research Evidence on Ways of Dealing with Offending Behaviour.* (Home Office Research Study No. 187.) London, UK: Home Office.

Wikström, P-O., R. Clarke and J. McCord (eds.) (1995). *Integrating Crime Prevention Strategies: Propensity and Opportunity.* Stockholm, SWE: National Council for Crime Prevention.

Wilkins, L. (1997). "Wartime Operational Research in Britain and Situational Crime Prevention." In: G. Newman, R.V. Clarke and S.G. Shoham, (eds.), *Rational Choice and Situational Crime Prevention: Theoretical Foundations.* Aldershot, UK: Dartmouth.

APPENDIX
THE CONJUNCTION OF CRIMINAL OPPORTUNITY (CCO) FRAMEWORK

This brief resume is intended merely to impart the flavour of CCO. Readers are referred to Ekblom (2000a) for a full version, and Ekblom (2001c) for a shorter, but more recent one. Since the framework is under continual development in terms of both content and usability, comments are welcome to the author.

The CCO framework is inclusive both of theories of crime, and of the range of practical methods of prevention — situational and offender-oriented, criminal justice-based and civil. It provides clear and logically-related definitions of crime prevention and reduction, and a whole body of key terms for systematically mapping out the immediate (or proximal) causes of criminal events, the interventions in those causes and the contextual conditions with which the interventions interact. (In this, it follows the spirit of the "systems" approach advocated by Wilkins, 1997.) It has been designed to fit in with the know-how stages of the Preventive Process, aiming to organise know-about, know-what and some aspects of know-who. It seeks to:

(1) Help practitioners both to give a systematic description of the crime problem, as in crime pattern analysis or wider assessment of risk and protective factors; and to clearly specify the objectives of the operation to tackle that problem (*"problem space"*).

(2) Provide a generic map of the causes of crime to help practitioners systematically consider what factors might be causing their particular crime problem in that context (*"diagnosis space"* — *Figure 1*).

The 11 generic, immediate causes are, on the offender side:

- *Criminality* — longer-term, personality-based influences predisposing offenders to crime.

- *Lack of resources to avoid crime* — e.g., for avoiding conflict or gaining a legitimate living.

- *Readiness to offend* — shorter-term influences — motives and emotional states, as determined by current life circumstances, conflicts and influence of drugs.

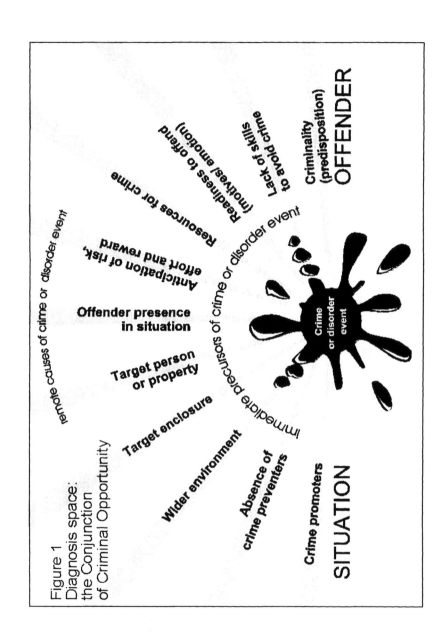

Figure 1
Diagnosis space:
the Conjunction
of Criminal Opportunity

OFFENDER

Criminality
(predisposition)

Lack of skills
to avoid crime

Readiness to offend
(motives/ emotion)

Resources for crime

Anticipation of risk,
effort and reward

Offender presence
in situation

Target person
or property

Target enclosure

Wider environment

Absence of
crime preventers

Crime promoters

SITUATION

remote causes of crime or disorder event

immediate precursors of crime or disorder event

Crime
or disorder
event

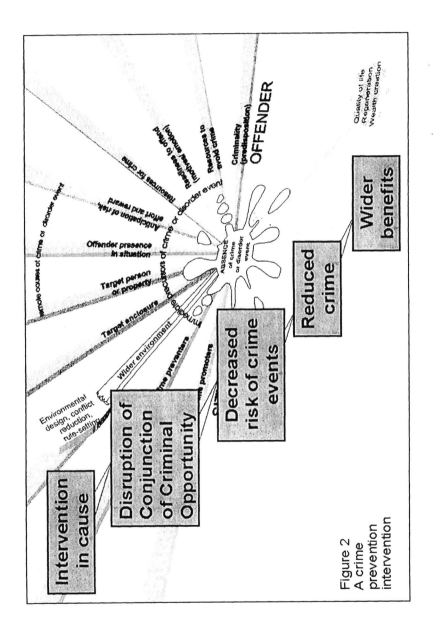

Figure 2
A crime
prevention
intervention

- *Resources for committing crime* — skills, courage, knowledge of targets, *modus operandi,* tools, weapons, access to networks of collaborators.

- *Immediate decision to offend* — anticipation/ perception of low risk and effort, and of high reward, and absence of attacks of conscience.

- *Presence* in the crime situation.

On the situational side:

- *Target* person, property, service, system or information that is vulnerable, provocative or attractive.

- *Target enclosure* — building, room, vehicle or container that is vulnerable to penetration and contains suitable targets.

- *Wider environment* that is logistically/tactically favourable for offenders and unfavourable for preventers, and which may attract or motivate the offence.

- *Absence of crime preventers* — people or organisations, formal or informal, who make the crime less likely whether deliberately or incidentally.

- *Presence of crime promoters* — who make the crime more likely, whether unwittingly, carelessly or deliberately — for example by supplying tools, information or other criminal services before or after the crime.

(3) Provide a generic map of intervention principles to help practitioners choose those which might work to block the causes of their particular crime problem, in that particular context ("*intervention space*" — *Figures 2 and 3*). The principles correspond to the 11 causes just identified. They can be cast at the very abstract, genotypic level ("target hardening"), or can be further differentiated like the twigs of the tree ("resistance to shearing force"; "resistance to drilling," etc.). In all cases these are "functional" descriptions, expressed in terms of the cause of crime that is to be tackled — usually relating to an offender's modus operandi.

Figure 3: Intervention Space: Crime Prevention and the Conjunction of Criminal Opportunity

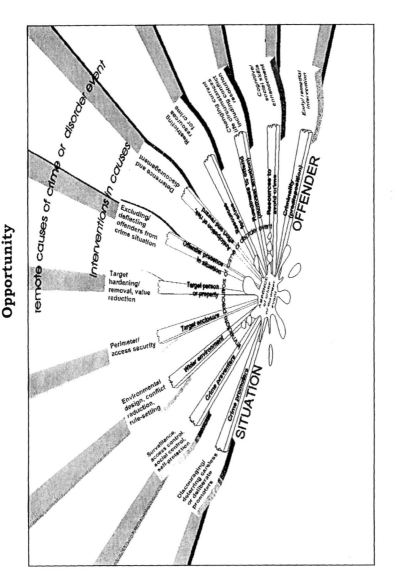

(4) Help in the clear specification of real-world, phenotypic, solutions — practical crime prevention methods, schemes and packages intended to bring about the chosen interventions ("*solution space*" — *Figure 4* — the spiders' webs cross-linking the branches of the tree of principles and mechanisms). Method statements etc., are linked to principles using a "by" phrase. For example, "target hardening through resistance to shearing, *by* using swivelling anchorages." This general clarity of what is being implemented and how it works makes for more reliable implementation, and supports monitoring for quality assurance and general project management. Both of these processes contribute to programme integrity — ensuring that what is delivered, and what continues to be delivered, is what was planned.

(5) Characterise the dynamics of criminal events, whether through scenes and scripts (Cornish, 1994) or through processes such as displacement, diffusion of benefit, offender replacement and arms races (Ekblom, 1997, 1999).

(6) Help select and mobilise other agencies that can play an effective part in reducing crime — *insertion* (Ekblom and Pease, 2001). This includes replicating the knowledge within them.

(7) Help feedback, adjustment, evaluation and measurement of cost-effectiveness ("*learning space*" — *Figure 5*). If the operation was well-implemented, then it is also worth evaluating. Because the framework has already been used to map out the causes of crime and the interventions, it provides a firm base for attributing cause and effect in order to evaluate the operation's impact on crime and the processes by which it achieved that impact.

(8) If we combine a clear *description* of the methods that were implemented, and the results of a good-quality process and impact *evaluation*, we have the material for a knowledge base of "what works." The framework gives us the structure for the efficient storage and retrieval of that information, and the synthesis of practical principles. It also facilitates the two-way flow of information between generic theory and specific practice — theory informs practice, and practice tests theory only if the one can be mapped clearly onto the other.

Figure 4: Solution Space: Methods and Packages

Figure 4: Solution Space: Methods and Packages

– 201 –

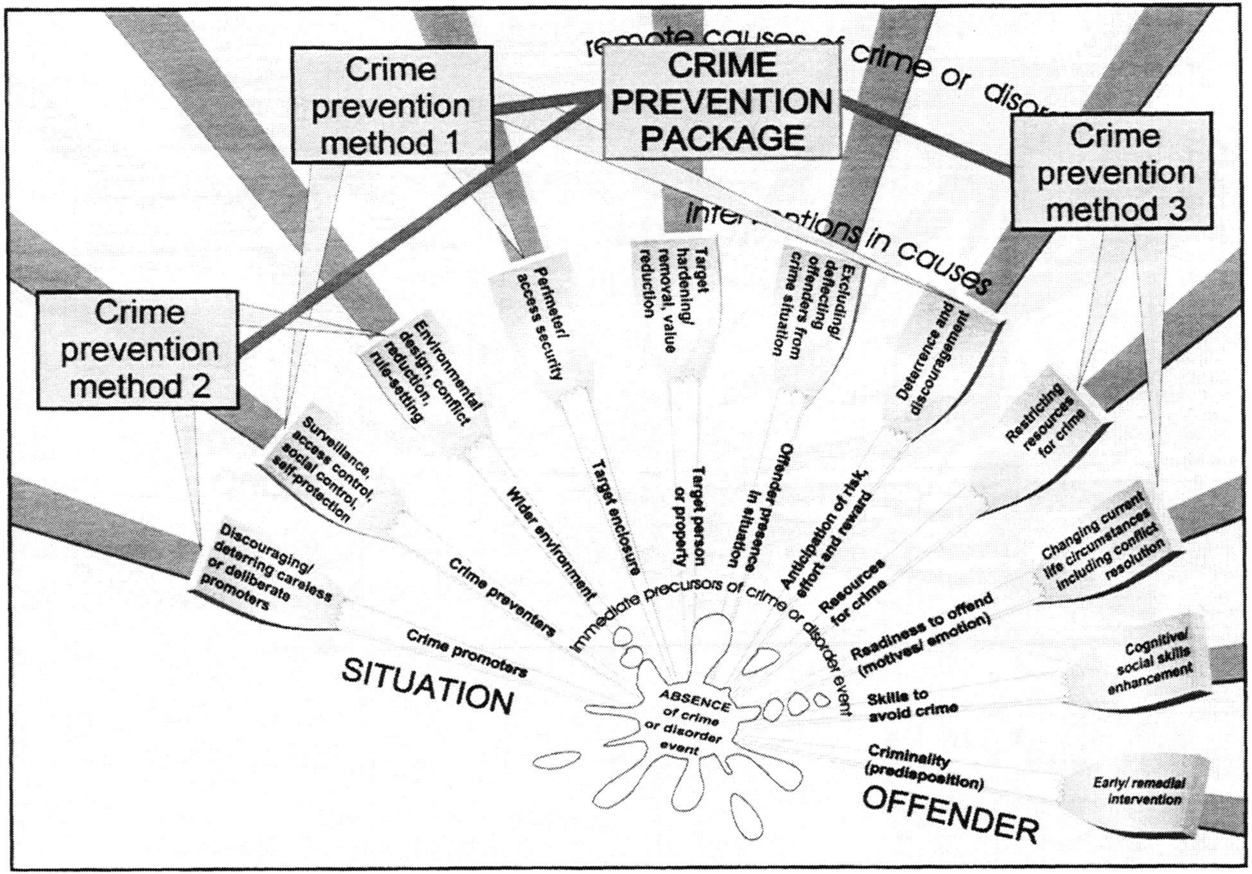

Figure 5: Evaluation: Additional Inputs and Attributable Effects of a Crime Prevention Scheme

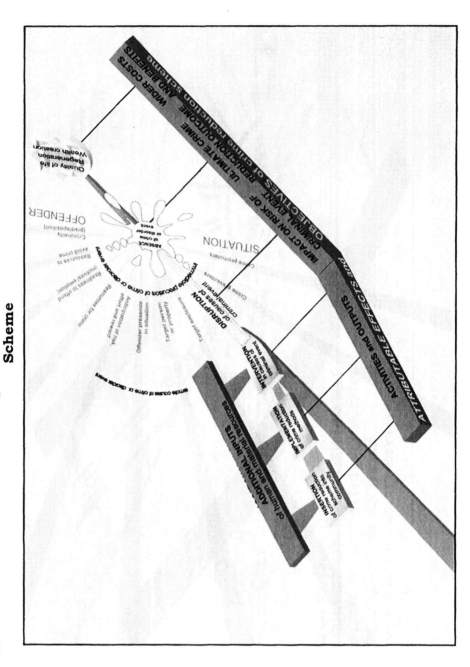

NOTES

1. Following the success of the Cochrane Collaboration in reviewing health care interventions, the Campbell Collaboration was founded in February 2000 to produce systematic reviews of social, educational and criminological interventions. The aim of the Campbell Collaboration is to make the best knowledge about "What Works" immediately available electronically (e.g. on the World Wide Web) to all interested persons, including scholars, practitioners, policy makers and the general public. These systematic reviews will be subject to rigorous quality control, will cover research throughout the world, will be regularly updated and will be revised in the light of cogent criticisms. The Campbell Collaboration further aims to stimulate higher-quality evaluations to feed the knowledge-gathering process in the future. Farrington and Petrosino (2001) describe the general background to Campbell and the aims of the Crime and Justice Group in particular. The website is http://campbell.gse.upenn.edu.

METHODOLOGICAL ISSUES IN WORKING WITH POLICY ADVISERS AND PRACTITIONERS

by

Gloria Laycock
University College, London

Abstract: *This chapter considers what policy advisers and practitioners arguably need from researchers, and what they can reasonably expect. It goes on to discuss the implications of these needs and expectations for the methodologies used in research. But we begin with some definitions — what we mean by policy adviser, practitioner and researcher in this context, and why they need definition.*

DEFINING TERMS

It may seem odd to begin a chapter with the definition of such basic terms as policy adviser, practitioner and researcher, but there are some specific characteristics of these individuals that are central to their expectations and their capabilities and it is, therefore, worth spelling these out. This is particularly true in the context of crime prevention, where the assumptions and beliefs of the general public form the backdrop against which policy makers and practitioners operate (Tilley and Laycock, 2000). They would not be performing their jobs properly if they were to ignore the public view. The same is far less true of the researcher, who, in theory at least, should be trying to acquire knowledge independently of the public's views.

So let us begin with the "policy adviser." In the United Kingdom we are talking about senior civil servants, in the United States of America, political advisers at federal, state or even local levels whose responsibility it is to advise the governors and legislators about crime and its control. They are one step removed from politicians but are nevertheless aware of the political pressures operating at that level and, therefore, well advised to attend to the expectations and beliefs of the public. In making sensible recommendations about crime prevention many will be conscious of the long held public view that the police, acting through the criminal justice system, can and should be expected to reduce crime. And some will share that view. It is an approach that generally leads to an expansion of the enforcement model — it fuels cries for more police officers on the streets, and for tougher and longer sentences. It does not point, naturally, to the notion that environmental measures play a major part in generating criminal or disorderly behavior. So any advice reinforcing, for example, the role of opportunity in crime control (Felson and Clarke, 1998), has to overcome these beliefs as a first step. This message has the added disadvantage that it is not cost-neutral to the recipients. The members of the public, and a wide range of agencies in commerce and industry, have to take some responsibility for crime control — they actually have to *do* something rather than sit back and expect the police and others to protect them (Laycock, 1996). This is not an easy message politically. It involves, at least partially, handing crime control back to the people from the State, with the accompanying responsibility (Christie, 1977).

The practitioner can be characterized as an individual who is expected to deliver the policies "on the streets." In the case of crime prevention, this is often the police, although, depending on the scope of the crime prevention effort, it might also include the other statutory or voluntary partners with whom they are now beginning to work (Crime and Disorder Act, U.K., 1998). They, quite literally, come face to face with the beliefs and expectations of the public in a way in which the more remote policy advisers do not. For the purposes of discussion in this chapter, we are restricting the definition to statutory police agencies — those whom the general public see as central to the delivery of safe and crime-free communities, although the extent to which these expectations can be met by the police alone has been challenged in official U.K. publications for about two decades and the idea that the police need to work in partnership is also central to the current "community policing" approach in the U.S.

Finally, the researchers — how are they to be described? There is a sense in which a wide range of activities can legitimately be called research. The work of a detective, for example, might be so construed. He or she will go through a systematic process of gathering evidence and apply various rules of logic or systematic review to try to achieve a satisfactory solution to a case. And a wide range of disciplines might claim to carry out research in the normal course of their work — the journalist, historian, or scientist — all use systematic processes, with claims to objectivity and the application of scientific method. In this chapter we are taking a fairly narrow definition. The researchers as discussed here will draw on the social sciences, will use some sort of data analysis, quantitative or qualitative, in the course of their investigations, and, importantly, will formulate and test hypotheses about crime and its prevention. They will be familiar with the research literature, or know how to access it. They will also draw on the various theories of human behavior from psychology, sociology or the behavioral sciences more generally in their efforts to describe, understand or test the crime prevention programs with which they may be associated. They will not, therefore, only be concerned with producing descriptive statistics, or even the evaluation of programs, unless there is a clear statement of the process or mechanism through which those programs might be operating. To do otherwise risks producing barren reports which tell the knowledgeable adviser or experienced practitioner what they already knew. The challenge to the research community is to tell the world something new and take the field forward, rather than looking back, as so often happens (Christie, 1997).

WHAT DO POLICY ADVISERS AND PRACTITIONERS NEED FROM RESEARCH?

Bearing in mind where these people are coming from, as they say, what might their needs be? Some suggestions are listed below under the separate headings of policy makers and practitioners, and the section concludes with a brief discussion of some of the constraints on the researcher in being able to meet the demands.

Policy Advisers

The world in which the policy adviser works is a fast changing and demanding one. This is a common feature of the scene in both the U.S.A. and the U.K., although there are some major differences between these two jurisdictions — in the U.S.A. senior policy advisers are often appointed by politicians and may, for example, have an implicit remit to support the politicians' re-election or at least to toe the party line. The advisers are, therefore, not only sensitive to whether the messages from research fit with the public's expectations, but they are also expected to address the extent to which research results are compatible with the political complexion of their patrons. In the U.K. the position is somewhat different. Although there are politically appointed advisers in all government departments, and they have grown in number over recent years, they are still vastly out-numbered by the permanent senior civil service whose advice is ex-pected to be politically impartial and factually based.

In both the U.S.A. and the U.K. recent administrations have be-gun to look for "what works" as a means of improving efficiency and reducing costs. This interest has been something of a two-edged sword. On the positive side, it has led to substantially increased de-mand for research, with the associated funding and implication that policy might finally be influenced by it (U.K. Home Office, 1999; U.S. National Institute of Justice, 1997). More unhelpfully, it has also ex-posed the amount of money that has already been spent on research, and the relatively little by way of firm evidence on effectiveness that it has produced (Sherman et al., 1997; Goldblatt and Lewis, 1998).

In both jurisdictions, however, it is probably fair to say that the advisers are looking for "good news," i.e., the policies that were effec-tive — in the crime prevention world, this means that crime went down, the public was less fearful, everyone was happy. So the first somewhat cynical requirement from research is that it produces what the politicians want to hear. And it needs to do so quickly. There is an impatience about the process of government that leaves research at the starting block. While the average university professor is begin-ning to contemplate the enormity of the research exercise facing him or her, the politician is expecting an answer, and an unequivocal one at that. Conclusions that "more research is needed" receive a very bad press.

Despite their wish for good news, and the rush to announce new initiatives, the policy adviser in this new and developing outcome-focused world will increasingly need to have confidence in the con-clusions of the research exercise, particularly if large sums of public money are at risk of commitment to new programs. In the "old days" it mattered less if decisions were made on the basis of political expe-diency rather than efficacy, but now, with the public, the media and others watching the public sector equivalent of the "bottom line," confidence in research conclusions matters. And an additional di-mension has been added with the interest in reducing the cost of central government activity — not only do policy advisers want to know what works, they want to know at what cost. Cost-effectiveness is increasingly being built into the evaluation plans for new studies (Dhiri and Brand, 1999; Colledge et al., 1999).

Next is the delicate matter of money. There is a tendency for policy advisers in central government to see themselves as the custodians of public money — and he who pays the piper expects to call the tune. In the U.S.A. the process is more directly dependent on the views of Congress, where research money is voted for specific purposes, with at present a relatively small amount for discretionary use. The degree of flexibility within the discretionary allocation varies, but the head of the federal government's criminal justice research agency in the United States is a presidential appointee, and is expected to take the government's priorities, and view of the world, into account when setting the agenda.

In the U.K. the position is again rather different. Here the money voted by Parliament for centrally funded criminological research has generally been for the support of the criminal justice policy process. The policy advisers were, therefore, seen as the customers for the work (although ministerial approval was generally expected) and felt that they should have the major say in research expenditure (Cornish and Clarke, 1987). More recently the picture has changed somewhat, with the "legitimate user" being expanded from the policy advisers to include the practitioners, and with more weight being given to the experience of the government researchers and their views, in setting the research agenda. The relationship is now better characterized as a set of partnerships between policy, practice and research (Laycock, 2001). Whatever the subtleties of the developing relationship between researcher and policy advisers, the policy advisers feel they have a significant role to play on both sides of the Atlantic — and that they should not, therefore, be ignored in determining the research agenda. While this partnership approach dilutes the political influence over the research agenda, in reality it does not remove it. Political ideology at least maintains a "filtering" role (Doherty, 2000) over what research is done, how it is presented publicly, and what influence it may have over future policy direction.

Finally, and in some ways this ought not to need saying, policy advisers need to be able to understand the results of a research project. Research papers that are written in obscure technical language, permeable to the chosen few, and covering reams of paper, are less likely to influence policy than a concise, crisp few pages which summarize the important points and spell out the implications for policy. Some researchers are distinctly uncomfortable with this scenario, particularly the idea that they should perhaps go somewhat beyond their data in spelling out the policy implications of what they have done.

The requirements of the researcher from the policy adviser can therefore be summarized as:

- Good news;
- Confidence in the results;
- Costs included in evaluations;

- A feeling of involvement in the agenda setting process;
- Timely production of results;
- The identification of "what works";
- Good communication skills; and
- A willingness to take risks in making inferences from their data.

Practitioners

The world is changing rapidly for criminal justice practitioners. It is no longer good enough to point to a list of outputs from the field — more tickets issued, more arrests made, more neighbourhood/block watch groups or partnerships established. The pressure is on for the delivery of outcomes. There are a variety of ways in which this is manifesting itself. In the U.K., for example, the Crime and Disorder Act requires the police and local government to work together and produce a strategic plan for the reduction of crime and disorder. There is an increasing expectation that this will be related to hard targets for reduction. Indeed the Government has set itself a target of reducing vehicle crime by 30% over five years.

In parallel, still in the U.K., a new regime of "best value" has been introduced under which police forces are expected to examine their policies and procedures on a regular cycle and demonstrate that they are achieving value for money. This does not mean going for the cheapest option necessarily, but going for the most cost effective (Leigh et al., 1999).

In the U.S.A., one of the more tangible manifestations of this move toward an outcome focus is through the Compstat process first used in the New York City Police Department and now being replicated in a number of police agencies across the country. Compstat is no more than a management tool forcing the attention of precinct commanders to the crime and disorder statistics in their area. Typically there will be a map of the precinct with the recent crime and disorder incidents displayed. The commander will be expected to give an account of what he or she intends to do about the offending pattern. How will it be reduced?

In both the U.S.A. and the U.K., there is also a significant move toward problem-oriented policing (Goldstein, 1979, 1990) — the police are expected to solve problems rather than to react continually to them. Again there is an expectation that what might have been a recurring problem will be addressed in such a way as to reduce the rate at which the incidents occur, or to eliminate them — a focus on outcome rather than output.

One collective consequence of all these developments is the increasing pressure on practitioners to implement cost-effective tactics to reduce crime. There is, therefore, a need for the practitioners to know what works, where, and at what cost. They are looking to the research community to provide some answers.

In this respect the picture has changed dramatically over the last five or so years. In the past, the researchers and practitioners could operate in independent universes for all practical purposes. The researchers could carry out their research *on* the police and report the results in their academic journals. The police could complain about the unfairness of the results and the frequent negative findings — nothing works — and ignore the outcome. This is clearly a caricature of the situation, but it is not that far off. If we calculate the amount of money spent on police-related research in the U.S.A. over just the past decade, and then look at how much it has impacted operational policing, then we might wonder where the money went. Although some commentators argue that the influence has been subtle but important, on, for example, police responsiveness and accountability (Bayley, 1998), the view taken in this chapter is that at best it provides poor value for money — if, that is, changing the way the police do business was the intention of the research, and it often was not.

Like the policy makers, the practitioner should be involved in the agenda setting process. Although they do not have resources to spend on research to the same significant extent, a great deal of research time can be saved if practitioners are involved in the process of agreeing to the research program from the beginning. Research hypotheses can be generated on the basis of their experience for example. In addition, because of their proximity to "the streets," they are often the first to become aware of a rising crime problem, which in the normal course of events might take months or even years to permeate the policy consciousness. An ability to pick up these emerging problems early would be one advantage of involving practitioners in determining the research program. Not only could the emerging problem be quantified and described, but a timely research-based response could nip it in the bud.

Many practitioners also appreciate some research support in tackling problems unique to them. They are on the receiving end of policy decisions, and are often ill advised on how, for example, the decisions might best be implemented and what others are doing to deliver the latest proposals in a cost-effective and timely manner. They need to know not only what works, but where and why. Neighborhood or block watch is a good example of an initiative that is highly sensitive to the context within which it is introduced in what it can deliver (Laycock and Tilley, 1993). Practitioners need to be aware of these subtleties.

Perhaps most importantly, what practitioners need to understand is *why* an initiative may or may not have worked. Knowing this will help them, and their research colleagues, in deciding where and how to replicate the initiative (Tilley, 1993), and ultimately to "mainstream" it. At some point the research process needs to lead to the articulation of the "mechanism" (Pawson and Tilley, 1997a) through which the initiative is presumed to be effective. This amounts to saying what the hypothesis is that might lead to a reduction in crime. In the U.S. literature this is called the "logic model" or "program theory" (Weiss, 1998a).

Like policy advisers, practitioners also need to be able to understand the results of the research process. Results need to be presented in plain English, with the practical implications of projects written clearly. Busy practitioners do not have the time, nor in many cases the interest to immerse themselves in the details of research. A different product is required which meets the needs of the practitioner audience.

Finally, and perhaps a relatively trivial point, practitioners appreciate (even if they do not "need") feedback when they have given their time, resources or effort to support a research exercise in their agency. Too often there are complaints that researchers come and go — collecting data, issuing questionnaires or generally making demands, without providing any feedback on the final results of the exercise.

To summarize the requirements of the practitioner, they need:

- To know what works, where and why;
- Help in replicating "what works" — understanding contexts and mechanisms;
- Help in generating testable hypotheses;
- Timely research;
- Involvement in setting the agenda;
- Reports and recommendations in plain English;
- To know of current good practice; and
- Feedback on the results of research in which they have participated.

None of the requirements outlined above are in any way illegitimate or unfair. They simply reflect the realities of life. If research is to be of use to policy advisers and practitioners then it needs to be attentive to the needs of these communities.

Constraints on the Researcher

If these expectations of research are fair and reasonable, why have they not been met as extensively as they might? There are a number of possible reasons, largely stemming from the way in which research is organized and funded both at national level (where decisions about expenditure are made and where the focus is on project management) and within the university or consultancy sector (where the bulk of the research is carried out). There are also reasons related to the way in which researchers in social science have typically been trained. Perhaps the primary reason, however, is simply that government-funded research was no more clearly outcome-focused than the processes and procedures that were the subject of that research. And there was no requirement that it should be.

The bulk of the research expenditure resulted in published articles, academic books, briefing notes, conference papers — all output measures, not outcomes. Indeed, outcome measures for research are particularly difficult to develop (Weiss, 1998b), not least because few research exercises have been designed explicitly to influence practice. Researchers, like policy advisers and practitioners, have been working to their own agenda. In their world, they are rewarded for articles published in refereed journals, for the number of citations they amass, and for attracting research grants. They are concerned with tenure policies and, at a professional level, are rightly expected to attend to the quality and professionalism of their work. There are no brownie points for sticking the academic neck out and speculating beyond the collected data set about the implications for either policy or practice of the research exercise on which they may have been engaged. And some might say quite right too.

Researchers are also wary of being seen to be "too close" to either the policy adviser or the practitioner. On the policy side they may be vulnerable to pressure to come up with a good news story, which supports the party line. On the practitioner side they may be influenced by personalities, be caught up in the detail of the local initiative or, for other reasons, simply find themselves investing personally in the outcome of the study and produce bias in their results as a consequence.

All of these issues and concerns affect the way in which researchers carry out their tasks, including their choice of methodology. The remainder of this chapter will discuss some of the methodological implications of what might be called a "new agenda" (Kennedy, 1999)

for researchers. This new agenda will need to meet researchers'
needs, but also those of their "partners." It will not consider some of
the other issues, which are equally relevant to the implementation of
research results, such as the commissioning process and the presentation and dissemination of results.

IMPLICATIONS FOR METHODOLOGY

By way of a reminder, we are looking at methodologies relevant to
determining what works (for the policy advisers) as well as where and
why (a major concern of the practitioner). These methodologies need
to be acceptable ethically and politically — by which we mean that
there is no sense in suggesting a randomized control trial on the deterrent effect of removing body parts of convicted offenders, no matter
how effective or even cost-effective such a process might be felt to be.

Practitioners want to feel part of the research process rather than
the remote subjects of it. They want to be included, not excluded,
and they want their views and experience taken into account. They
do not want to be told, at the end of a two-year evaluation, that there
was an implementation failure from day one — but nobody told them.
And the policy advisers do not want any surprising bad news — if
things are going badly then the sooner they hear about it the better
— and in any event they do not want to read about the bad news (or
even the good) in their morning paper.

Policy advisers, in particular, are concerned to know as quickly as
possible whether or not an intervention is proving effective. This is
because they are often under pressure to "mainstream" the initiative
almost as soon as the pilot site has been announced. This expectation needs to be "managed." Interim results might be helpful, for example, or at least some early lessons on implementation.

Against this background, the remainder of this chapter first considers "experimental methods" (randomized controlled trials and
quasi-experimental designs), which have been described as setting
the gold standard for evaluation. It then goes on to consider some
alternatives to experimental methods, which, it is argued, better meet
the needs of the time.

Experimental Methods

Experimental methods have an impressive pedigree. The advancement of knowledge in the field of medicine, for example, owes
much to designs of this type, where the question is the extent to
which particular medical treatments may or may not "work." As
such, these designs are obvious candidates for transfer into other

areas of social policy where similar "what works?" questions are being asked. The medical experience is often seen as setting the standard to which other social policy research exercises might aspire. There are, though, some major differences between the way in which medical issues can be addressed and the problems faced in other social policy areas. In medicine, the treatments themselves have, traditionally, been fairly readily defined in most cases — dosages can be prescribed, for instance, so as to make "implementation failure" unlikely. Also, although the picture is now becoming more complex, there is generally a relatively clear outcome — the patients' conditions improved or they did not (defined as mortality, morbidity, quality of life and/or patient satisfaction). In addition, the unit of analysis is typically an individual, and it is feasible to allocate individuals to treatment, control or placebo groups on a random basis. The sample sizes can be manipulated to reflect the expected effect, with large samples being used, for example, where treatment effects are expected to be marginal. It is also feasible to carry out more than one such randomized controlled trial (RCT) in any given research field. Furthermore, there is a reasonable degree of certainty that sufficient numbers of patients will follow the treatment regime to make the trials viable.

Furthermore, it is sensible to test the hypothesis that treatment X, a particular dosage of medication, will be to some degree effective across all patients. While there is assumed to be individual variation in the appropriateness of the treatment, the assumption is that it will be more effective than not on aggregate. In other words, there will be a relatively small number of patients for whom it may be marginally less effective, but they will be sufficiently small in number not to affect disproportionately the outcome when compared with the untreated control group. Where the delivery of the treatment is heavily dependent upon the skills of an individual — in surgery, or psychotherapy, for example — the experimental procedure may need to be more complex, and larger samples may be required, if the effects of the different individual styles are to be controlled for.

It is probably also fair to say that in many if not most of the early clinical trials, researchers were comfortable with the notion that the mechanism through which the treatment was expected to exert its effect was unknown, and it was not necessary that it should be known in order for the experiment to be carried out "successfully." So, for example, the efficacy of penicillin could be tested using randomized controlled trials without any real understanding of *how* it was delivering its effect. As knowledge develops in relation to such mechanisms, it becomes possible to test efficacy in a more sensitive manner: hypothesizing, for example, that the effects may be greater for some sub-sets of the population than for others. And since samples can be relatively large, it is also possible to test for interaction effects in the course of a standard experimental trial.

Whilst RCTs might, to varying degrees, be an appropriate research model in the medical arena and in some other areas of public policy, there are some major differences in the crime prevention/policing fields, which raise serious doubts about their usefulness there. First, the unit of analysis is often not an individual; it may be a store, community, housing area or parking lot. Random allocation of a sufficiently large sample of stores, communities etc. to a treatment and control group is, generally, quite impractical.

Secondly, RCTs are "black box" experiments where the mechanism through which the effect is taking place is not necessarily known. So even if we were able to allocate randomly a large sample of communities to treatment and control groups, such allocation would not necessarily provide any information on *why* the initiative may have been successful. The outcome of the experiment is, therefore, along the lines that treatment X may have worked, but we do not know how or why. A conclusion of this kind is not what is required at this stage in the development of knowledge about policing and crime prevention.

Thirdly, RCTs assume that there is relatively little risk of implementation failure, or if it does happen it is in sufficiently small a proportion of the experimental population as to be irrelevant. In policing and crime prevention at the community level, implementation failure is a significant possibility, and major efforts have to be made to ensure against it (Laycock and Tilley, 1995).

Finally, in RCTs the experimental treatment has to be maintained throughout the experiment, as originally intended; learning from experience, or making ongoing improvements or adjustments is not permitted. While these assumptions and constraints are plausible in the medical field, with sufficiently large samples, they are not tenable in communities where there is far less control. Crime moves, evolves and develops with the opportunity structures offered by the immediate situation within which the potential offender finds him or herself, and which are beyond experimental control. For all these reasons, then, true experimental designs of the kind ideally deployed in the medical field are generally neither practical nor desirable in the real world of policing. There are far too many variables to even pretend that they can be controlled.

Quasi-experimental Designs

Quasi-experimental designs, employing experimental and control neighborhoods, and where there is no attempt at random allocation, are a rather different matter, although even here the reality necessarily falls somewhat short of the ideal. These designs require a control area, and possibly a displacement area, with which to compare crime rates in the experimental area where the innovation under investigation is taking place. The control area is meant to be comparable to the experimental area in social composition etc., but is expected to remain free of any innovation or other attempts to affect the dependent variable (the crime rate). The displacement area, usually adjacent to the experimental zone, is meant to test for the possibility that instead of reducing crime, the experimental effect was merely to relocate it (Barr and Pease, 1990). Crime figures over a reasonably long period are collected before and after the experimental intervention in all three areas.

There are some conceptual difficulties with such an approach. First, it is assumed that nothing other than the experimental treatment will affect the dependent variable in the experimental area, and nothing at all will happen in the control or displacement areas that might affect the dependent variable — or that if anything does affect the dependent variable it does so in all three areas (experimental, control and displacement) in equal measure. This is an almost impossible condition to guarantee in most real world experiments in communities where there are all sorts of changes and dynamics operating.

It also assumes that the crime rates in all three areas — experimental, control and displacement — are reasonably stable over time. Too much random fluctuation, or "noise" would make any empirical investigation questionable. In reality, the relatively small areas that are usually subject to experimental investigation are susceptible to random fluctuation, and are very difficult to control in the sense of ensuring that no other relevant activity is spontaneously occurring at the same time as the experimental investigation. Thus, it is not that unusual to find that crime has been reduced more in the so-called "control" area, for reasons that may well be beyond the experimenter to explain. And, as with true experimental designs, the experimental treatment has to be maintained in its original form throughout the exercise and not modified in the light of experience.

To make matters worse, the notion of "diffusion of benefits" has been developed in recent years (Clarke and Weisburd, 1994). Instead of crime moving from the experimental area to the adjacent "displacement" area, the benefits of the experimental intervention may spread into the displacement area and reduce crime there too. It is possible to offer some plausible speculations as to why this may happen, but the fact that it is a possibility produces problems for quasi-experimental designs.

Finally, the kinds of interventions which practitioners are now claiming might be effective in reducing crime or in improving policing are often multi-faceted. They suggest that a package of interventions is required in order to turn around disadvantaged communities. Approaches of this kind are particularly difficult to evaluate no matter what the approach, since it is not possible to determine which, if any, of the experimental interventions produced the observed changes; but they are certainly not susceptible to evaluation using quasi-experimental designs.

The criticisms of experimental and quasi-experimental designs have not, so far, been directly related to the extent to which they can provide the kind of information that is required by policy advisers and practitioners. They fail on a number of criteria in this area also. These designs are expensive and time consuming, but they are also unrealistic in expecting the control and displacement areas to remain intervention-free, and in expecting practitioners to ignore the incoming feedback — which may suggest the need for changes to the project — as an intervention begins to take effect. Finally, by their very nature they are not able to explain why an initiative might be working or what the context sensitive dimensions of it might be. All these issues go some way toward explaining the relative rarity of such experimental projects in the criminal justice field, and their inappropriateness.

This is a fairly depressing picture for those aspiring to evidence-based policy and practice. The picture is not, however, as gloomy as it may appear. Over the past few years a number of alternative approaches have been developed in other disciplines which are transferable to policing, and new approaches have also been tried within the criminal justice field itself, as discussed below.

Alternative Approaches

There is a huge range of alternatives to experimental methods. It is beyond the scope of this paper to go into the detail of how each of these might be used to develop and evaluate programs and projects; there are, however, three techniques, which seem particularly well suited to the kinds of evaluations now required. They have certain features in common, and after a brief description of each approach, their common features are discussed.

Theory of Change Approach

This approach has a fairly long history; indeed it could be described as experimental psychology. In recent years it has taken on a new label and has been adopted beyond psychology as an approach to evaluation more widely. A complex discussion of "theory-driven evaluations" is provided by Chen (1990), which draws on earlier work by Chen and Rossi (1987) and which has much in common with the theory-of-change approach more simply described by Weiss (1972, 1998a) and later by Fulbright-Anderson et al. (1998).

The impetus for the present incarnation of this approach derives from the need to evaluate comprehensive community initiatives (CCIs), which the traditional experimental approaches are ill designed to do (Kubish et al., 1995). CCIs are difficult to evaluate because they are complex, they are trying to solve a number of possibly related problems at once; they are flexible and evolve as the problems themselves change, and there are no control groups with which they can be sensibly compared.

In order for these complex interventions to be evaluated, the program manager or sponsor has to be specific about how and why the program, in its various aspects, might work (Weiss, 1995). The evaluator, with help from the program staff, has to be able to articulate the theories, assumptions and sub-assumptions that might be built into the program. It is these that form the hypothesis or set of hypotheses, which the evaluation will go on to test. Some of these theories can be complicated and inter-related, making firm conclusions and generalization difficult. In some cases, the practitioner may not be clear about how or why the program is expected to work, and they may need help in working through the possible alternatives. They may just *know* it is the right approach and resent the analytic approach taken by evaluators in pressing them to work through the underlying theories. There may also be some disagreement among practitioners or between them and the program sponsors. Finally, there is a possibility that being explicit about just how something might have an effect may be politically problematic. For instance, the mechanism may be interpreted as divisive of the community, or may appear to favor one sub-group over another. Whilst such possibilities can be glossed over when the program assumptions are not brought out, it is much more difficult to do this when they are on the table for all, including the media, to see.

If, on the basis of a number of specific theories, a program appears to have worked, how far can we generalize to other communities in what might be quite different areas? The fact that the theory has been set out is helpful in answering this question, and the extent to which it is capable of generalization depends upon the theory it-self. If, for example, it relates to some very specific attribute of the particular community, or to the skills or inter-personal relationships of central players, then the scope for generalization may be less. If the initiative is to be shown to be more generally applicable then it will be on the basis of its replication in other areas. In order for repli-cation to occur, the theory has to be clearly stated. Replications are notoriously susceptible to replicating the wrong thing (Tilley, 1993).

Let us take a specific example from the U.S. literature. Weiss (1998a) describes the program theory behind the proposal that higher teacher pay may increase student achievement. There are a number of possibilities why this may work, as set out in Figure 1.

To quote Weiss (1998a:57) directly:

> program theory, ...refers to the *mechanisms* that mediate be-tween the delivery (and receipt) of the program and the emer-gence of the outcomes of interest. The operative mechanism of change isn't the program activities per se but the response that the activities generate (original emphasis).

Her decision to emphasize the word "mechanisms" is significant, as we move on to look at scientific realism.

Scientific Realism

Pawson and Tilley have fully described scientific realism in their book *Realistic Evaluation* (1997a). It makes use of four concepts — embeddedness, mechanisms, contexts and outcomes. "Embedded-ness" refers to the wider social system within which all human action takes place. Much of it is taken for granted — it is implicit. As an ex-ample, they give "the act of signing a check is accepted routinely as payment, only because we take for granted its place within the social organization known as the banking system. If we think of this in causal language, it means that causal powers do not reside in par-ticular objects (checks) or individuals (cashiers), but in the social re-lations and organizational structures they form" (Pawson and Tilley, 1997b:406). This notion is important to the understanding of pre-cisely what a "program" comprises. It is not, simply, a target hard-ening initiative or a block watch program: "a program *is* its person-nel, its place, its past and its prospects."

When turning to *how* a program might exert its effect, Pawson and Tilley use the notion of "mechanisms." It is directly analogous to the notion of program theory as described by Weiss and others. De-scribing the mechanism means going inside the black box. As Paw-son and Tilley say, we can never understand how a clock works by looking at its hands and face, rather we need to go inside the works. It is through the process of understanding, or hypothesizing about mechanisms, that we move from evaluating whether a program works or not, to understanding what it is about a program that makes it work.

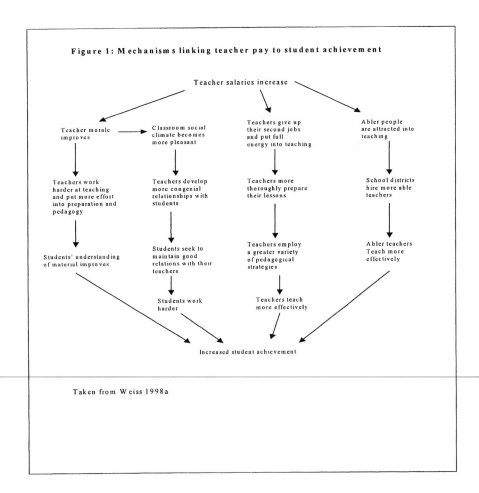

Figure 1: Mechanisms linking teacher pay to student achievement

Taken from Weiss 1998a

But whether it "works" or not will also depend on the "context" within which it is introduced. Solutions to crime problems are often context-dependent. What might work in one place could be disastrous or prohibitively expensive in another.

As an example, let us look more closely at block watch. If block watch were to reduce crime, how would it do so? What is the "mechanism"? And how is it related to the context within which it may be introduced? The bottom line seems to be that residents agree to "watch out" in their neighbourhood, and call the police if they see anything unusual, particularly an offence in progress. Another way in which it may work would be, through the window decals, to alert would-be offenders to the fact that they are entering an areas where residents care about their neighborhood (whether they do or not) — so offenders better look out! There may, of course, be other reasons for block watch, with other mechanisms coming into play — perhaps it is going to improve police/public relations for example, but that would be a different outcome measure. Let us stick with crime reduction for now.

So we have two hypothesized "mechanisms," and both may be correct and contribute to any observed effect. We also have to ask ourselves to what extent the mechanisms behind block watch may be operating anyway, whether or not we introduce the scheme in a particular area. For example, in low crime middle class areas if residents see a crime in progress they already call the police. So what would we be testing? — perhaps the marginal effect of the window decals and street signs. In this case, we are saying that the mechanism is context-dependent.

So the evaluation of block watch has now become quite complex. We may need a high crime area, where residents would not normally call the police, and we may need to do some very specific things to make sure the residents feel comfortable with doing that — providing telephones for example, and some degree of protection against bullying or threats. We also need to take note of the fact that in areas of this kind it is probably the neighbors who are burgling each other, so looking out for strangers may not be so important as providing a socially acceptable and safe way for residents to call the police. We may also need a low crime area where we are fairly confident that residents do call the police, but we are interested in the effect on burglary of street signs and window stickers — i.e., publicizing the fact to the would-be offender that the neighborhood is cohesive and working against crime. And we may be interested in the effect of publicity alone in high crime areas, regardless of whether the community members sign up to block watch. By setting up a set of interrelated projects, each with a specified mechanism in different contexts, we can begin to see how a body of knowledge can be built up. The picture is set out in Table 1.

Table 1: Mechanisms Operating in Block Watch Crime Reduction Program

Context	Mechanism	
	Call police when crime in progress or when seen a suspicious stranger	**Window/door decals Street signs**
Low crime area	Already operating	New measure introduced
High crime area 1	Special measures taken by program staff to support this	No decals or street signs
High crime area 2	No measures taken to support this	Decals and street signs introduced in the area
High crime area 3	Special measures taken by program staff to support this	Decals and street signs introduced in the area

The mechanism, then, is hypothesized to have a particular effect, in a given context, which will lead to an observed "outcome," in our current discussion, a reduction in crime. This can be summarized as Outcome = mechanism + context, or in prose:

The basic task of social enquiry is to explain interesting, puzzling, socially significant outcomes (O). Explanation takes the form of positing some underlying mechanism (M) that generates the regularity and thus consists of propositions about how the interplay between structure and agency has constituted the outcome. Within realistic investigation there is also investigation of how the workings of such mechanisms are contingent and conditional, and thus only fired in particular local, historical, or institutional contexts (Pawson and Tilley, 1997b:412).

By operating in this way, and being prepared to replicate our results in other areas, a body of knowledge can be built up which enables the better understanding of the various methods of crime control.

Rival Explanations

Yin presents his ideas for "Rival Explanations" as a methodology for evaluating complex community-based programs (Yin, 1999, 2000), although they are equally appropriate for testing more modest community or policing initiatives. Yin describes the features of CCIs as typically involving:

- Systemic change (e.g., in the norms, infrastructure or service delivery of an agency or set of agencies), not just change in individual behavior;

- Multi-faceted intervention, not just a single variable;

- Unlikely to be standard across sites;

- Multiple, not single outcomes of interest; and

- Idiosyncrasies of communities reduce validity of defining "comparison" sites.

Yin's argument is that a complex set of activities is introduced into a community; there is a desire to attribute subsequent change to those activities (i.e., to say that they caused them); the threat to this attribution is that some other event or set of events may have been the cause; therefore, let us test plausible rival hypotheses or explanations for the observed changes and see if we can eliminate them. He likens this approach to that or the journalist, detective, forensic scientist or astronomer.

Yin notes that traditional experimental designs try to rule out rival explanations through randomization or the use of control groups, without specifying what the rival explanations might be. Although Yin's rival explanations methods rule out only those rivals that are named and tested for, the process is more transparent. His main argument, however, is that this approach has greater applicability in that it can address more complicated social change, including CCIs.

The steps are fairly straightforward: define the problem; hypothesize about the main effect and any other possible reasons which may explain any observed change (the rival hypotheses); collect evidence, and assess the evidence in support of the main and rival hypotheses. Yin lists a number of possible rival explanations, which may apply in a fairly wide range of community-based evaluations. These are:

- Direct rivals in practice or policy — another intervention which was introduced at the same time *caused* the change;

- Commingled rival — another intervention *contributed* to the change;

- Implementation rival — the initiative was *not implemented* properly and could not have caused the change;

- Rival theory — the change was caused by the intervention but for *other theoretical reasons* than those hypothesized;

- Super rival — some new innovation, but external to the project and applying more generally caused the change; and

- Societal rival — things are changing anyway.

All these various options may need to be considered in any given evaluation, and the program evaluator can never, in theory, rule out every alternative potential cause of change. But by making the alternatives explicit, and collecting data relevant to testing them, the process becomes transparent and challengeable as a result.

Commonalities and Differences

There are some common features to these approaches, which make them attractive. First they unpack the "black box." They require a statement of the causal mechanism between what is being done and what is expected to change. Weiss and her colleagues call this "program theory," Pawson and Tilley call it "mechanisms," and Yin calls it an "explanation." It is one of the most important improvements on the traditional experimental methods approach, and is essential if we are ever to build up a body of knowledge about what works, where and why. It also has other advantages. If, for example, the causal chain is long, or tenuous, then this might cast doubt on the likelihood of the intervention generating a measurable effect, or may lead policy advisers to question its cost-effectiveness.

"Program theory" and "rival explanations" approaches have relatively little to say directly about "context," which is given considerable weight in the discussion of "scientific realism." This concept is important in surfacing the relationship between *what* is being done in a program, which may cause the hypothesized effect, and the *circumstances* or social context within which it is being done. These relationships take on an increased significance when the question of generalizability is raised. It then becomes important to know the extent to which the particular characteristics of the project site were essential to the salience of the mechanism, in order to replicate the results. And this issue becomes even more relevant with the increasing interest of policy advisers in cost-benefit or cost-effectiveness analysis.

To take the Perry Preschool Program (Barnett, 1996) as a concrete example, this involved exposing a group of youngsters at high risk of school failure, involvement in crime and delinquency and so on, in a high quality intensive preschool support program, which included their parents and teachers. The project was highly successful in achieving a number of aims, including less involvement in delinquency, better school performance and reduced teenage pregnancy.

The cost-benefit ratio is quoted as 1:7 — for every dollar spent, seven dollars were saved. So does that mean that the Perry Preschool Program should be implemented nationwide? Would the same benefits accrue? The answer is no. The Perry Preschool Program was introduced in a high crime disadvantaged area of Chicago. The context was right for such a program and the potential payoff was high. Introducing a similar scheme in Bethesda, or Hampstead, both upper middle class areas where the involvement of young people in crime is already low, and teenage pregnancies are not a major social concern, would not be cost-effective. There would be too many false positives in the population — children who were not going to get into trouble whether they were in the (expensive) program or not. Looking at the mechanism through which the Perry Preschool Program was supposed to be effective, and realizing that in many other contexts those mechanisms, or better, are already in place, leads to the realization that mechanisms and context are inter-related.

The rival-explanations approach stands out from program theory and scientific realism in offering an alternative to the "control group" used in traditional experimental paradigms. The program theorists note that it is almost impossible to find a control community with which to compare the CCIs, but they do not say how they cope with the criticism that any observed changes in their program area could have been caused by something that was operating outside the program, perhaps in the whole city or state within which the community was located. Yin's approach to this is highly pragmatic. To take a straightforward example from policing, let us assume that we introduce a crime reduction project in a public housing complex, and we subsequently find a reduction in crime. Was the reduction due to our intervention? Following Yin, we may then look at crime rates in the whole police precinct, or the neighboring areas, to test the rival hypothesis that crime was reducing generally, and for other reasons than our intervention. We would not, in this case, characterize the precinct or neighboring areas as *control* areas with the implication that they are somehow comparable.

In various combinations, these three approaches constitute a viable alternative to the experimental methods traditionally adopted by social science researchers. The extent to which they, and some of the other approaches discussed, meet some of the criteria relevant to delivering what is required of social science research methods is summarized in Table 2 below.

Table 2 requires some explanation. Working across the categories at the top of the table — "*Theory-based*" means that the evaluative approach requires the description of a theory or mechanism through which change will be achieved. Program theory and scientific realist approaches clearly state the mechanism, but experimental designs do not.

The production of *"timely results"* clearly depends upon the scale of the evaluation. Data can only be collected as fast as they become available. If a program requires the determination of reconviction rates following release from prison, for example, then there may be a built in delay of some years. RCTs are classified as lacking timeliness because the emphasis on the sampling frame, and getting that right, can lead to long delays in establishing the project.

The extent to which project evaluations are *"real-world sensitive"* is an assessment of the extent to which they may make unreasonable or simply undeliverable demands on the practitioners or policy advisers with an interest. For example, the requirements for random allocation can sometimes be quite unacceptable politically, and the need for a program to be "set in concrete" and not to change, develop or evolve in the interests of the evaluators, is in many cases impractical and unrealistic. Experimental methods come out badly here.

The *"user-friendliness"* of an approach does, to some extent, depend on how the results are written up and presented to policy advisers and practitioners. The experimental methods are at greatest risk of being less well understood by non-specialists, since they can often involve fairly sophisticated sampling strategies or statistical analyses.

"Internal validity" relates to the extent to which any changes in the dependent variable — i.e., the thing the program is intended to change (in our case the rate of crime or disorder) — can be unambiguously attributed to the program or project activity. It is here that the experimental designs come to the fore. They are specifically intended to cope with threats to internal validity. Program theory and scientific realist approaches are acceptable, if combined with the rival hypotheses approach.

"External validity" is an assessment of the extent to which the evaluation findings can be generalized to other places, times or populations. Most approaches do not do too well on this criterion, which serves to illustrate the importance of replication as a means of establishing principles of effectiveness, and of teasing out the relationship between contexts and populations.

Table 2 covers a selection of the kinds of criteria that practitioners or policy advisers might be interested in when considering the various types of evaluation, but it does not cover all of their interests, nor does it work systematically through their "needs" more generally, as were discussed above.

Table 2: Research Methods and Delivery of Results

Approach	Theory-based	Timely results	Real-world sensitive	User-friendly	Internal validity	External validity
Program theory	✓	✓	✓	✓	✓	?
Quasi-experimental designs	✗	✓	✗	✗	✓✓	✗
Randomized trials	✗	✗	✗	✗	✓✓	✗
Rival hypotheses	✓	✓	✓	✓	✓	?
Scientific realism	✓	✓	✓	✓	✓	?

Table 3 below summarizes the needs that were identified (without distinguishing between practitioners and policy advisers) and comments on how they might be met.

Table 3: Meeting the Needs of Practitioners and Policy Advisers

Needs	How will the needs be met?
To know what works, where and why	More investment in experiments with an outcome focus and more use of research designs which are explicit on mechanisms and contexts.
Help in replicating "what works" — understanding contexts and mechanisms	Greater preparedness on the part of funding agencies to support replication of apparently effective projects in different contexts. Inclusion of these concepts in training programs for practitioners and researchers.
Cost included in evaluations	Encouragement by central funding agencies to include at least basic cost measures in new projects.
Help in generating testable hypotheses	Closer working relationships between evaluators and practitioners before evaluations are commenced to ensure that the hypotheses being tested are clear and agreed.
Timely research	Funding arrangements, which do not lead to excessive delays in commissioning "hot topics." Tight management of research contracts to minimize delay in completing work and a clear publication or dissemination strategy aimed at getting results out quickly.
Involvement in setting the agenda	Mechanisms in place to ensure that policy advisers and practitioners are involved in the research agenda-setting process.
Reports and recommendations in plain English	Advice to report writers on "house style" and training in report writing where appropriate.
To know of current good practice	Regular reviews of "what works, where and why." Support for the Campbell Collaboration and similar activities. Attention to the means through which good practice is developed and disseminated.

Needs	How will the needs be met?
Feedback on the results of research in which they have participated	Routine mechanism established to ensure that research results are reported back to those who have contributed to their development.
Good news	Sensitive drafting, and early warning of potential bad news. Essentially managing the expectations of the recipients of research results.
Confidence in the results	External scrutiny of research reports; publication of results; transparency; high standards in training and support for researchers.
Risk taking in making inferences from data	Specific encouragement for researchers to explain the implications of their work for policy and practice. This may require them better to understand the constraints under which policy advisers and practitioners operate, which in turn may require specific training opportunities for researchers. A clear statement should also be required of the extent to which any advice is speculative rather than deriving directly from the research data.

Some of the approaches suggested in the table are already operating or are being developed. They are not solely related to the methodology of choice, but where they are relevant to methodology, they are not necessarily compatible with the tradition of experimental design.

CONCLUSIONS

This chapter has argued that the research community has not served the advancement of evidence-based policy and practice for a number of reasons. It has also argued that the current interest in evidence means that the situation has got to change. Not only will the policy advisers and practitioners need to pay more attention to research, but the researchers will need to be more sensitive to the needs of these two groups, who are increasingly being conceptualized as partners rather than "experimental subjects" in the case of practitioners, or "disinterested funders" in the case of policy advisers.

The kinds of approaches advocated here as more methodologically appropriate pay greater attention to the realities of community crime control. They are not necessarily cheaper, because of the need for replication, but they should lead to a body of knowledge in which we can have greater confidence. They are also addressing the right questions — what works where and how? There are, however, some caveats to the enthusiastic adoption of a closer working relationship between policy advisers and practitioners, which need to be noted. First, attention needs to be paid to the testing of rival hypotheses. The difficulty of identifying control groups for many of the community-based interventions, which are increasingly being proposed as offering the best hope of longer-term crime control, are particularly difficult to evaluate, but this should not rule out the testing of at least the most obvious rival hypotheses.

Secondly there are a number of issues, which can loosely be related to "integrity," which also demand attention. One set of problems can arise if researchers are close to policy advisers, and a related but different set can arise from closer working with practitioners.

It would, of course, be a mistake to assume that researchers using experimental designs are invulnerable to pressure, and that they somehow hold the ethical high ground. There are numerous cases where results have been manipulated and scientific processes ignored during randomized controlled trials — held out as the gold standard in experimental design. Scientists, including "pure" scientists, are as vulnerable to pressures as the next person; what differs is the source of the pressure. In academia, for example, there is pressure to publish research in journals, and this leads to a reinforcement of critical, generally negative findings, and a fiercely competitive context within which research is being carried out; the prize goes to the first in print.

There are essentially two dimensions in this debate: ethics, or integrity and the extent to which researchers and practitioners are working together. Ideally these two dimensions would be orthogonal, but we have no evidence that they are. But neither do we have any evidence of a necessarily high positive correlation, as is implicitly assumed by those who criticise close collaborations of researchers with policy advisers or practitioners.

It is, nevertheless, probably true that proximity to policy advisers risks exposure to pressure to come up with good news, fast. And the notion that researchers might also offer opinions, as is suggested in the last row of Table 3, invites them to go beyond their data. If they were to do this, then they would need to be very clear on the boundary between fact and opinion, both in their own minds and in their communication with their partners.

Working closer with practitioners risks emotional involvement in the results of the research exercise. Sympathy toward hard working and committed colleagues, who are trying their best in difficult circumstances, risks researchers putting a positive spin on the results which is not justified by the data (see Stake, 1997, for an example).

Some options for handling these difficulties have been suggested by Weisburd (1994), whose starting assumption is that the researchers will not pull any punches in their evaluations. He sees the key issue as how best to manage the role tensions that inevitably exist between the practitioners and researchers. Weisburd recommends: carefully mapping out the research design from the outset, with the practitioners fully involved; clear statements made (and agreed) about how emerging information will be handled as the evaluation progresses; a clear definition of what constitutes "success" and how that will be measured; and agreement on how the results will be disseminated and how (if at all) program reports might differ from research reports. This is good advice. The process of working effectively with practitioners (and policy advisers) is as much about managing their expectations as anything else. If they believe that the researchers are there simply to rubber stamp the project efficacy, then they are operating under an illusion and it is important to make the terms of engagement clear. An evaluation is an attempt at an objective assessment of a program or project. Unfortunately this is not always as clear as it might be. As Sherman (2000) remarked at an NIJ seminar: "If you put forward a hypothesis you are presumed to support it." And therein lies the problem.

If, however, we start with the proposition that the researchers are vulnerable to being "soft" on the practitioners — as Scriven (1997), for example, tends to assume — then a rather different set of options emerges. First, the outcome measure needs to be valid, reliable and independent of the evaluators. If the outcome measure is crime-related, for example, then short of actually fiddling the figures, there should be less of a problem than if the study is reporting on a process, or using some other measure, which is dependent upon interpretation. So that is a first step in the corrective direction — choose outcome measures that are valid, reliable and open to independent scrutiny.

The same potential difficulties arise for researchers working close to policy advisers, where there are similar pressures to "prove" that the latest policy initiative works well. Campbell, in his seminal paper "Reforms as Experiments" (1969:409-410), discusses the relationship between the researcher and political expectations of the research:

... specific reforms are advocated as though they were certain to be successful. For this reason knowing outcomes has immediate political implications.... If the political and administrative system has committed itself to the correctness and efficacy of its reforms, it cannot tolerate learning of failure [original emphasis].

In this new, outcome-focused world the policy advisers are in a major bind. On the one hand they still want the "good news" story — the confirmation that the already announced new initiative works — but they also want a valid assessment of the value of the program: *Did* it "work"? Campbell offers a way out of this bind in his 1969 paper, which is as relevant today as it was then, but only marginally more likely to happen. He suggests that we need a shift in political posture away from the advocacy of a specific reform and toward the advocacy of the seriousness of the problem:

The political stance would become: This is a serious problem. We proposed to initiate Policy A on an experimental basis. If after five years there has been no significant improvement, we will shift to Policy B [1969:410].

Unfortunately, Campbell seems to ignore the probability that politicians do not normally work to five-year time frames. If Policy A is really going to take five years to test, then by the time the results arrive there could well be a quite different administration in place, or at least different individuals, with their own prejudices and concerns. The answer, as with the practitioner, is to be clear at the outset that the results will be what they are, and they may or may not confirm the program as a complete or partial success. If the political position is that regardless of the evaluation results the program will be expanded and declared a winner, then the best advice to the politician is to save the money and not bother with the evaluation in the first place.

Perhaps the most direct and important means of guarding against threats to objectivity is through transparency — the results should be published unless pre-publication peer review suggests that there are methodological flaws which cannot be corrected. The availability of a report on a study should be a requirement regardless of the methodology used, but is less likely to happen if the study is carried out by a consultancy company, not-for-profit organization or professional evaluator with no personal or professional investment in publication. Academics, on the other hand, have a vested interest in ensuring publication. Sufficient detail to enable replication is also important. Publication and scrutiny of results by the academic community and by the critical and independent media should help to offset any tendencies toward partiality, exaggeration or significant departures from the "truth."

One final, perhaps overly defensive point: This chapter is not saying there is no place for experimental methods in crime prevention or policing research. But it is stressing the need better to understand the methodological choices and to make these choices on the basis of a thorough understanding of the research questions being addressed, and the policy and practice context within which they are being made. The "gold standard" should not be any *particular* methodology, but a process of informed decision making through which the *appropriate* methodology is chosen.

Address correspondence to: Professor Gloria Laycock, Director, The Jill Dando Institute of Crime Science, School of Public Policy, University College London, 29/30 Tavistock Square, London WC1H 9QU. E-mail: <g.laycock@ucl.ac.uk>.

Acknowledgements: This project was supported by grant number 1999-IJ-CX-0050 awarded by the National Institute of Justice, Office of Justice Programs, U.S. Department of Justice. Points of view in this paper are those of the author and do not necessarily represent the official position or policies of the U.S. Department of Justice.

REFERENCES

Barnett, W.S. (1996). *"Lives in the Balance: Age-27 Benefit-Cost Analysis of the High/Scope Perry Pre-School Program."* (Monographs of the High/Scope Educational Research Foundation, #11.) Ypsilanti, MI: High/Scope Press.

Barr, R. and K. Pease (1990). "Crime Placement, Displacement, and Deflection." In: M. Tonry and N. Morris (eds.), *Crime and Justice: A Review of Research*, vol. 12. Chicago, IL: University of Chicago Press.

Bayley, D.H. (1998). "Policing in America: Assessment and Prospects." *Ideas in American Policing*. Washington, DC: Police Foundation.

Campbell, D.T. (1969). "Reforms as Experiments." *American Psychologist* 24:409-429.

Chen, H-T. (1990). *Theory Driven Evaluations*. Newbury Park, CA: Sage Publications.

—— and P.H. Rossi (1987). "The Theory Driven Approach to Validity." *Evaluation and Program Planning* 10:95-103.

Christie, N. (1997). "Four Blocks Against Insight: Notes on the Oversocialization of Criminologists." *Theoretical Criminology* 1(1):13-23.

—— (1977). "Conflicts as Property." *British Journal of Criminology* 17(1):1-15

Clarke, R.V. and D. Weisburd (1994).. "Diffusion of Crime Control Benefits: Observations on the Reverse of Displacement." In: R.V. Clarke (ed.), *Crime Prevention Studies*, vol. 2. Monsey, NY: Criminal Justice Press.

Colledge, M., P. Collier and S. Brand (1999). *"Programmes for Offenders: Guidance for Evaluators."* (Crime Reduction Programme Guidance Note 2.) London, UK: Home Office.

Cornish, D. and R.V. Clarke (1987). "Social Science in Government: The Case of the Home Office Research and Planning Unit." In: M. Bulmer (ed.), *Social Science Research and Government*. Cambridge, UK: Cambridge University Press.

Crime and Disorder Act, U.K. (1998). "Chapter 37." London, UK: The Stationery Office.

Dhiri, S. and S. Brand (1999). *Analysis of Costs and Benefits: Guidance for Evaluators*. (Crime Reduction Programme Guidance Note 1.) London, UK: Home Office.

Doherty, J. (2000). "Housing: Linking Theory and Practice." In: H.T.O. Davies, S.M. Nutley and P.C. Smith (eds.), *What Works? Evidence Based Policy and Practice in Public Service*. Bristol, UK: The Policy Press.

Felson, M. and R.V. Clarke (1998). *Opportunity Makes the Thief: Practical Theory for Crime Prevention*. (Police Research Series, Paper no. 98.) London, UK: Home Office.

Fulbright-Anderson, K., A.C. Kubish and J.P. Connell (eds.) (1998). *New Approaches to Evaluating Community Initiatives: Volume 2 — Theory, Measurement and Analysis*. Washington, DC: The Aspen Institute.

Goldblatt, P. and C. Lewis (eds.) (1998). *Reducing Offending: An Assessment of Research Evidence on Ways of Dealing with Offending Behaviour*. (Home Office Research Study No. 187.) London, UK: Home Office.

Goldstein, H. (1990). *Problem-oriented Policing*. New York, NY: McGraw Hill.

—— (1979). "Improving Policing: A Problem Oriented Approach." *Crime & Delinquency* (April):236-258.

Kennedy, D. (1999). *Research for Problem Solving and the New Collabora-tions in Viewing Crime and Justice from a Collaborative Perspective: Plenary Papers of the 1998 Conference on Criminal Justice Research and Evaluation.* Washington, DC: U.S. Department of Justice.

Kubish, A.C., C.H. Weiss, L.B. Schorr and P. Connell (1995). "Introduc-tion." In: P. Connell, A.C. Kubish, L.B. Schorr, and C.H. Weiss (eds.), *New Approaches to Evaluating Community Initiatives — Con-cepts, Methods and Contexts.* Washington, DC: The Aspen Institute.

Laycock, G. (2001). "Hypothesis Based Research: The Repeat Victimisa-tion Story." *Criminal Justice* (London: Sage) 1(1):59-82.

—— (1996). "Rights, Roles and Responsibilities in the Prevention of Crime." In: T. Bennett (ed.), *Preventing Crime and Disorder — Tar-geting Strategies and Responsibilities.* University of Cambridge Press.

—— and N. Tilley (1995). "Implementing Crime Prevention Programs." In: M. Tonry and D. Farrington (eds.), *Building a Safer Society: Crime and Justice, A Review of Research,* vol. 19. Chicago, IL: University of Chicago Press.

—— and N. Tilley (1993). *Policing and Neighbourhood Watch: Strategic Issues.* (Crime Prevention and Detection Paper No. 60.) London, UK: Home Office.

Leigh, A., G. Mundy and R. Tuffin (1999). *Best Value Policing: Making Preparations.* (Police Research Series, Paper 116.) London, UK: Home Office.

Pawson, R. and N. Tilley (1997a). *Realistic Evaluation.* London, UK: Sage.

—— and N. Tilley (1997b). "An Introduction to Scientific Realist Evalua-tion." In: E. Chelimsky and W.R. Shadish (eds.), *Evaluation for the 21st Century.* Thousand Oaks, CA: Sage Publications.

Sherman, L. (2000). Seminar at the National Institute of Justice. Wash-ington DC, April, 2000.

—— D. Gottfredson, D. MacKenzie, J. Eck, P. Reuter and S. Bushway (1997). *Preventing Crime: What Works, What Doesn't and What's Promising A Report to the United States Congress.* Washington, DC: U.S. Department of Justice.

Scriven, M. (1997). "Truth and Objectivity in Evaluation." In: E. Chelim-sky and W.R. Shadish (eds.), *Evaluation for the 21st Century.* Thou-sand Oaks, CA: Sage Publications.

Stake, R.E. (1997). "Advocacy in Evaluation: A Necessary Evil?" In: E. Chelimsky and W.R. Shadish (eds.), *Evaluation for the 21st Century.* Thousand Oaks, CA: Sage Publications.

Tilley, N. (1993) *After Kirkholt: Theory, Methods and Results of Replication Evaluations.* (Crime Prevention Unit Paper 47.) London, UK: Home Of-fice.

—— and G. Laycock (2000). "Joining Up Research, Policy and Practice About Crime" *Policy Studies* 21(3):213-227.

U.K. Home Office (1999). *Reducing Crime and Tackling its Causes — A Briefing Note on the Crime Reduction Programme.* London, UK: Home Office.

U.S. National Institute of Justice (1997). *Criminal Justice Research Under the Crime Act — 1995 to 1996.* Washington, DC: U.S. Department of Justice.

Weisburd, D. (1994). "Evaluating Community Policing: Role Tensions Between Practitioners and Evaluators." In: D.P. Rosenbaum (ed.), *The Challenge of Community Policing: Testing the Promises.* Thousand Oaks, CA: Sage.

Weiss, C.H. (1998a). *Evaluation* (2nd ed.). Englewood Cliffs, NJ: Prentice Hall.

—— (1998b). "Have We Learned Anything New About the Use of Evaluation?" *American Journal of Evaluation* 19(1):21-33.

—— (1995). "Nothing so Practical as a Good Theory: Exploring Theory-based Evaluation for Comprehensive Community Initiatives." In: J.P. Connell, A.C. Kubish, L.B. Schorr and C.H. Weiss (eds.), *New Approaches to Evaluating Community Initiatives: Concepts, Methods and Contexts.* Washington, DC: The Aspen Institute.

—— (1972). *Evaluation Research: Methods for Assessing Program Effectiveness.* Englewood Cliffs, NJ: Prentice Hall.

Yin, R.K. (2000). "Using the Rival Explanations Method for Evaluating Complex, Community-based Programs." Paper presented at the Annual Conference on Criminal Justice Research and Evaluation, Washington DC, July 2000.

—— (1999) *Rival Explanations as an Alternative to Reforms as Experiments.* Bethesda, MD: Cosmos Corporation.